AF541766

To
The Victims of Terrorism

Terrorism in South Asia : Views from India

Editor
A. Subramanyam Raju

India Research Press
B-4/22, Safdarjung Enclave,
New Delhi – 110 029.
Ph.: 24694610; Fax : 24618637
bahrisons@vsnl.com
www.indiaresearchpress.com
contact@indiaresearchpress.com

ISBN : 81-87943-49-1

Cataloguing in Publication Data
Adluri Subramanayam Raju
Terrorism in South Asia : Views from India
by : Adluri Subramanyam Raju

ISBN : 81-87943-49-1

Includes bibliographical references and index.

1. Terrorism - India / South Asia 2. Politics - India / South Asia
3. Security - India / South Asia
I. Title II. Author

Printed in India at Focus Impressions, New Delhi – 110 003.

Contents

Foreword

It gives me great pleasure to write a Foreword to this important book, **Terrorism in South Asia : Views from India.** At the turn of the new millennia terrorism has emerged as the most important security issue facing not just South Asia but the entire international community. From the perspective of New Delhi it is not 9/11 that heralded terrorism in the new era, but it is when the rest of the world joined India in recognizing this new challenge. Indeed for several decades before the attack on the World Trade Centre at New York, India has faced terrorism in all its different manifestations. Various forms of terrorism sponsored externally have plagued not merely Jammu & Kashmir, but other provinces of the country as well. Periodic attacks by terrorist groups at population centres, places of religious worship and numerous acts of sabotage have been common occurrences around the country. Consequently, there is in India today a much greater awareness and reflection on terrorism than perhaps in other regions of the world. That is why I am particularly glad that Dr. Subramanyam Raju has brought together such a distinguished group of experts to reflect and write on terrorism and provide this view from India.

Terrorism is a complex issue and it requires reflection and analysis to understand its various contours. Not only is one man's terrorist another person's freedom fighter, the international community has not yet been able to satisfactorily define what is meant by terrorism. In turn this has made it difficult to evolve common approaches and actions to root out this evil in our midst. This should not, however, serve as an excuse. There are international norms to define non-acceptable use of violence by non-national entities. These are covered under various Geneva Conventions, international customary law and humanitarian laws. Indiscriminate violence, whatever be their reason or cause, targeting innocent unarmed civilians, can never be accepted as legitimate action and is entirely unacceptable to the world. Whoever undertakes such acts commits a gross violation of all such laws and deserves to be dealt with seriously by concerted action of the international community. Countering terrorism in one form in one particular region or against a particular country is not sufficient. This evil has to be countered in all its manifestations in all parts of the globe if we are to deal with this phenomenon comprehensively and in its entirety. The response is neither simple nor one that should be formulated without due care and deliberation.

The book has dealt with these major issues comprehensively. From a theoretical perspective in the first section, the book goes on to examine the various facets of terrorism in South Asia in subsequent parts. I am particularly happy to see an examination of the linkages between terrorism and violence and links with political Islam. Issues of bio-terrorism have received attention. The contours of terrorism, its causes and implication have been discussed in other sections. Terrorism in Kashmir has been considered in three separate articles. Finally, a number of very useful appendices have been included which provide the necessary background factual information so necessary in a book of this type.

A critical question that emerges is how does one counter this menace in a liberal and democratic society? For this one has to understand clearly the nature of terrorism, its genesis and causes, its motivations and preparations, its support base and origin and the manner in which it actually perpetrates these heinous acts. To counter the phenomena one will have to address the issue both strategically and operationally.

International terrorism today is a response to many wrongs particularly as perceived by significant groups around the world. It is not often relevant whether these are actually true. As long as they are perceived to be so, these acquire a salience in the minds of people that needs to be addressed. In this era of globalization, happenings in one part of the world has immediate impact elsewhere and one cannot shut one's eyes and hope that their effects will remain localized. Then there is the stark reality of gross inequities within nations and between countries. Globalization, necessary and inevitable though it may be, has adversely affected several people in far too many countries without any hope of an improvement in their lives in the near future. A determined global effort will be required to rectify these and other serious wrongs in our midst. A task, which is more easily written about than actually achieved, given the nature of international relations today. Yet, even as we move towards addressing these fundamental causes that lead to terrorism, it is nobody's case that forceful countermeasures are not initiated to deal with the overt nature of this form of violence.

An area that will require our early attention concerns an issue of some delicacy. This is the link that has come to be established between terrorism and certain religious orientations. While religion has always been and will remain central to the lives of people, this should not be allowed to impinge on state functions or be used to further political objectives. This is what allows religion to be misused to perpetrate terrorism. A central cause of these developments has been the rapid spread around the world of a form of fundamental religious assertion through its primitive school system. These pseudo- religious institutions then become centres through which violence is perpetrated. These will need to be dismantled around the world and soon as possible to counter terrorism. This will require complex responses. At one level it would mean strengthening the state's capability to provide reasonable and relevant education to its citizens. At another level it will mean stringently rooting out the whole back-up system that allows transfer of international funds, resources and teachers to sustain these seminaries. Indeed it may well mean addressing the causes, which permitted such a colossal accrual of funds in some regions, which were then available to be diverted to such a purpose in the first place.

Several operational measures will have to be considered as well both within nations and internationally. These will require a redirection of effort from developing combat capabilities to counter conventional war to a more focused attempt to counter terrorism. A major military reorientation is required to bring this about, for most countries resources will not permit both to be addressed simultaneously. The requirements are substantially different and will need not only newer forms of surveillance and weaponry, but also new tactics and training. Altering this will require a new way to think about conflict and hence to reorient people's thinking, a most difficult issue at the best of times and particularly so when it comes to dealing with traditional organizations.

This is a fairly substantial agenda for the international community and one that will require several decades of effort to achieve. What is apparent, however, is that India will remain at its forefront. With the help and support of the international community as long as possible and alone, if necessary. When the rest of the world and perhaps even the US has done what is necessary and perhaps disengaged from this war or counter it at a low key, India will have to commit itself for the long haul.

Once again I would like to congratulate Dr Subramanyam Raju for his pioneering effort in this direction. He has indeed done commendable work in establishing the RCSS Hyderabad Chapter. His dynamism and enthusiasm has enabled the Chapter to function with meagre resources and minimal support and yet contribute so substantially to fulfil its objectives. As the former Executive Director of the RCSS, I would like to wish him every success.

Dipankar Banerjee
Major General (Retd)
US Institute of Peace
Washington, DC

January 2003

Acknowledgements

It is my foremost duty to express my sincere gratitude to the Regional Centre for Strategic Studies (RCSS), Colombo, which was the major sponsor for the seminar. I express my deep sense of indebtedness to Major General (Retd) Dr. Dipankar Banerjee, who was the Executive Director of the RCSS during 1999-2002 and presently Fellow at the US Institute of Peace, Washington, DC, for his encouragement and help in organizing the seminar. But for his wholehearted support this seminar would not have materialized. I would be failing in my duty if I do not acknowledge the contribution and support of Indo-American Centre for International Studies (IACIS), Hyderabad; Indian Council of Social Science Research (ICSSR), New Delhi and Southern Regional Centre, Hyderabad and Forum for Policy Promotion (FPP), Hyderabad, which co-sponsored the seminar. I must express my gratitude to Prof. Isaac Sequeira, Acting Director of IACIS; Dr.Y.R.K.Reddy, Chairman of FPP; Mr. Shankar Bose, Deputy Director and Mrs. Ramesh Madan, Asst. Director of ICSSR and Prof. Kousar J. Azam, Honorary Director of Southern Regional Centre of ICSSR who were instrumental in making the seminar a success.

I would like to express my gratitude to General K.V. Krishna Rao, Mr.Vijay Kumar, I.P.S, Commissioner of Police of Chennai; Mr. P.S.V. Prasad, I.P.S, Additional Director of National Police Academy, Hyderabad, who have extended their cooperation and help. It is my bounden duty to thank Dr.J.L.N. Rao, Dr.G.B. Reddy, Mr.S.Srinivas Rao and Mrs. Ann Kumaraswamy, who helped and stood by me in times of need. I wish to thank my friends Ravinder Reddy, Sanjay and Raj Reddy for their timely help.

Introduction

A.Subramanyam Raju

"When you are ignorant of the enemy but know yourself,
your chances of winning or losing are equal.
If ignorant both of your enemy and of yourself,
you are certain in every battle to be in peril"-Sun Tzu

Terrorism has been spreading its tentacles to all aspects of human life thus eroding the quality of life. Hardly a day passes without a terrorist incident somewhere or the other.[1] It is an unacceptable affront on society, disrupting the very foundations upon which it is based. Responding to terrorism is difficult because the threat is usually not constant. What the terrorist does is kill, maim, kidnap and torture. Terrorism is not the problem of its victims or victim societies alone but its impact reverberates across the globe. A victory for terrorism anywhere in the world is a victory for terrorism everywhere. Many individuals and organized groups use terrorism for several purposes. Terrorism is used as a strategic weapon in creating disorder and anarchy in the international system. In the post-Cold War period it is increasingly assuming transnational dimension, making it difficult for states to curb terrorist activities. No single state is in a position to combat terrorism. Hence this evil must be fought collectively by all states. A comprehensive understanding of the phenomena demands examination of not only visible violence and subversion, but also analyzing the ideologies that propagate violence both at the national and international levels, state-sponsored terrorism and use of conventional/ non-conventional weapons.

Technology has enhanced the lethality of terrorists' activities. Their access to weapons transformed the conflicts from low-intensity to high-intensity. Other lethal instruments such as nuclear devices, biological and chemical weapons, most of which could be procured, stolen or manufactured can be operated from remote areas. International travel and proliferation of information technologies – satellites, television, fax, internet, mobile phone – enhanced terrorist communication and intelligence capabilities with their members and supporters internally and worldwide. Technology facilitates to operate beyond the national boundaries of their target states.

Terrorism is the use or threatened use of violence for a political purpose to create a state of fear, which will aid in extorting, coercing, intimidating or causing individuals and groups to alter their behaviour. A terrorist group does not need a defined territorial base or specific organizational structure. Its goals need not relate to any one country. It does not seek a popular base of support. Its operations are very secret and its activities do not conform to rules of law or warfare. Its targets are civilians, non-combatants and its victims generally have no role in either causing or correcting the grievance of the terrorists. Its methods are hostage-taking, hijacking, sabotage, assassination and indiscriminate bombings or suicide bombings.

There are rules that prohibit taking civilians as hostages, hijacking and indiscriminate bombings. But terrorists recognize no such rules. A terrorist act is intended to produce effects beyond the immediate physical damage it causes. Terrorism is a problem of the mindset of individuals who claim to be aggrieved. In law, an aggrieved person brings his grievances to the court of law and seeks justice by tribunal. A terrorist, however, is one who has lost faith in all existing systems of conflict resolution. Unlike wars, terrorism has neither a fixed set of enemies nor the prospect of coming to closure, be it through a win or some other kind of denouement. Threats may come in different forms – some are waxing, some are waning; some are old and others are very new. It can occur anywhere. Terrorists appear to be increasingly successful because they are targeting relatively unprotected public individuals. They want to make government docile in responding to the cause of the public's safety. Any person or place becomes a potential target. Meeting the terrorist threat is a difficult challenge for many reasons: the terrorist is usually a member of a small, insular group; he may not have a criminal record to track him and terrorist activities are neither spontaneous nor random. He wants many people watching and listening and intends to produce fear in someone other than the victim.

Terrorism is a politically loaded term. It created not only definitional problem for society but has also confused the debate on how to characterize acts of political violence. The difficulty in coming to grips with terrorism is the problem of determining its nature and scope. For instance, the Indian government did not consider the LTTE as a terrorist organization till 1988, whereas the Sri Lankan government treated it as such an organization. Similarly, India considered the militant activities in Kashmir as terrorist activities, whereas Pakistan has been considering the militants as freedom fighters.

Terrorism can be defined by the quality of the acts and not by the identity of the perpetrators or the nature of their cause.[2] Howe defines "The one element common to the various kinds of terror is the wish to create unmanageable fear through a use of violence that breaks down traditionally accepted distinctions between combatant and civilian."[3] Further, Leiser states that

> Terrorism is any organized set of acts of violence designed to create an atmosphere of despair or fear, to shake the faith of ordinary citizens in their government and its representatives, to destroy the structure of authority which normally stands for security, or to reinforce and perpetuate a government regime whose popular support is shaky. It is a policy of seemingly senseless, irrational, and arbitrary murder, assassination, sabotage, subversion, robbery, and other forms of violence, all committed with dedicated indifference to existing legal and moral codes or with claims to special exemption from conventional social norms. The policies of terrorists are pursued with the conviction that the death and suffering of innocent persons who have little or no direct connection with the causes to which the terrorists are dedicated are fully justified by whatever success terrorists may enjoy in achieving their political ends.[4]

Terrorism in South Asia

South Asia has been experiencing terrorist activities for a long time. Hundreds and thousands of people are getting killed in the region. Violence and atrocities on people have become the order of the day. A collective effort by the South Asian states and civil societies against terrorism is yet to be made. Following the 11 September 2001 attacks on the World Trade Centre, the Indian Parliament also become a target for the terrorist attack, thus making South Asia more vulnerable to the terrorist activities. Violence has been with us since the beginning of history. Earlier it was limited but now the terrorists have access to weapons of mass destruction that can bring nations into total wars. The phenomenon of terrorism thus provokes urgent response. In that case we have to probe into: What are terrorist acts? Can we protect ourselves against terrorists? In this context, the Hyderabad Chapter of Regional Centre for Strategic Studies (Colombo) organized a two-day seminar on *Terrorism and Security in South Asia* in Hyderabad on 21-22 March 2002. The main objective of the seminar was to make an attempt to probe into ideological nuances, legal, diverse motivations, complex interrelationships and patterns of terrorist activities.

There are seventeen papers, which are divided into seven sections. It is difficult to maintain a strict distinction between the papers as their contents overlap. The editor gratefully acknowledges the cooperation and support of the authors of these papers.

Section-I : Theorizing of Terrorism

Shibashis Chatterjee, in his paper entitled "State, Terrorism and Violence: A Theoretical Engagement", maintains that more substantial theorization of terrorism requires problematization of several issues: a) terrorism has to be situated in the wider context of theoretical debate on political violence in order to distinguish terror and violence and thereby locating the specificity of the former; b).Theorization also demands liberation of terrorism from a specific arena orientation as terrorism cannot be explained adequately with reference to the State; c). The fact that comparable empirical circumstances of exploitation, oppression and anarchy do not necessarily produce similar levels of terror indicates the limits of a purely objectivist understanding of terrorism. The paper tries to theorize contemporary terrorism along some of these much-neglected axes of contestation.

Secion-II: Terrorism and Violence: New Trends

T. Sreedhar, in his paper on "New Trends in Terrorism and Violence: Pakistan-Taliban-Al-Qaeda", explains that terrorism is not going to be the same in the coming years. He argues that the Al-Qaeda phenomenon has considerably altered the face of terrorism and violence. The militant organizations have recruited cadres and established networking in sixty countries. He explains about Al-Qaeda networking with similar organizations in the world and recruitment of its cadres. The article focuses on the Al-Qaeda's connections with the narcotic mafia and their acquisitions of weapons of mass destruction. Kousar J. Azam's paper on "Political Islam and Terrorism in Contemporary Times" deals with Islam and the rise of terrorism. She maintains that though there are many religious groups, which are terrorizing the people, the 11 September incident came to be associated with Islamic fundamentalism. She maintains that there should be a distinction between terrorism and Islam. And also there is a need for the Muslims to reassess their perception of the essence of a faith. Failure of the political institution in the Arab countries is the major cause for the rise of militancy, she argues. Mohd. Moazzam Ali, in his paper on "Tackling Terrorism: Fight Disease Not Just the Symptoms", stresses the necessity to concentrate not just on the symptoms of terrorism but on the disease of which terrorism is just a symptom. He argues that an indiscriminate war against terrorism without addressing the root cause of terrorism would make the world a more volatile place to live. He adds that different types of terrorism need to be tackled differently. The mishandling of terrorism could lead to more violent multiplication of the acts of terrorism.

Section-III: Bio-terrorism

Pushpa Bharagava, in his paper on "Biological Warfare, Bio-terrorism, the World and Us", argues that contrary to the popular perceptions a biological weapon is a poor man's atom bomb. He refers to various misconceptions on biological weapons such as the difficulty involved in manufacturing the biological weapons. He argues that terrorists in future might use biological weapons, as they are easily available to them. Ravindra Nath's paper on "Bio-terrorism: A Threat to National Security" deals with the importance of bio-terrorism as a means of threat to national security. The likely misuse of advances in technology would pose a real threat to cripple the economy of a nation and global peace. Tackling the threat with efficient management strategies could minimize the severity of the epidemics caused by bio-terrorism.

Section-IV: Terrorism in South Asia

In this section there are four papers. P.V.Rao, in his paper on "The Global Contours of Terrorism: South Asian Predicament", discusses the dynamics of internal conflicts in South Asia and the difficulties in the resolution of conflicts due to the internationalization of their internal conflicts and due to the proliferation of small and light weapons in the region. He maintains that South Asian states find difficulty in identifying and controlling the proliferation of illicit arms, which fuel the ongoing ethnic war in the region. He concludes that no single state in the region can control such a nourished phenomenon of violence unless there is going to be a regionally coordinated mechanism to combat the lethal sources of support to the terrorist outfits in the region. He examines the difficulties in the resolution of conflicts such as encountered by India and Sri Lanka owing to the indiscriminate proliferation of small weapons. J.L.N.Rao's paper on "Jihad and Cross-Border Terrorism in South Asia" explains that terrorism is the result of the policies followed by Pakistan and Bangladesh during the Zia ul-Haq and Zia ur Rahman regimes respectively. During their regimes both of them used madrassas to create the Mujahideen and right-wing elements in their countries. In the case of Pakistan the regime used the Mujahideen to fight the Soviets in Afghanistan. The paper provides a linkage between the rise of madrassas, mujahideen and jihad leading to the spread of terrorist activities in South Asia. He argues that terrorism is encouraged and supported by the South Asian states to pressurize the neighbours. In due course of time terrorism has become a Frankenstein monster challenging the very basis of South Asian societies. M.J.Vinod, in his paper on "Financing Terror: Dealing with Transnational Networks", argues that the fight against terrorism and the fight against drugs are interlinked. He explains that the Taliban could not have existed, if the opium trade was not there. He maintains that terrorism has to be fought on different fronts such as the trafficking of narcotics and arms and the large reserve of religious mercenaries. Suba Chandran explains, in his paper on "Suicide Terrorism: An Enquiry", that the two countries of South Asia –India and Sri Lanka – are facing suicide bombings. These bombers have come from an educational and higher economic background. He elaborates the features of suicide terrorism in the 1980s and 90s and concentrates on suicide terrorism in India and Sri Lanka.

Section-V: Legal Regime and Terrorism

Nageswara Rao's paper entitled "Elimination of International Terrorism : International Legal Regime and Perspectives" focuses on international terrorism and the legal regime that is being sought to be evolved to define it and to suppress and eliminate it. His paper analyses the definitional problems of international terrorism. He discusses other factors such as the acts of private actors or the State also amount to terrorism. The paper discusses the targets of terrorism, manifestation of international terrorism and dilemma faced by the international community in arriving at an agreed definition of an international terrorism with adequate enforcement mechanism. G.B.Reddy, in his paper pertaining to "Indian Legal Regime and Prevention of Terrorism", gives a detailed exposition of various organic laws that have been passed by the Indian state to deal with terrorism, the use and misuse of some of those legislations, judicial interpretation thereof and more particularly the impact of such extraordinary laws on the fundamental rights of the Indian citizens. His paper analyses the police power of the State on one side and the limitations in the form of the inalienable rights of the citizens on the other side, with a focus on the recently promulgated Prevention of Terrorism Act. Satya Narayan Pradhan, in his paper on "Akshardham and Beyond: Redefining Police and Public Order Maintenance in the Face of Terrorist Hyper-Violence", maintains that public order maintenance has come to acquire primacy in day-to-day policing. The entire structural and functional focus of policing has shifted in a major way to public order maintenance. The paper focuses on issues such as Public Order maintenance and national security concerns; transnational terrorism and its attendant challenges and transnational policing as the cutting edge of public order maintenance and control of terror. His paper elaborates on these aspects and presents a scenario and possible approaches and strategies for contemporary public order maintenance in the face of the challenges of terrorist hyper-violence.

Section-VI: Terrorism in Kashmir

P. Sanjay, in his paper entitled "Kashmiri Ethnic Identity and Terrorism", examines the Kashmiri ethnic identity and its mutation. The paper examines various factors that resulted in Kashmiri ethnic identity expressing itself in virulent form in the late 1980s and the rise of terrorism due to the de-institutionalization of democratic institutions. Finally the paper provides a glimpse of the impact of terrorism in transforming the Kashmiri ethnic assertion into an Islamic Jihad. B. Krishnamurthy's paper on " European Union's Response to Terrorism in Kashmir" explains that European countries understood India's concern and felt that Pakistan is responsible for the insurgency in Kashmir. The paper discusses the European Union views on terrorism in Kashmir and elaborates the factors, which made European countries change their policy towards India.

Section-VII: Women and Terrorism

In his paper entitled "Women and Terrorism in South Asia: Some Observations", A. Subramanyam Raju discusses the impact of violence and terrorism on women and women's involvement in the violence against the state. This paper argues that women are victims either being involved or not being involved in the conflict. They are more affected than men in the conflict. In his brief paper, he tries to see women as victims and warriors in Sri Lanka, India and Nepal. Rashmi Bhure, in her paper on "Terrorism: The Enduring Saga of Women in Kashmir", focuses on the impact of terrorism on women in Kashmir such as displacement and psychological trauma due to violation of human rights. They are the worst sufferers of terrorism. The emotional and economic rehabilitation of women in the male-dominated society becomes very crucial. She emphasizes the role played by women persistently in restoring peace in Kashmir despite all odds.

Terrorism constitutes a threat to all: what is being inflicted on one country today can be inflicted on another tomorrow. The South Asian states should realize that they couldn't reduce terrorist activities unless they are able to devise a common strategy to fight the ideologies of terrorism in the minds of people. They should develop a worldwide counter terrorism network and should exchange intelligence, cooperation with other governments, put economic, political and diplomatic pressure on terrorism-sponsoring states. No two states will react in the same way to the threat posed by the terrorists because of deficiencies in existing policies, lack of adequate resources and loopholes in the adopted measures. The states cannot curb terrorism completely by using traditional methods hence terrorism is here to stay. Special laws are required to tackle the terrorist menace. However, such laws must take cognition of individual liberties. Regular training programmes for law enforcement agencies should be carried out as such measures would not only help in evolving effective counter-terrorist tactics but also in protection of human rights. Since terrorism has a transnational dimension, cooperation at bilateral as well as multilateral levels is needed to combat the threat from terrorists. There is a need for comprehensive national legislation that provides a clear definition of terrorism and concrete measures to deal with it. Every state has the duty to refrain from assisting terrorists in another state or within its territory. There is a need for unified rules governing global finance so that terrorists and other outlaws do not exploit loopholes in law in some countries. Prior to this, the South Asian countries should solve their disputes. The South Asian states must strive to provide good governance and improve the quality of life of all citizens. Civil societies in South Asia must unite to fight terrorism. People should play a significant role in countering terrorism. They have to understand some of the complications in tackling terrorism. Their support is most essential for countering terrorism effectively. People are suffering due to the terrorist activities not only economically but also psychologically. Finally it is for the people to decide whether they will suffer in silence or will fight against the perpetrators of violence with the aid of the government.

Notes

1. For threats posed by terrorists, see Juliet Lodge (ed), *The Threat of Terrorism* (Boulder, Colo: Westview, 1988); Walter Laqueur, *The Age of Terrorism* (Boston: Little Brown, 1987); Christopher C. Harman, *Terrorism Today* (London: Frank Cass, 2000); Lawrence Freedman and Yonah Alexander (ed), *Perspectives on Terrorism* (Delhi: Hindustan Publishing Corporation, 1985); Harvey W.Kushner (ed), *The Future of Terrorism: Violence in the New Millennium* (Thousand Oaks, Calif: Sage Publications, 1998); K.P.S.Gill and Ajai Sahini (ed), *The Global Threat of Terror: Ideological, Material and Political*

Linkages (New Delhi: Bulwark Books and The Institute for Conflict Management, 2002); Neil C. Livingstone, *The War Against Terrorism* (Lexington, Mass: Lexington Books, 1982); Neil C. Livingstone and Terrell E. Arnold (ed), *Fighting Back: Winning the War Against Terrorism* (Massachusetts: Lexington Books, 1984).

2. Brian M.Jenkins, "Statements about Terrorism", in Marvin E. Wolfgang (ed), *The Annals*, Vol. 463, September 1982, p.12.

3. See Irving Howe, "The Ultimate Price of Random", *Skeptic*, no.11, January-February 1976, p.15, cited in Louis Rene Beres, *Terrorism and Global Security: The Nuclear Threat* (Boulder: Westview Press, 1979), p.140, f.n.

4. Cited in Burton M. Leiser. "Terrorism, Guerrilla Warfare, and International Morality", *Stanford Journal of International Studies*, vol.12, Spring 1977, p.39.

Section-I : Theorizing of Terrorism

State Terrorism and Violence : A Theoretical Engagement

Shibashis Chatterjee

Introduction

It is widely recognized that terrorism, be it national or international, constitutes perhaps the most potent threat to human security. Yet, it is surprising to see that there is little agreement amongst people at large about the definition of terrorism, although, virtually every major state of the world in the recent epoch has suffered significant casualties owing to terrorist attacks. The problem is extended into the global arena due to the failure of the United Nations to agree upon a working definition of terrorism in international law and thereby distinguish terrorism from other forms of armed conflict. There is another dimension to the problem, which has confounded the matter even further. Although terrorism is usually recognized as organized or systematic use of violence or terror against the state, or some legitimate public authority or government, there are frequent cases of state involvement in terrorist activities, and the state can hardly claim any immunity against the legitimate allegation of deliberate perversion of its coercive monopoly for ulterior ends, and even for perpetration of genocidal crimes against humanity. Even otherwise, the issue of terrorism and the centrality of the state therein are too closely related to be treated separately. It is true that in normal circumstances, democratic states have nothing to do with the exercise of indiscriminate violence against a select body of subjects. But the state might cultivate connections with terrorist organizations or groups for other purposes. States often sponsor terrorist organizations that are active against enemy states, or might use these organizations to destabilise a hostile neighbour, or might still find investing in global or regional terrorism useful for a whole gamut of foreign policy goals. In brief, although states are seldom terrorist by themselves, the culpability and clandestine involvement of states in forming, encouraging, sponsoring and sustaining terrorist groups are too self-evident to be denied by an impartial analyst.

In the present study, we take up three problematics related to the state and terrorism. In the first section, we look into some of the legal and theoretical perspectives of terrorism and advance a critique of such perspectives. In the second section we take up the issue of political theory of violence and revolution. In the final section, we deal with some of the ethical dilemmas underlying the relationship between terrorism and the modern state, and address the issue of how to deal with such dilemmas.

Finally, this essay is not meant for any specific understanding of terrorism in South Asia. This essay attempts an exposition of the theory and philosophy of terror and political violence independent of time and space. We do not claim that the specificity of terrorism do not afford any temporal and/or spatial variation. Our central contention is that the fight against terrorism can hardly be effective if our understanding of what we are fighting against remains somewhat vague and indeterminate. It may well be the case that we have to combat here a notoriously elusive enemy. However, the greater the extent of ambiguity which is structural to the phenomenon, more pressing is the need for a theoretical engagement. For without some clarification of the vexing imbroglio, concrete policy prescriptions, which would not perpetuate the cycle of retributive terror and punitive counter-terror but turn it into a virtuous cycle of peace and order, can never be evolved. This essay is unable to suggest any macro blue print for the eradication of terrorism. Rather, it engages in some form of clearing exercise, so that the authority, whose responsibility is to conceive policies and implement them, might deliver more meaningful discourses which would go a long way to exorcise the manifest predisposition in a section of humanity to engage in mindless violence and terror.

I

Terrorism: Problems of Definition

Despite the scale of violence and destruction that inevitably accompanies any terrorist attack, the international community is yet to agree on a universal definition of the phenomenon. The difficulty presents itself at various levels. At the level of international law, despite steady attempts to codify some of the recognized practices dealing with the case, there is still no manifest agreement about what terrorism definitionally constitutes. The primary reason for this legal predicament is the failure to distinguish terrorism from war or war - like conditions, particularly, to conceive terrorism as an unjust war model. Moreover, states have been so inconsistent and blatantly hypocritical in their anti-terrorist fulmination and discourses on the one hand, and in their clandestine support for and, at times, open encouragement of terrorist groups on the other, that any systematic anti-terrorist legal regime has not yet taken concrete shape. At the level of theory, the problem involves several structural dilemmas in which the issues of terrorism and legitimate (or illegitimate) political authority get inextricably intertwined, with very little possibility of any meaningful breakthrough. The problem of an insufficient theoretical distinction between terrorism and other forms of political violence and armed rebellion has never left the members of the international community. The fact that many terrorist groups and organizations espouse fidelity to causes, which are intrinsically, recognized as just or legitimate further compounds the theoretical predicament. Even at the level of policy making, one fails to witness the articulation of a coherent and unified policy paradigm, that would not only bring policy coordination closer and turn it into more effective, but would ultimately pave the way for a global counter-strategy against the menace of terrorism. Partly, the policy failure sterns from *real political* consideration of states, who are, expectedly perhaps, victims, sponsors and silent spectators of terrorism at various times. Although, there is at present an international consensus against the threat of terrorism as never before, there are huge differences among states over definitions, the extent and character of anti-terrorist measures, the role of international agencies or institutions in combating terrorism, the legitimacy of coercive or enforcement strategies adopted against terrorist groups and "states" by big powers, and the nature of modalities to be decided to fight terrorism as a common threat to the survival of states and the safety of the international community.

We intend to look into these issues *seriatim*. First, even a cursory glance into the practices of international law at present shows us that the legal regime is gradually hardening against terrorism.[1] International law, particularly laws of war and international conflict, have come a long way since the days of a recognized incognoscenti of the field, L. Oppenheim categorically defined war as a "contention of States *through their armed forces*". (Emphasis in the original).[2] The modern development of legal restrictions on the right to resort to war and the use of armed forces have made important shifts in the laws of war. As Tim Hillier rightly argues, "(the) law of war is now less regarded as an alternative to the law of peace and more regarded as a device for alleviating the suffering caused by war".[3] The law regulating armed conflicts grew out of the law of war. War was, by definition, a dispute between states, and thus unquestionably a matter of international law. With the growth of laws of armed conflict, new problems emerged. For historically, internal and civil wars were matters of exclusive domestic jurisdiction. The application of international law to such disputes led to a new controversy that such an application contravened the principle of non-interference in the domestic affairs of sovereign states. This controversy not withstanding, the general tendency has been towards the strengthening of a new branch of law, known as International Humanitarian Law. Both the four Geneva Conventions of 1949 and the Geneva Protocol-II relating to the Protection of Victims of Non-International Armed Conflicts (1977) have contributed significantly towards this end. Although the purpose of this essay is not to analyse laws of armed conflict in general, some observations in the matter are thought to be necessary as a connecting link with the issue of terrorism.

Non-international conflicts are defined in Article-I of Protocol-II as

"(Conflicts) ... which take place in the territory of a High

Contracting Party between its armed forces and dissident armed forces or other organized armed groups which, under responsible command, exercise such control over a part of its territory as to enable them to carry out sustained and concerted military operations and to implement this Protocol. The Protocol shall not apply to situations of internal disturbances and tensions, such as riots, isolated and sporadic acts of violence and other acts of a similar nature, as not being armed conflict..."

The requirement set by Protocol-II is definitely more rigid compared to Protocol-I, wherein a national liberation movement is not required to control any part of the national territory in order to be recognized as an international armed conflict. Significantly enough, control here does not refer to conventional administrative or governmental control; control connotes the ability "to carry out sustained and concerted military operations". The upshot of this is quite self-evident. The definition of a non-international armed conflict in Protocol-II has such a high threshold that it would seem to exclude most revolutions and rebellions, and would probably not apply in a civil war until the rebels were well-established and have set up some kind of a *de facto* government. This clearly reveals the inherent weakness of the existing legal regimes to provide protection to civilians and others in situations of non-international armed conflicts. It can only be said in defense of the existing regime that all parties involved in any insurrectionary conflict (that does not satisfy the Protocol-II threshold) remain bound by the minimum conditions laid down in Article 3 common to the Geneva Conventions as well as any human rights agreements to which the government involved had been a party, or any human rights principles which had hardened into *jus cogens* or customary law.[4]

The fact that even modern International Humanitarian law affords insufficient protective coverage in cases of international and non-international armed conflicts short of war is a pointer to the kind of weaknesses that plague legal principles and regimes dealing with international terrorism. Attempts at defining international terrorism in the past do not seem to guide us anywhere. Partly, this is because of the varied and changing social context of the phenomenon itself, a variation that also extends to its forms, manifestations, intensity, magnitude, timing and the nature of incidence. From the days of the Greek city states and the age of Reformation in Europe, the American Revolution and the Latin American wars of Liberation, the French Revolution, the killings during Metternich's Congress of Vienna, the resistance movements during and between the two World Wars in the occupied territories and in the European dictatorships in the inter-war period, the Cold War context of political rivalry and socialist rebellions in Asia, Central and South America and some African states, the violence associated with the terminal phase of the decolonization struggles in Asia and Africa, the intense and protracted West Asian crisis involving Israel and the various Arab states revolving around Palestine, and down to the post-Cold War contexts of ethnic cleansing in various parts of Africa and Southern and Central Europe, anti-US attacks, in primarily the Islamic parts of the world, the intensification of violence throughout South Asia in general and various forms of terror unleashed in India in particular, terrorism has remained a living force within the international system. As these diverse contexts would most obviously suggest, the terror associated at various epochs and in different parts of the world had their unique purposes, which were paraded as self-justification(s) of such acts of violence. While in previous times, the acts of terrorism were essentially acts of political murder or assassination of political dignitaries or diplomatic personnel, the 1960 and the 70s saw a great upsurge in the manifestations of terrorism in the forms of hijacking of aircrafts, killing of civilian and non-military public officials, acts against various categories of diplomatic personnel, murder and abduction of businessmen and other important personalities, and the massacre of ordinary civilians, including women and children, for creating an environment of generalized terror and fear. Although, apparently, the admission of a political motive behind each and all terrorist strikes seem to be the continuing link between such disparate events, the nature of the political motive and the justification of terrorist violence in terms of such motives, have also undergone substantial modification in recent times.

What makes terrorism so difficult to define is the range of issues and components it has to cover by way of such an exercise. Needless to say, nearly all components that might enter into a definition (and there is much debate about the nature of the components and their mutual relations or priority) are problematic. Some of these components include actors (private or public?), range of acts, the determination of the international component, underlying motive and intent, and the nature of victims involved.[5] The dilemma on actors is simple: Whether the definition should include acts of private individuals or those representing some political motive? States suffering from unjust exploitation at the hands of superior powers naturally privilege the case for state terror. They argue that individual terrorism is of international concern only when it is employed solely for personal gain or caprice as distinguished from acts committed in furtherance of a political cause especially against colonialism and for national liberation. The standard Western practice in the past took the diametrically opposite view. They did this not because state acts, however punitive or cruel, are sacrosanct, but for the opposite reason: that adequate international law already restrains state violence.[6] In recent times, the Western perspective has changed. The West now considers itself the victim of state-sponsored terrorism, and although individuals are still held responsible for acts of terror, and given the density and sufficiency of international norms in binding states to abjure violent practices, there is now a felt need to legally prohibit "states" from assisting and even encouraging the cause of such terrorism. Needless to say, that some states harbour an antithetical sentiment on the issue, and continue to link terrorism with unjust / unfair practices of the powerful states.

The dilemmas underlying the range of acts, determination of the international component and victims are less pressing. The range of acts have gone on increasing, given the steady rise in the intensity of lethality of terrorist attacks and the vast magnitude of devastation caused by them. The scale of devastation in the cases of attacks against American embassies in Dar-e-Salam and Nairobi, the complete decimation of the Twin Towers in New York and the attack against the Pentagon in Washington DC, or the scale of violence unleashed continuously in Sri Lanka by the Tamil militant outfit, the LTTE, or the magnitude of suffering in Bosnia, Croatia and elsewhere in the war-torn former Republic of Yugoslavia, and the wanton killings in Russia, Georgia, in the South Asian subcontinent, particularly in the provinces of Kashmir, Punjab, Assam and Manipur in India, have driven home the gigantic scale of global terrorism as a genuinely devastating phenomenon. The debate on deciding the international component, right from the start, was rather academic. It is true that certain terrorist predispositions are generated and sustained purely by national means. But these are exceptions. On a closer scrutiny, terrorism, particularly the terrorism of the 1990s and of the first years of the new millennium developed as an international nexus, with terrorist organizations operating in widely divergent areas, collecting financial resources globally and recruiting soldiers from different states. In any way, the international component of the terrorists can easily be determined by reference to the motive, the states of the victim, and by emphasizing the territorial and jurisdictional aspects of the act.[7]

The determination of victimhood in terrorism is both simple and difficult. At the level of identifying people whose lives are indiscriminately claimed in an incessant cycle of terrorist violence, there is no need to classify the victims. Modern weapons do not usually discriminate targets, and terrorists often engage in mindless violence that makes no distinction between combatants and non-combatants, or give any thought to the considerations of age and motive of potential victims. On the other hand, and at a different level, nearly all-contemporary approaches to the study of terrorism remain nearly exclusively subject or actor-oriented with little or no regard shown to the agonizing trauma of victimhood. In fact, the absence of a victim-oriented reading of terrorism remains a crippling limitation of our understanding of the phenomenon itself. The problem here, however, is much deeper. In a sense, unless one grants the possibility of some legitimate victimhood for terrorism, terrorism cannot be compared or viewed as a war model. There is no reason why terrorism has to be viewed as a war model; but in the event of repeated attempts to model terrorism on war, this issue of victimhood assumes great significance. We would return to this issue in the final section.

The question of motive is undoubtedly the most vexing and elusive of components that go into the definition of terrorism. One way to avoid this problem is to replace motive by intentionality.[8] The idea here is that to define terrorism by criminal intent regardless of motive drives home the point that it is the intent to commit the act and not the reasons that led to its commission that has to be the governing factor. On the other hand, states have generally defined terrorism by motive. Thus, it is widely held that the most specific attribute of terrorism constitutes of its political motive, for otherwise, terrorism cannot be distinguished from large-scale violence used for private commercial purposes. Therefore, terrorism seems to damage the interests of and claims concession from its enemy, which may either be the state or some non-state actor. To incorporate the considerations of damage and concessions is to immediately place at front stage centre all the perplexing problems of the political, ethical and legal legitimacy of every cause espoused by each actual or potential terrorist group.

It is perhaps to axiomatic to mention that unless the international community can decide a satisfactory basis of delinking terrorism from political motivation, this excruciating dilemma would never be resolved. The only possible manner in which to achieve this is to define terrorism as ordinary criminality and deny any ethical defence of the terrorist's cause from the very outset. In the final section of the essay we would take up this proposition and explain the inherent difficulties of such an exercise from the standpoint of applied ethics.

If terrorism is difficult to be defined at international law, its theorization has proved to be even more slippery.[9] One regularly comes across scholarly discourses on terrorism, which are vague and open-ended, with little conceptual clarity of the underlying ethical considerations and without affecting any meaningful contrast of terrorism and other forms of political violence, such as armed conflicts and political murders.

In fact, there are several levels at which terrorism has been theorized, and accordingly, diverse accounts of the phenomenon are available. Of these diverse tracts, we concentrate on three studies to reveal some of the problems emerging out of them. To begin with, there are contributions that emphasize the psychological attributes of the terrorist and reduces his predisposition to use violence to such pathological traits. Thus Lawrence Zelic Freedman identifies four essential features of a terrorist, which are, without exception, psycho-pathological in orientation.[10] The terrorist engages in terrorism in search of a reaffirmation of his self-esteem, which was denied to him in his pre-terrorist stage, in the form of severe blows to his self-image and ego; terrorism involves the depersonalization of the individual, in the sense of abandonment of individuality (as individuality creates a burden of responsibility, a sense of impotence and an impoverishment of the ego) and merger of the individual into a larger group without any distinctive evidence of personhood; terrorism is also, like violence in general, a method of building intimacy with the enemy. A terrorist might suffer from a sense of nothingness, which is overcome only by his fearful presence within the mental horizon of his real and potential victims. Terrorism finally, believes in the magic of violence. Violence becomes a form of "terrorist sacrament". But killing and murder are not sacraments where human powers are dedicated in the service of the divine — rather, it is a sacrament that compels God's divine energy to human (the terrorist's) service.[11]

The attempt to explain terrorism by psychological attributes or pathological derivatives fails to relate the phenomenon to wider social forces and contexts. Surveys of state practices and tendencies within international law seem to converge on the point that the right to act on a political purpose and the right to use violence under certain circumstances are rights of states, and not of individuals or groups of individuals. It is true that terrorists operate generally as groups of individuals and are seldom directly employed, controlled or operated by states. Yet, states are recognized as the most effective counter-terrorist agents. The laws of war, through its myriad practices, have further reinforced this trend. The significant point here is that one requires to anchor any theorization of terrorism within the practices of the modern state. To delink terrorism from structural factors and view it as aberrant behaviour of abnormal, schizophrenic individuals is therefore to discount perhaps the most abiding aspect of the phenomenon itself.

Accordingly, most academic treatment of terrorism has proceeded generally along the accepted binary of state morality and terrorist dehumanization. A classic illustration of such a perspective comes from Ted Gurr, the celebrated American political scientist of political conflict and revolution. For Ted Gurr, terrorism consists of three distinct objective elements, namely the peculiarity of the method, whereby terrorists use explosive and incendiary instruments, along with other strategies or methods to achieve their end; the second attribute of terrorism resides in the specificity of its target, which are political in nature. Public or political targets include public buildings, political figures, and groups including the military and the police. Private targets may also be selected by terrorists primarily because of their political linkages or because of personal considerations. The final element identified by Gurr consists of the nature of action of terrorism, which involves perpetration of violence by individuals or groups in a sporadic and clandestine manner.[12]

Ted Gurr's efforts to sketch a structural account of terrorism is undoubtedly far superior than the psychological theories or biological explanations of the same. The problem with Gurr's analysis, however, is that it fails to distinguish sufficiently terrorism from other forms of collective political violence. Such a perspective therefore conflates terrorism into a generalized account of anti-state practices, thereby blurring the boundary between terrorism and revolutionary political violence. Secondly, this also encourages terrorism to be defined solely by direct violence, and thus generate a perspective, which is invariably actor-oriented. In Gurr's defence, it must be said that he did refer to the structural dimensions of collective violence explicitly in his accounts. In fact, his model sought to link up individual propensities for violent behaviour with larger material and political factors, which transform the aggressive potential of such individuals into definite forms of collective political violence.[13] In one of the most outstanding contributions to the dynamics of collective violence, Johan Galtung explained the mechanisms, which generated violence through their contribution of victimhood in the forms of repression (loss of freedom of various kinds including freedom of choice), misery (deprivation of basic human needs), and alienation (non-material deprivation leading to the loss of identity).[14]

Paul Wilkinson's seminal work on terrorism provided a useful classification of the phenomenon into revolutionary, sub-revolutionary and repressive terrorism, each with a set of distinguishing features. Revolutionary terrorism was defined as the use of systematic tactics of terrorist violence with the objective of bringing about a political revolution.[15] Its defining features included a group character, a revolutionary ideology as a justification of terror, the presence of effective leaders capable of collective mobilization and a certain demonstrated capacity for alternative institutionalization. The objectives of such terrorism need not end with successful capturing of political power; revolutionary terror might continue to be used against the enemies of the revolution and to consolidate the new regime. Sub-revolutionary terrorism, on the other hand, is a sporadic and indeterminate phenomenon in terms of strategies, targets and victims, employed for political purposes other than capturing state power or for repression of political opponents. Wilkinson's most significant contribution was to create the category of repressive terrorism which he defined as the systematic use of terrorist acts of violence for the purposes of suppressing, putting down, quelling or restraining certain groups, individuals or forms of behaviour deemed to be undesirable by the repressor.[16] Needless to say, Wilkinson's repressive terrorism takes care of the controversial issue of state terrorism, and thereby liberates the definition of terrorism as being necessarily anti-establishment and revolutionary. Yet, a closer look into the typology and the attributes suggested by Wilkinson reveals its most obvious shortcoming: there is hardly any specification identified by the author that renders terrorism distinct from other forms of collective political violence. In fact, Wilkinson's treatment blurs the distinction between terrorism and revolutionary violence, for he prepares an exhaustive genealogy of terrorism in terms of the received heritage of political philosophy on revolution itself.

The failure to define terrorism, whether in international law or in terms of political philosophy, is explained primarily by a deep and in pervasive moral dilemma underlying the phenomenon itself in relation to the state. In a way, the battle over definition of terrorism at heart is an ethical battle, which is not only about contrasting morality and immorality but also between the determining priority of moral worth of various forms of violence. Second, the standard understanding of terrorism as particular acts of violence committed in violation of accepted norms, rules, standards and legal principles of international diplomacy and warfare fails to provide a universally accepted, clear criterion and definition of the substance of terrorism both during war and peace. The difficulties of placing terrorism in relation to the practices of modern warfare and its laws tend to negate any conceptualization of the former as an unjust war model, although it is not quite certain what alternative conceptualization might better describe the phenomenon. To define terrorism by "acts" would make a terrorist of many "advanced" states if an objective and unbiased account of their past conduct in international affairs is put in a proper perspective. Indiscriminate killing of innocents and non-combatants is not an exclusive preserve of the terrorist; many states in the past engaged in and at present use repressive terror against their political opponents, and their record of public morality, when it comes to their dealings with adversaries, might put the record of many organised crime syndicates to shame. It is, nevertheless, clear that states are not yet prepared to countenance such a possibility or willing to factorize self-culpability as an essential ingredient of any working definition of international terrorism. Again, to define terrorism by motive is notoriously elusive, for it opens up a virtual Pandora's box. Not only is the issue of legitimate authority contextually problematic at times, the confrontation between a just cause espoused by the terrorist groups in defence of liberation and the counter claims of the legitimate public authority to constitute the only custodian of its 'subject's' liberty and well-being seems endemic. The only possible way out of this dilemma seems to deny terrorism the defence of a just cause; given the tradition of revolutionary political philosophy, this is and remains, an exceedingly difficult theoretical exercise, whose normative desirability, once again, is itself not beyond contestation.

II

Revolutionary Violence and Political Philosophy

This section primarily looks into the tradition of Western political philosophy to probe the relationship between politics and violence. This is deemed essential for two reasons. First, the first section of the essay has shown the definitional ambiguity of the idea of terrorism, which tends to imperceptibly glide into the notion of collective political violence and/or revolutionary violence. Second, the contemporary global mood against international terrorism has further reinforced the conflation of the term's original meaning into some thing far too wide, thereby implying that the use of any violence by some individuals and groups, regardless of any motivation whatsoever, is ethically impermissible and non-representative of the ideal of politics. In simple words, is violence necessarily antithetical to politics? How then are we to understand revolutions, where the use of violence might be a strategic or tactical imperative? Do we then close the issues of social transformation for ever, since it can be plausibly demonstrated or argued that radical social change, despite it infallible normative desirability, might be prevented by status quo-ist forces for the unrestrained perpetuation of their parochial self-interests and domination, thereby making violence inevitable? Understandably, it is not possible to engage with all dimensions of such basic issues within the limits of the present exercise. Instead of any lengthy and sustained treatment, we propose to examine the tracts of three influential philosophers of the previous millennium, whose contribution to the subject is not only recognized as seminal but is more relevant to the problems raised by the present essay itself.

We begin by drawing upon the work of Hannah Ardent, who distinguished clearly between the ideas of politics and violence, particularly in her celebrated essay *On Violence*.[17] According to Ardent's argument, politics deals with power, while violence is apolitical. Violence and politics cancel out each other: 'where the one rules absolutely, the other is Ardent's.[18] The contrast between violence and politics by the use of power, sounds strange and unfamiliar, primarily because Ardent's terminology builds upon continental philosophy as against the dominant Anglophone version which equates a policy of power with power politics qua realism. Ardent distinction rests on a contrast between *potentia (Vermogen) and potestas (Macht*). Roughly speaking, the contrast here is between power understood as ability and power thought as domination. Ardent uses the initial idea of power conceived as 'the human ability not just to act but to act in concert'.[19] For Ardent this ability is the key to politics, and she goes to the extent of using the term action as synonymous with political interaction, given the high degree of correspondence between power and ability. Power as ability is continuous and can enhance the capacity of a human being for a better and wholesome life. In sharp contrast, power as domination threatens to approximate to violence, and Ardent is emphatic in her cautious insistence of the inherent precariousness of a political regime premissed on the threat of violence alone. Violence is apolitical since it fragments and atomises individuality, whereas power (or ability) is both the condition and result of politics conceived as a mode of dialogic interaction of capacitious individuals. Ardent's central idea of interactive empowerment is sound. However, her political conservatism comes out in the open when she draws a harsh and unequivocal wedge between violence and politics, by denying any role of the former in the constitution of the latter.[20] This is perhaps best exemplified in her book *On Revolution*, where she, somewhat dubiously, compares a successful American with an unsuccessful French Revolution on the basis that the former, unlike the latter, was not compelled to engage with the violent demands of the poor. Significantly, Ardent's idea of politics seems to rule out any politics of the poor, for their demands, which inevitably enters into the political arena and gets quickly politicized, are non-negotiable, zero-sum demands of material means of existence, including the most basic demand for food. The non-negotiable nature of such demands denies their political character and turns them into apolitical or anti-political, thereby exposing itself to the real possibility of violence. The problems of such an understanding are self-evident. It drives the whole exercise towards embracing an impossible formulation that anything that is non-political must be violent. It is somewhat surprising to find Ardent making an extraordinary claim that it is completely futile and absurd to liberate mankind from the grip of poverty by political means. A part of such a bizarre conclusion stems from the author's inherent conservatism. But this is hardly a complete explanation. In fact, given the innumerable instances of Ardent's delicate espousal of a political and ethical sensibility of the highest order, it is highly debatable that her delinking of politics and poverty eradication followed from her innate aversion to welfare politics.[21] Ardent's liberalism cannot be equated with the hard liberalism of Hayek or Nozick. It is perhaps more meaningful to argue then, that her conclusion followed more from her harsh distinction of politics and violence, and less from any other normative consideration which she might have believed in. There is an unmistakable hint of Weber in Ardent's formulation. Both viewed violence instrumentally. But whereas Weber thought that a rational administration could reform a corrupt politics, and thereby redeem society of violence, Ardent categorically denied politics of any such capability. By definition, Ardent's understanding of politics decapitated itself to engage with any form of violence.

In sharp contrast to Ardent one finds in the writings of Franz Fanon a passionate and tragic justification of violence.[22] A victim of intense and tortuous pains of colonialism, Fanon looked upon violence as an indispensable component of his theory of liberation. Fanon has emphasized the cathartic or rejuvenating dimensions of violence throughout his writings. He described violence as rehabilitative and healing, and this followed naturally from Fanon's concern with health, both physical and mental. A doctor and a psychiatrist, he was sensitive to the fact that the social environment was often the primary hindrance to mental health, and if it is, one had to use violence if necessary to escape from it. The goal was not merely to save the individual; it was not less than remaking society into a healthy place for all to thrive mentally and physically.[23] Fanon understood that colonialism was not only a physical threat; it was above all an elusive but monstrous mental enemy, one that "poisoned" the colonial subjects with the 'toxic" of the colonial syndrome. He therefore wrote: "The independence of Algeria is not only the end of colonialism, but the disappearance, in this part of the world, of a gangrene germ and the source of an epidemic".[24]

Fanon's classic work in liberation theory offered a double critique: it was a virulent critique of both colonialism and its neo-colonial mutation. He was concerned with the theorization of mediation involved in the transition from colonialism to post-colonialism. His theorization of violence has to be located in this context. His answer is most uncomfortable to the liberal, Western psyche. His treatment cannot be appreciated unless the two significant aspects to his thought, one his existential-phenomenological humanism and the other the role of tragedy as a human signifier are properly accounted for.[25] He was deeply influenced by the whole tradition of anti-humanist European philosophers, particularly the works of Nietzsche, and the existential philosophy of Jean- Paul Sartre. In his dual theory of liberation, Fanon argued that the colonized, exploited subjects experience psychological liberation through the use of violence against the oppressor. This for Fanon is the indispensable first step towards social liberation, for without the catharsis of the self, there cannot be any meaningful transition to the higher level of action. Once psychologically catharcized, the helpless, exploited masses would settle into more organized modes of collective violence, which is indispensable for the creation of a new, liberated social order.[26] The tragic discourse in Fanon's prose saw violence as the very condition of liberation of the ideal of highest humanism. Tragedy is thus indispensable to Fanon's ideal of violence. In revolution or violence the human being tragically emerges out of a violent situation of "Gods" and the "downed". Violence is fundamentally the subjectification of an objective reality. Therefore, to deny subjectivity is to deny violence. It is when violence is associated with the innocent that there is victimization, and when linked to the guilty, retribution.[27] Fanon saw no possibility of equalizing matters short of violence. For, if the colonizer perceived the very idea of a post-colonial society as a violent condition (in the sense of his own displacement), his insistence for non-violence was nothing short of a strategy for colonialism, or its subtle mutation into neo-colonialism without a structural break.

A pivotal point, which Fanon brought out to the open concerned the notion of "death" –the eternal nothingness and the passive anonymity of countless deaths of the coloured and the oppressed stand in sharp contradistinction with the hallowed celebration of life of the white. Such is the enormity of their mutual distance in terms of recognition of worth, that while life is the natural metaphor for the Western, European oppressor, death is the normal fate of his innumerable other, the millions of colonized, oppressed individuals counting days in a nauseating slaughterhouse of abject dehumanization that ultimately bereft them of the ability to distinguish their anonymous existence from that of the array of other animals that sink each day with the belly of consumption, death and irrelevance.[28] While the death of a colonized, black man never unsettles the overdetermined silence of a nature-like existence, in times of trouble, security is monopolized for the white. Amidst countless coloured deaths, the loss of life of a single European can change the course of world politics by exploding the consciousness of the world. Fanon found such dehumanization contra-civilization and anti-liberation. In order to transform this unimaginably horrifying world, the oppressed must squarely face the reality. If the post-colonial, post-racist world is to emerge, it can only emerge through a long and violent battle culminating in the eventual submission of the colonizers and racists. For Fanon, the tragedy of a colonial and post-colonial society lies in the enormous price that all must pay for its complete transformation. Violence is the only weapon of the slave, if he is to immune against the reformist liberation (enslavement?) via his master's values.[29]

There is sufficient illustration of rehabilitation or even celebration of violence in the history of Western political philosophy, which refutes the Aristotelian-Hobbesian-Arendtian line of dismissing violence as apolitical. In fact, in the writings of Sartre, Fanon and George Bataille, in more recent times, violence was not only recognized as a justified method of political transformation, but was even redefined as a condition of politics. Sartre, for instance, bluntly claimed that violence could be a 'practical bond'.[30] In a more serious note, Sartre's major political and philosophical treatises endowed violence with enviable communicative and political resources. And in fact, Sartre, who influenced Fanon so markedly, formed his challenge to instrumental conceptions of politics by freely drawing upon a highly efflorescent passage of Hegelian thought. Hegel, in his personal life, did not support the cause of revolutionary violence. And yet, Hegel's treatment of the subject was far from being equivocal. In a section called "Absolute Freedom and Terror" of his *Phenomenology of Spirit,* Hegel exposited on the renovative capacities of violence in a political manner.[31] Either this is interpreted as meaning that politics becomes a perversion of violence in its ultimate project of human liberation; or this means that politics can, however fearsome this might seem, be sustained through terror. Whether one considers the redemptive role of violence as a method to correct unjust practices, or look for the sources, origins and sustenance of politics, there is little to escape the uncomfortable conclusion of the close, internal relationship between politics and violence. As the ontological distinction between instrumental and communicative modes of action does not coincide with the ethical distinction of (good) politics and (bad) violence, the uncomfortable implications of this non-coincidence would continue to disturb the more peaceful and pacific understanding of the said relationship.

III

Models of Terrorism and International Relations

Political violence and revolution are certainly not pariahs to political philosophy. Can the rehabilitation and justification of violence extend to the cause of terrorism? If the international community (on the debatable assumption that there is one) feels strongly that international terrorism, in all forms or manifestations, must be outlawed and collectively resisted, how are they to conceptualize it? In this brief final section, we look at certain alternative conceptualizations or modelling of terrorism and show why the phenomenon has proved so stubbornly intractable to academic analysis.

In simple terms, terrorism can be conceptualized as two distinct models.[32] The first of these Paul Gilbert describes as the unjust war model. According to this model terrorism is viewed as a method of war, which deliberately obliterates the conventional distinction of its victims into combatants and non-combatants. Terrorism is unjust because it deliberately or intentionally targets people who should not be targeted in any war. Terrorism is also dehumanizing for it withholds respect for the life of other fellow human beings. This model compares terrorism with warfare. Just war theory, the bedrock of modern legal practices regulating warfare, provides a set of rules, which make any war appear just. Terrorism is an unjust war model in as much as it indicates serious departures from those accepted norms and rules, thereby making the activities terrorist. Just war theory has two components - namely, enumeration of conditions, which make recourse to war "just"; and specifying what kind or degree of violence is tolerable under such circumstances. Just war theory, however, is inconsistent. Its incoherence inheres in two opposite tendencies originating from the doctrine. One tendency justifies action in self-defence, the other, and the more aggressive tendency, advocates punitive action. Terrorism is found to accord to the unjust war model not because it lacks a just cause, but due to its advocacy of indiscriminate and unlawful violence against unspecified targets.[33]

This characterization becomes problematic given the death of innumerable innocent men, women and children even during a "just" war. Moreover, the punitive version of the just war theory demands target fixation by the source of injustice of the aggressor. Injustice, however, does not necessarily result only from overt aggression. Therefore, it is quite plausible that many individuals might be legally targeted in a war if their association with the guilt can be established, even when they did not actively take part in military operation. Targets, in brief, are not coterminous with those who pose a direct military threat; targets extend to all those who planned and helped organize the injustice in question. In both cases, the result is to broaden the list of legitimate targets to include even those who did not directly take part in military activities. Now if this is justified in the case of war why is this defense not available to terrorism? Why criticize terrorism for its use of indiscriminate violence, when war can be shown to be equally, if not more, extensive in its choice of targets? The simple argument is that "if the parallel between war and terrorism is to hold, terrorism must be provided with some legitimate "targets" as is the case with a just war. To deny this is to logically refute the description of terrorism as a possible war model.[34]

The crime model of terrorism denies the parallelism between war and terrorism from the very outset.[35] It equates terrorism with ordinary criminality. It defines terrorism as the use of violence for political ends by "unauthorized, non-governmental actors" in breach of accepted codes of behaviour regulating the life of a society or a community.

The notion of violence employed here is evidently criminal in the sense that it involves commission of crimes contrary to the existing laws against murder, kidnapping, etc. The crime model describes terrorist acts as criminal rather than political offences, and demands appropriate persecution of such actions. To make the model operational, it is needed to contrast crimes for the commission of which some political motivation is essential, and crimes, which are independent of such a motive. The crime model therefore has to locate the criminal character of a terrorist act outside the structure of political motivation.[36] In effect, two things are involved in this exercise. The first is to distinguish terrorism from recognized political crimes (such as treason) and ordinary acts of criminality (like murder) and treat terrorist acts as instances of the latter. Second, and more significantly, the crime model can become functional provided it negates the application of arguments upholding the political justification of terrorist acts. Justification is negated simply by arguing that terrorism is not a political crime, and further by emphasizing that criminality has to be judged by intention and not by motive.

The problem with the crime model is that it fails to persuasively argue why terrorism cannot be treated as illustrative of political crime. If one has to describe terrorist attacks by victims, the distinction between terrorism (as ordinary criminality) and political crime seems to break down. The matter is further compounded by the fact that motives of terrorism often do not look very different from those of the war – to deprive a government control ever some particular territory on the ground of illegitimacy, unlawful occupation, repression and exploitation, or a combination of all. The predicament is exposed by three other considerations. First, in liberal democracies, at least, anti or counter terrorist measures must evolve strictly in conformity with the established legal codes. If excessive force is used, the methodological distinction between terrorism and counter-terrorism in the context of a democratic political order might collapse.[37] Secondly, the state might deny terrorism the status of political crime, but its response might be self-defeating. States often recognize that they need to militarily engage terrorists who might seek to dislodge them from power through insurrectionary attempts. As the state veers towards a military response from a conventional constabulary one, it unconsciously brings in the considerations and standards of war in its own dealings with the terrorists. Finally, the state's terminology of accusation against terrorist violence claims the victims of the latter as innocent. Once again, the point is not that these victims are "not" innocent. The point is that to argue in this manner is to countenance the possibility of distinguishing victims into innocent and something else, which in turn, imputes a war-like motivation on part of the terrorists and this, paradoxically enough, is recognized by the state in order to reinforce its own case of following accepted codes of behaviour within a legitimate political system.[38]

The argument advanced here is that the central moral issue raised by terrorism cannot be non-combatant immunity. B. T. Wilkins, for example, has argued: "Perhaps the main obstacle to any agreement that terrorism may in some circumstances be morally justifiable lies in claim that it involves the violation of the right of the *innocent persons*" (My emphasis).[39] Yet, to regard terrorism in this way is to make an enormous moral concession, since it necessarily involves the extension of the distinction made originally in war between combatants and non-combatants to terrorism itself. Not only do terrorists affirm their right to wage war to elevate their acts of killing from the unlawful category of criminal acts into the lawful category of acts of war, even the custodians of rule of law and authority often acknowledge, at least implicitly, the terrorist's possession of the right to war and therefore the uncriminal character of their activity.

The criterion of legitimate authority can hardly salvage the situation, given the difficulty of establishing who constitutes legitimate authority in conditions of civil strife or political conflict involving many contending groups. Moreover, the equation of legitimate public authority and a just cause is unwarranted, and often proper authority might apply to both sides of a civil conflict as in the case of an external war between two states. Moreover, in conditions of civil conflict, the determination of legitimate public authority in association with a proper representation of community interests is also exceedingly difficult. In cases of intractable civil strife, which party properly represents the community can hardly be established, as their definition of what the concerned community that they propose to represent is non-identical. Even in cases, where groups converge on their understanding of the community they serve, the issue is complicated as one has to guard against the possibility of mixing up which of the group has the authority to represent the community from the one having the support of people.[40] Most crucially, the criterion of legitimate public authority is most unserviceable in cases of state terrorism, even in the context of democratic states. The formal test of legitimacy in a procedural democracy has a simple enough threshold, which is not difficult to satisfy in most cases. Once public choice freely constitutes the government, the actions of the public authority will be legitimate to the extent of conforming to constitutional rules. Despite this formal stipulation, which is not very difficult to satisfy, democratic states have been in the past, and continue to be at present, ruthless in their denial of any concession to their political opponents. In conditions of contested authority, the fact that a public authority is democratic can hardly satisfy the test of legitimacy in its dealings with its contenders.

Despite such difficulties, the issue of terrorism has to be addressed primarily through the criterion of legitimacy. An objective analysis of the rise of terrorism throughout the world reveals that the phenomenon has grown inevitably in conditions of relative deprivation, unjust domination and relentless exploitation of the weak and the voiceless people by the strong and the resourceful ones. West Asian terrorism grew out of the womb of the Israel-Palestinian conflict and the historical bias of the United States to underwrite Israel's security with scant regard to the legitimate demand for independent statehood by the Palestinians; the strategic and political stranglehold of the United States in the Middle East to guarantee an unrestrained flow of oil to itself and to West Europe coupled with its iron determination to resist any radicalization of these backward societies through mass political mobilization; the failure of the Islamic societies to imbibe modern cultural values even while embracing modern science and its technical artifacts; the peril of an uncompromisingly conservative strand of Islam in the face of globalization of Western cultural forms; the pent-up dissatisfaction of the Arab masses given the ruthless denial by the political elite of any meaningful democratization of political power; the paradoxical situation of affluence in a condition of cultural void; and the steady growth of a fundamentalist, belligerent and non-liberal political Islam as a guiding force of a decadent social mosaic. All these have turned Islamic terrorism into a potent force of an enormous destructive potential.

It is a truism to suggest that the West, in general, and the United States in particular, cannot claim immunity from being responsible in a large way in creating a Frankenstein for themselves. The threat emanating from Islamic terrorism became global, given the international spread of the faith, and the historical centrality of ortho-praxis therein. And yet, as the analyses of radical humanists / socialists such as Noam Chomsky and Edward Said have shown, the terrorism of the Islamic fundamentalists and the domination of the United States are mutually constitutive of each other. Unless the dominant powers recognize this, their collective crusade against global terrorism might, temporarily at least, make their societies safe against terrorist violence, without making the others secured against the threat of Western military, political, economic and cultural dominance which is at the source of many forms of terrorism operating against Western interests. The West might mitigate the symptoms successfully; but in order to target the disease they need to face up to the charge of a legitimacy deficit in their external conduct across the world. Unless they agree to do this, the world will not be safe from the scourge of terrorist violence.

(The funding of this research came from UGC-DSA programme (phase-III) of the Department of International Relations, Jadavpur University)

Notes

1. Some of the important Conventions, Declarations and Protocols adopted by the United Nations to combat terrorism include, Convention for the Suppression of Unlawful Seizure of Aircraft, Hague, 16, December 1970; Convention for the Suppression of Unlawful Acts against the Safety of Civil Aviation, Montreal, 23 September 1971; Convention on the Prevention and Punishment of Crimes against Internationally Protected Persons, including Diplomatic Agents, adopted by the General Assembly of the United Nations on 14 December 1973; International Convention against the Taking of Hostages, adopted by the General Assembly of the United Nations on 17 December 1979; Protocol for the Suppression of Unlawful Acts of Violence at Airports Serving International Civil Aviation, Supplementary to the Convention for the Suppression of Unlawful Acts against the Safety of Civil Aviation, Montreal, 24 February 1988; Convention for the Suppression of Unlawful Acts against the Safety of Maritime Navigation, Rome, March 10, 1988; Protocol for the Suppression of Unlawful Acts against Safety of Fixed Platforms located on the Continental Shelf, Rome, 10 March 1988; International Convention for the Suppression of Terrorist Bombings, adopted by the General Assembly on 15 December 1997; International Conference for the Suppression of Financing of Terrorism, adopted the United Nations General Assembly in Resolution 54/109 of 9 December 1999; and the Declaration on Measures to Eliminate International Terrorism, adopted under the General

Assembly Resolution 49/60, 1995. Apart from many such efforts, there are countless measures undertaken by individual states. Perhaps, it is most appropriate to look into the resolution adopted by the General Assembly of the United Nations on the report of the Sixth Committee:

i) Strongly condemns all acts, methods and practices of terrorism as criminal and unjustifiable, wherever and by whosoever committed;

ii) Reiterates that criminal acts intended or calculated to provoke a state of terror in the general public, a group of persons or particular persons for political purposes are in any circumstances unjustifiable, whatever the considerations of any political, philosophical, ideological, racial, ethnic, religious or other nature that may be invoked to justify them;

iii) Reiterates its call upon all states to adopt further measures in accordance with the Charter of the United Nations and the relevant provisions of international law, including international standards of human rights, to prevent terrorism and to strengthen international cooperation in combating terrorism and, to that end, to consider in particular the implementation of the measures set out in paragraph 3(a) level to eliminate international terrorism.

2. L. Oppenheim, *International Law: A Treatise*, vol.II (London: Longmans, Green & Co., 1952), p.204.

3. Tim Hillier, *Sourcebook on Public International Law* (London: Covendish Publishing Limited, 1988), p.625.

4. For a detailed treatment of the subject, see L. C. Green,

The Contemporary Law of Armed Conflict, (Manchester: Manchester University Press, 1993), pp.63-66.

5. Thomas M. Franck and Bert B. Lockwood, Jr., "Preliminary Thoughts Towards An International Convention on Terrorism", *American Journal of International Law*, vol. 68, no.1, January 1974, pp.72-82.

6. *Ibid.*, p.74.

7. *Ibid.*, p.78.

8. Article 2(1) of the Draft Articles of the International Law Commission for the protection of diplomats recognises the element of intentionality but not of motive, while speaking of the "intentional commission, regardless of motive..." The commentary explained that "(w)hile criminal intent is regarded as an essential element of the crimes covered by Article 2, the expression 'regardless of motive' restates the universally accepted legal principle that it is the intent to commit the act and not the reasons that led to its commission that is the governing factor". See *ibid.*, pp.78-79.

9. For standard theoretical expositions on terrorism, see Grant Wardlaw, *Political Terrorism: Theory, Tactics, Counter-Measures* (Cambridge: Cambridge University Press, 1989); David E. Long, *The Anatomy of Terrorism* (New York: The Free Press, 1990); Paul Gilbert, *Terrorism, Security and Nationality: An Introductory Study in Applied Political Philosophy* (London: Routledge, 1994); Lawrence Z. Freedman and Yonah Alexander, (eds.), *Perspectives on Terrorism* (New Delhi: Hindustan Publishing Corporation, 1985); Michael Stohl (ed.) *The Politics of Terrorism* (New York: Marcel Dekkar Inc,

1985); Paul Wilkinson, *Terrorism and the Liberal State* (London: MacMillan, 1986); and B. T. Wilkins, *Terrorism and Collective Responsibility* (London: Routledge, 1992). For an excellent introduction on the problems of definition of terrorism, see Anindya Batabyal, *Studies in Terrorism-I,* Occasional Paper, no.2, UGC-DSA Programme, Department of International Relations, Jadavpur University, January 2002, pp.1-21.

10. Lawrence Zelik Freedman, "Terrorism: Problems of the Polistraxic" in Freedman and Yonah (ed), *ibid.*, pp.3-12.

11. *Ibid.*, pp.4 -5.

12. Robert Ted Gurr, "Some Characteristics of Political Terrorism in the 1960s", in Stohl, (ed.), no., pp.31-33.

13. For details, see Robert Ted Gurr, *Why Men Rebel* (Princeton: Princeton University Press, 1970).

14. Johan Galtung, *Transarmament and the Cold War: Peace Research and the Peace Movement* (Copenhagen: Christian Ejlers, 1988)

15. Batabyal, n.9, p.4. For details, see Paul Wilkinson, *Political Terrorism* (London: MacMillan, 1974), pp. 36-40.

16. *Ibid.*, p.5.

17. Hannah Ardent, "On Violence", in Hannah Ardent, *Crisis of the Republic* (Harmondsworth: Penguin Books, 1973).

18. *Ibid.*, p.123.

19. *Ibid.*, p.113.

20. Richard Gunn, "Politics and Violence", in Richard Bellamy (ed.), *Theories and Concepts of Politics* (Manchester: Manchester University Press, 1993), p.267.

21. *Ibid.*, p.268.

22. Franz Fanon's major works include, *A Dying Colonialism*, translated by Haakon Chevalier (New York: Monthly Review Press, 1965); *The Wretched of the Earth* (London: MacGibbon and Kee, 1965); *Black Skin, White Masks*, translated by Charles Lam Markmann (New York: Grove Press, 1967); *Toward the African Revolution*, translated by Haakon Chevalier (New York: Monthly Review Press, 1967/68).

23. Gail M. Presby, "Fanon on the Role of Violence in Liberation: A Comparison with Gandhi and Mandela", in Lewis R. Gordon, T. Denean Sharpley-Whiting and Renee T. White, (eds), *Fanon: A Critical Reader* (Cambridge: Blackwell Publishers, 1996), p.284.

24. Fanon, *Towards the African Revolution*, n.22, p.64.

25. Lewis R. Gordon, "Fanon's Tragic Revolutionary Violence", in Gordon (eds), n.23, p.298.

26. *Ibid.*, pp.298-299.

27. *Ibid.*, p.304.

28. *Ibid.*, p.303.

29. *Ibid.*, p.305.

30. Jean-Paul Sartre, *Critique of Dialectical Reason* (London: New Left Books, 1976), as quoted by Gunn, n.20, p.283.

31. *Ibid.*, p.285.

32. This is suggested by Paul Gilbert. He develops two comparisons of terrorism with unjust war and political crime respectively. For details, see Gilbert, n.9

33. *Ibid.*, pp.7-10.

34. *Ibid.*, pp.11-13.

35. *Ibid.*, pp.47-51.

36. *Ibid.*, p.49.

37. *Ibid.*, pp.50-51.

38. *Ibid.*, p.50.

39. Wilkins, n.9, p.65.

40. Gilbert, n.9, pp.31-32.

Section-II: Terrorism and Violence : New Trends

New Trends in Terrorism and Violence : Pakistan-Taliban-Al Qaeda

T. Sreedhar

The Pakistan Taliban-Al Qaeda phenomenon has considerably altered the face of terrorism and violence. What was considered as a hypothetical scenario in the 1980s and early 1990s, like nuclear terrorism, became a reality. In addition, the organized manner in which they have conducted their recruitment of cadres and the networking done with similar outfits in 60 countries, show terrorism will not be the same in the coming years. This paper highlights some of these new trends.

The Pakistan- Taliban- Al Qaeda phenomenon that started in 1994 has brought in seven new dimensions to the politics of global terrorism during the last seven years. To understand these new dimensions, a quick survey of Taliban's birth and growth needs to be taken. After the Soviet withdrawal from Afghanistan, the task of rebuilding the war-ravaged country was handed over to Pakistan, a close ally of the US during its proxy war with the Soviet Union. For its own strategic reasons, Pakistan wanted an amenable government in Kabul. It tried various permutations and combinations with the existing leadership among the Afghan refugees turned (holy warrior), but could not succeed. Finally, in early 1994, the then home minister of Pakistan came to the conclusion that there is a need to create an independent entity away from the traditional leadership of the Afghan polity.[1] By the time the Pakistani ruling elite came to this conclusion, its own polity was cracking up due to four and a half decades of mismanagement. Therefore, Pakistan going through the process of a failing state, began looking for shorter routes to achieve its own strategic objectives. These included strategic depth against India in the event of an Indo-Pak war, and resolving the vexed issue of the Durand Line with Afghanistan. These apart, an interesting dimension to the Pakistan-Taliban relationship was put forward by Musa Khan Jalalzai, an Afghan journalist based in Peshawar North-West Frontier Province I (NWFP). According to him:

> "...their (Pakistan's) goal was at once ideological and economic. Some (Pakistan armed forces) set their sights on detaching Central Asian Republics from the CIS, which they hoped would lead to disintegration of the Russian Federation itself and the emergence of a new space dominated by conservative Islamic regimes. From this point of view, the return to power of the neo-communists in Dushanbe was a reversal for Islamabad, hence its support, through Afghanistan, for the Tajik rebels."[2]

On the economic level, Pakistan sought to make itself the Central Asian Republic's main route of access to the Indian Ocean. It, therefore, launched a huge roadway construction programme in the summer of 1993, which was to link Karachi and the ports of the Indian Ocean with Central Asia via Peshawar and Afghanistan. According to Musa Khan Jalalzai, Maj. Gen. Naserullah Babar, interior minister in Benazir Bhutto's government, thought of two routes for Central Asia. 'If the route from Peshawar through Kabul and the Salang Highway to Tashkent was blocked by war in Kabul, Pakistan should seek to open the western route, from Quetta through Kandahar and Herat to Turkmenistan.[3]

If this objective of Pakistan is correct, it is operating on the assumption that having defeated the Red Army of the Soviet Union once, it is not difficult to defeat the disintegrated Soviet Union's armed forces guarding the Central Asian Republics again. This also raises the question as to whether Pakistan is planning to convert its Taliban forces into a jihadi Islamic army. One can notice a particular pattern to this effect in the Pakistan- Taliban-Al Qaeda combine actions.

After giving support to the Tajik rebels, the Pakistan-Taliban-Al Qaeda combine target has been Uzbekistan. The leadership of the Islamic Movement of Uzbekistan (IMU) attempted to assassinate Uzbek President Islam. A. Karimov in February 1999, when six bombs in Tashkent killed 16 people and wounded 128. The leader of the IMU, Tahir Yoldassev, then fled to the Taliban-controlled Afghanistan. In May 1999, the Taliban allowed Yoldassev to set up military training camps in northern Afghanistan, just a few miles off the Afghan-Uzbek border. Unconfirmed media reports say that he was training several hundred Islamic militants from Uzbekistan, Tajikistan and Kyrghyzstan, as well as Uighurs from the Xinjiang Autonomous Region in China. Initially, the Taliban denied having extended any help to the IMU. But in June 1999, when the Uzbek government requested the extradition of Tahir to Tashkent, it was rejected by the Taliban.

In August 1999, another IMU leader, Juma Nanangani, entered southern Kyrghyzstan with about 800 militants, seized villages and threatened to invade Uzbekistan. All this resulted in Uzbekistan severely condemning Pakistan for supporting the dissident movements in Uzbekistan.

According to Ahmed Rashid, what brought in a new dimension was that:

> "...although the IMU are not Deobandis, they are influenced by Wahhabism and have tried to impose the Taliban code in their areas of influence. Although the Uzbeks have historically been suspicious of the Pushtulfs, the Taliban offer IMU a sanctuary from the Karimov crackdown with weapons, and the means to finance themselves through the drug trade."[4]

With these objectives in mind, Pakistan became a guiding spirit and mentor of the Taliban till about mid-1996. The arrival of Osama bin Laden in May 1996 to Kandahar, and his assuming the leadership of the Taliban transformed Pakistan's role from that of a guardian to a partner of the Taliban outfit. By 1998, Taliban became synonymous with bin Laden's Al Qaeda movement and Pakistani soldiers began participating in Taliban-AI Qaeda activities. From 1996 onwards, the Taliban became a pressure point for Pakistan to pursue its foreign policy objectives in its immediate neighbourhood.

Providing Legitimacy

The fall-out of this extraordinary policy towards terrorism and a terrorist outfit like the Taliban resulted in their achieving a certain amount of legitimacy and recognition. Pak-Afghan's smaller neighbours in Central Asia even opened channels of communication on the assumption that Pakistan- Taliban-AI Qaeda are a combination created by the Great Powers. The arrival of Osama bin Laden, first in the 1980s and later in May 1996 to Afghanistan, was seen as a tacit approval of the custodian of the Holy Shrines of Islam, Saudi Arabia. The recognition of Taliban the government in May 1997 by Pakistan, Saudi Arabia and the UAE further reinforced their perception. Till 10 September 2001 Saudi Arabia never passed a judgment on Osama's activities, and though the US accused Ohim as a prime suspect in the al-Khobar attacks, Saudi. Arabian law-enforcing agencies exonerated him. In addition, countries like Turkey and China, two close allies of Pakistan, even started providing economic aid to the Pakistan-Taliban-AI Qaeda combine. China went a step further. It purchased unexploded Cruise missiles, fired by the US on Khost terrorist training camps of Al Qaeda in August 1998, from Taliban.

Only three explanations can be given for this extraordinary behaviour of nation- states in the south-west and Central Asia. First, some states found in the Pakistan Taliban-AI Qaeda combine a convenient conduit for pursuing their own agenda. Second, most of the nation-states in the vicinity and in the Islamic world felt ideologically drawn to the Pakistan-Taliban-Al Qaeda's philosophy. Finally, some small neighbours lacking resources to confront this nexus, subtly accepted its existence.

Networking with Other Organizations

The Pakistan- Taliban-AI Qaeda combine, for the first time indulged in extensive networking with similar organizations across the globe. In the past, terrorist organizations networking have been limited to within the country or, at best, with their ethnic groups living abroad. The Liberation Tigers of Tamil Eelam (LTTE) and the Palestine Liberation Organization (PLO) in its 1960/1970s incarnations are two examples. According to various assessments, the Pakistan-Taliban-AI Qaeda combine spread its network over 60 countries in four continents. This networking is made possible due to poor law and order enforcing machinery in some countries, while others states have blatantly collaborated for a number of reasons (ideological, financial considerations, etc.) with the Pakistan-Taliban-Al Qaeda and have allowed them to prosper.

This networking has resulted in organized gangs that have emerged in the name of a particular faith, and have manifested themselves through acts of terror and violence. The IMU that operated in the Central Asian Republics is one example. A close scrutiny of the network reveals three basic characteristics of the countries where this networking has succeeded: These countries are underdeveloped; have many social inequalities and have dissident movements against the ruling governments. Such movements have surfaced repeatedly in the Central Asian Republics and Philippines and, have found favour with a section of the local population. As the current Afghan war has shown, there is a certain amount of solidarity among these networked organizations. For instance, the Arab cadres would go to Central Asia to fight along with IMU cadres for the latter's cause.

Interestingly, countries like Pakistan, and to a lesser extent China, have started using these terrorist organizations as pressure points to achieve their foreign policy objectives. Every one in the Afghanistan neighbourhood was hesitant to address these organizations as terrorist outfits. Some countries like China have even started doing business with them and are offering economic aid to maintain good relations. Doubts arise from the peculiar Chinese behaviour from 1998 onwards, causing one to wonder whether the

Taliban was created by one of its closet allies Pakistan, or whether there was a Sino-Pak collusion. This extraordinary behaviour of China—one of the permanent members of the UN Security Council—with a terrorist organization surprised every nation-state in south and south-west Asia.[5] Apparently, this must have resulted in many others perceiving the Pakistan-Taliban-Al Qaeda combine as part of a greater game played by the great powers.

This indeed is a unique situation, where the Pakistan-Taliban-Al Qaeda combine is being patronized by one of the permanent members of the Security Council. The question that arises is what punitive action should be taken against this act? This cannot be brushed aside by saying that the Chinese were trying to reform the Pakistan-Taliban-AI Qaeda combine.

Systematic Recruitment of Cadres

Unlike in the past, with other terrorist organizations, the Pakistan- Taliban-Al Qaeda combine started a phased programme for new recruits for their organization. When the "volunteers" are spotted, they are first given indoctrination in the ideology. If the recruit is too young, about 6-7 years, he is asked to spend some years in a "seminary" studying under the close supervision of senior cadres. A chain of "seminaries" were established both in Pakistan and Afghanistan, (estimated to be around 4,000), with a curriculum so as to give it a semblance of an institution of learning. This has resulted in places of worship and institutions of learning emerging as the focal points of terrorist recruitment and training in countries like Pakistan. The physically fit are picked up for weapon training ranging from two to 12 weeks. They are then slowly inducted into battle training under the supervision and guidance of seniors. Those physically not so fit are used for running errands and working as porters, guides and so on.

All of them receive remuneration from the organization to which they are affiliated. In fact, if they are killed in action, the families are paid money for the "sacrifice" made by their family member. Interestingly, to make the work more attractive, these terrorists are called Mujahideen, and their acts of terrorism and violence were described as part of a jihad (holy war). The impressionable young minds get affected and even children/youth from affluent families have begun joining these organizations. The best example is that of the "Saudi-nationals" who participated in the attacks on the World Trade Centre and the Pentagon on 11 September 2001. They all came from affluent families and were a well-educated lot too.

This institutionalized training of terrorists has few parallels in the contemporary history of terrorism.

Regular Armed Forces Supporting Terrorists

Along with this regular recruitment, Pakistani military personnel have also been involved in the Pakistan- Taliban- AI Qaeda combine. According to the anti- Taliban forces estimates, at least a brigade level force (4000-5000 men) of the Pakistani army worked with the Pakistan-Taliban-Al Qaeda. Whether these military personnel were hired by the Pakistan- Taliban-AI Qaeda combine, or whether they joined voluntarily or were assigned by Pakistan is not completely clear as yet. From the data available it appears that the last factor resulted in this development. The involvement of these Pakistani military personnel included training of the

Pakistan-Taliban-AI Qaeda cadres, extending diplomatic support to them and facilitating their financial activities. They even provided logistic support to the Taliban campaigns to occupy places like Kabul and Mazar-e-Sharif.[6]

This is the first time that the armed forces of a nation-state have become part of a terrorist outfit, and have provided a direct or indirect support in the activities of the outfit. If the regular armies get converted into terrorist organizations or collaborate with them, then the attack on the WTC or the Pentagon can become a common occurrence.

Ethnic Cleansing as an Instrument of Consolidation

The Pakistan- Taliban-Al Qaeda combine has also introduced two new variables to terrorism and violence. They have started ethnically cleansing the society. The best example is the killings of non-Pushtun people in the Bamiyan province in January 2001. One possible explanation for this brutal behaviour could be that the Taliban had planned to rule a nation of ethnic homogeneity. At different points of time they seem to have debated and come to the conclusion that people who oppose their regime have no place to stay within the territorial limits of Afghanistan; and since the majority of the people opposing them are non-Pushtuns, they can be physically eliminated. Other ethnic/religious groups who accept their dictates can be allowed to live separately, but as second-class citizens. One of the *fatwas* (ruling) issued by the Taliban said that Hindus living in Afghanistan must wear yellow badges to identify themselves as non-Muslims.[7]

In the same breath, the Taliban-Al Qaeda decided to dispense with the pre- Islamic history of Afghanistan. The destruction of the Bamiyan Buddhas in March 2001 is one example. Similarly, artifacts belonging to the pre-Islamic period in the Kabul National Museum were dumped in a basement to deny any links with the pre- Islamic Afghan history. According to some commentators, the Taliban sold the artifacts in the international market. Some have argued that the Taliban has resorted to this unprecedented action since idol worship is against the basic tenets of Islam. But most of the learned men of the Islamic theology felt that the destruction of pre- Islamic relics was not ordained in Islam.[8]

Whatever be the motives of the Taliban-Al Qaeda, they, in the name of achieving religious homogeneity, have indulged in vandalism unparalleled in history.

Partnership/Liasion with Narcotics Mafia

Another new trend introduced by the Pakistan-Taliban-Al Qaeda combine in global terrorism is the close nexus they have developed with the narcotic mafia. Though, this is not a new phenomenon among the terrorist groups operating in various parts of the world, it was always a subtle and low-key operation. The Taliban, however, have openly cultivated poppy and have used the income generated from poppy cultivation as the principle source of revenue by the state to maintain a subsistence level economy in Afghanistan.

The UN Drug Control Programme (UNDCP) estimates that in 1999 opium production in Afghanistan reached an all time high of 4,600 metric tones (MT). This is more than double the estimated production of 2,100 MT in 1998. The UNDCP also estimated that poppy cultivation has increased from 64,000 hectares in 1998 to 91,000 hectares in 1999, and 97 per cent of the cultivation has occurred in Taliban-controlled areas.

Table-1: Opium Production in Afghanistan (1995-99)

Year	Opium Gum (MT)
1995	1,230
1996	1,230
1997	1,265
1998	2,100
1999	4,600

As can be seen from Table 1, opium production has registered a continuous increase in Afghanistan after the arrival of the Pakistan-Taliban-Al Qaeda combine, and has continued to do so till 1999. In 2000, poppy cultivation was reduced not because of any change of heart by the Taliban but due to earlier years of excess production bringing down the international prices in narcotics. In the process, the entire neighbourhood of Afghanistan, being under-developed economies and neglected by the international community, readily accepted the income from the narcotic trade. In other words, it is more of a supply and demand in narcotics and less of an international condemnation that resulted in reducing the area under the poppy cultivation by the Taliban. This also shows that the Pakistan-Taliban-Al Qaeda has acquired a near monopoly of the world narcotics market.

What is alarming is that the narcotics money has been liberally used to acquire arms and ammunition from the grey international arms bazar.

Acquiring Weapons of Mass Destruction

For the past decade or so, the international nuclear nonproliferation lobby has talked in terms of hypothetical cases of terrorist outfits laying their hands on nuclear weapons. The available evidence has shown that the Pakistan- Taliban-AI Qaeda have not only thought in terms of acquiring nuclear weapons devices but have also put it into action. They have used their money power to buy nuclear weapon casings from a former Soviet Republic. Their creator and mentor, Pakistan, is suspected to have provided nuclear laboratories like A.Q. Khan Research Laboratories in Kahuta to reprocess uranium to the weapon grade level. The trained nuclear scientists from the Pakistani nuclear establishment, in the name of serving the cause of Islamic jihad, have started providing the necessary expertise.[9]

If they had a little more time, the Pakistan- Taliban-AI Qaeda left to themselves, would have acquired nuclear weapons. In fact, the ruthlessness with which they have dealt with their opponents, prompts one to conclude that they were not acquiring nukes as a deterrence, but to use them in order to achieve their political objectives. They would not have hesitated to use them against say, the US, Israel, Iran or even against India.

The Pakistan- Taliban-AI Qaeda have demonstrated that given adequate resources they can acquire nuclear weapons and other weapons of mass destruction, and make nuclear terrorism a reality.

How to dismantle this elaborate network is going to be an immediate problem. Two decades of their existence, first as Mujahideen fighting the Red Army and later as an organized force, has created a number of vested interests in a number of countries. How to bring back the young minds indoctrinated by the madrassas to the normal educational system are some of the questions that need to be addressed by the international community. The response of the Islamic countries to the 11 September incidents makes it abundantly clear that the ruling elites in these countries are afraid of a backlash in case they are too harsh on them. Their emphasis on "caution and restraint" by the US in dealing with the Taliban-AI Qaeda shows the extent they are willing to go to.

Against this backdrop, the next question that arises is what do we do with nations that have supported the Taliban-Al Qaeda? The culprits are far too many. To begin with, Pakistan and a several other states involved in creating Taliban-Al Qaeda. It is not possible to declare all of them as "rogue" states. One possible way could be to bring those responsible for the creation of the Taliban and Al Qaeda to trial in the International Court of Justice. For instance, the Inter Services Intelligence (ISI) agency of the Pakistani armed forces along with former interior minister, Naserullah Babar, should be made to stand trial along with the Taliban's supremo, Mullah Umar and Al Qaeda founder Osama bin Laden. This is certainly not an easy thing to do, given the fact that there are a number of countries (including Pakistan) who have found in the Taliban- Al Qaeda a useful instrument for pursuing their interests.

India: Tackling Terrorism

After 11 September, a section of the Indian intelligentsia began a debate on the country's response to terrorism and violence. Like the US attacked Taliban-Al Qaeda camps and hideouts in Afghanistan, India should attack terrorist hideouts in Pakistan-occupied Kashmir and if necessary, Pakistan itself. The Indian Air Force has the range and capabilities to undertake such a mission if the political leadership wants it. But is this the correct approach?

India started experiencing terrorism and violence, sponsored across its borders, from 1947 itself. First, it was Pakistan in Jammu and Kashmir and, later, it was China in the north-east. International security managers called them insurgency movements and proxy wars or low intensity conflicts. The security managers looked at these developments through the spectrum of desalinization and the ideological framework of the Cold War. In fact, they were doing similar things in some of their former colonies.

Since unity in diversity and pluralism are the ideological cornerstones of the Indian Republic, as long as territorial integrity was not affected any amount of dissent was accommodated. The government made periodical assessments and deployed the security forces not to allow any untoward development, which could disturb the social order. Whether it was Mizoram or Nagaland or Manipur in the 1960s and the 1970s or Punjab in the 1980s, force was used but to a limited extent.

The 11 September attacks are unfortunate and should be condemned strongly. Strangely enough, the people who executed the 11 September incidents and their ideologues were hailed as "holy warriors" less than 15 years ago by the US.

Equally strange is that five years before 11 September, the US was hobnobbing with the ideologues of those responsible for 11 September and advising countries such as India to recognize them and do business with them. In the Indian context, terrorism and violence prior to or post-11 September are not different. The terrorists killed in Jammu and Kashmir by the Indian security forces include people from Sudan, Iraq, Palestine, Yemen, China and Pakistan. The indigenous involvement in terrorism, which was at its peak in the early 1990s, came down drastically by the late 1990s. According to various Kashmir watchers, now terrorism is being sustained by mercenaries and diehard followers of Osama bin Laden and the Taliban with sanctuaries in Pakistan. The empirical evidence collected about the suicidal attacks from 1990 to 2001 in India shows that only in one incident was a local involved and the rest were all mercenaries.

Much before the US realized that regimes such as the Taliban were a threat to any civil society, India refused to do any serious business with them. In fact, India was trying to sensitize the international security managers to the dangers of such regimes and their mentors. Interestingly, not a single Indian is reported to have been involved with the Taliban-Al Qaeda network.

The US security apparatus, with its state-of-the-art technology, could not save the Pentagon from being attacked on 11 September. On 13 December 2001, a group of terrorists from Pakistan attacked India's Parliament, ultimate symbol of the Indian Republic. The republic mobilized its armed forces to convey to Pakistan and its supporters that it meant business. This deterrence worked.

Where do we go from here? In spite of a sustained campaign from a section of the intelligentsia, the Indian Republic refused to internationalize the terrorism issue like the US and Israel are doing. After the US President's statement that he was fighting a "crusade" in September 2001, India's political leadership quietly distanced itself from the US-led coalition's war against terrorism.

Since then, the Indian participation has been restricted to sharing of intelligence and other related activities with the US within the overall framework of improving bilateral relations. Otherwise, the political leadership has repeatedly emphasized that India has to fight its own battle against terrorism. India refuses to accept the US theory that if a terrorist attacks security personnel, he and the nation that sponsored him must be attacked. That approach can never be an answer to the problem of terrorism.

The US experience of more than one year of the war on terrorism has shown that it can never work. Similarly, the Chinese and Israeli models of physically eliminating the terrorists and changing the demographic composition of a region to achieve ethnic homogeneity and isolate problem ethnic groups have not resolved the issue. The Indian approach of keeping the issue localized and finding a political solution did work in the past and may work in the future. The October 2002 elections in Jammu and Kashmir and the ongoing negotiations with Nagas are the basis for this optimism.

(This is a revised version of the article published in *Strategic Analysis*)

Notes

1. There are a number of versions about the birth of the Taliban, see Ahmed Rashid, *Militant Taliban: Islam, Oil and Fundementalism in Central Asia* (New Haven: Yale

University, 2000), William Malay (ed), *Fundamentalism Reborn? Afghanistan and the Taliban* (Lahore: Vanguard. 1998), Sreedhar and Mohinder Ved, Afghani-Buzkashi, *Power Games and Gamesmen* (New Delhi: Wordsmiths, 2000), Musa Khan Jalalzai, *Taliban: The Great Game in Afghanistan* (Lahore: Hanguard, 1999).

2. Jalalzai, *ibid.*, p. 195.

3. *Ibid.*, p. 196.

4. Ahmed Rashid, "Talibanisation", *The Nation*, 18 November 1999. Also see "The Ferghana Valley", *Jane's Intelligence Review*, September 2001, p. 24.

5. See Ahmad Lufti, "Blowback: China and the Afghan Arabs", *Issues and Studies*, vol. 37, no.1, January-February 2001, pp. 160-214.

6. In interviews with Indian journalists who were in Kabul in 1996 and Mazar-e-Sharif in November 2001.

7. M.L. Khan, "Death by Taliban", *The Herald*, April 2001, pp. 37-38.

8. IIyas Khan, "Desperate Iconoclasm" and "History for Sale", *The Herald*, April 2001, pp. 32b-36.

9. See T. Sreedhar, "New Threat from Taliban", *The Hindu*, 19 May 2001.

Political Islam and Terrorism in Contemporary Times

Kousar J. Azam

Terrorism as a mode of protest in one form or the other has been inherent in all forms of political organizations. It has acquired a form and a character in contemporary times that seems to strike at the very roots of all social and political organizations and thereby at the foundations of civic rule and civil societies.

Beginning as an articulation of protest against perceived and real injustice, terrorism has manifested itself in different forms at different levels, ranging from individual, local, national and international. Perceived as a violent mode of political coercion by marginalized people to force societies to consider their political, economic and social priorities, terrorist violence has been justified by ideologues on the ground that it wakes up the despotic regimes to become aware of their civic obligations, which are also their moral obligations.

The roots of modern terrorism are to be traced in the anarchist thought that was a part of the revolutionary agenda of large sections of societies all over the world during the 19th and early 20th centuries. Late imperialism and early colonialism were equally implicated in the revolutionary fervour that changed the face of much of Europe and saw the rise of the modern nation-state on the rubble of autocratic and absolutist monarchies. This was also accompanied by the struggle of forces of socialism and capitalism, to capture the imagination of emerging elites.

International terrorism is generally described as an act when the terrorists decide to dramatize their plight and obtain international visibility, recognition, acceptance of their creed and support. Such international terrorist groups have been inclusive of not just the Islamic groups but also Armenians, the Ustasha and so on. Though described as international, most terrorist groups have indigenous roots, like the IRA, the German Role Army Fraktion, the Italian Brigade Rose, the neo-fascist Ordine Nuvo, the French Action Directe, the Basque ETA and so on. These groups have roots and purposes that are inherently national, even though they enjoy some reciprocal international support. Political terrorism endures as the weapon of groups that have neither the capacity, nor the will or the patience to pursue their goals and implement their strategies.

Passing through different historical phases, at the earliest stage of terrorism was marked by the use of assassinations for politico-religious ends, including tyrannicides of Greece and Rome, to the 19th century use of violence by anarchists and the nationalists. The assassination of Czar Alexander II in 1881 and of Archduke Franz Ferdinand in 1914, were two very visible acts of terrorism in the 19th century. It became a more complex phenomenon after the end of the Second World War. During the phase of decolonization and nationalist struggles, it became a part of the nationalist struggles in most of the Third World countries like Kenya, South Yemen, Cyprus and Algeria when officials and citizens of the colonial state were attacked as part of what in the end were successful campaigns for independence. Terrorist tactics did not succeed in some countries like Argentina, Brazil, and Uruguay. Terrorists made their presence felt even in some of the established democracies like the Red Brigades in Italy and the Basques in Spain. While most of these were associated with the political left, the notable right wing terrorist campaigns were active in France and Italy.

During the Cold War, the real issue of terrorism was obscured because of the public concerns generated by the binaries of Cold War, visible in ideological, military and political rivalries between the Western capitalist democracies and the socialist bloc. Though terrorist activities rooted in the specific awareness of religion have been active during the Cold War, these expressions were exploited by both the capitalist and socialist states in their mutual confrontations. It was not just the religion-based articulations of terror that became the tools of perpetuating the binaries of Cold War but also the disaffection caused by suppressions of ethnic, tribal and lingual identities – that became the tools for the cold warriors for mutual accusations. Both the 'Godless Empire of Evil' and the architects of the 'City on the Hill' discovered the use of Islamists as a tool to perpetuate their strategic, political, economic and ideological interests.

Though different religions and ideological and ethnic groups use terror, the events of 9/11 have focused mostly on one religion – Islam, on one perceived victim – the Western society (now inclusive of Russia!), on one region – the Middle East. While this kind of profiling may have an immediate relevance, terrorism itself has always defied the tenets of religion, the confines of geography and has ignored reason. The fact that the acts of 9/11 were perpetrated by Islamists to be justified later by their ideological gurus in the name of Islamic faith, leading to a flurry of activities of accusations, justifications, denials, apologies, anger, indignation, anguish, fear, hatred, distrust, disgust and dismay. This makes it imperative that we take a look at what has been generally perceived as the main cause behind the acts of 9/11 – the assertion of political Islam.

The term political Islam has been generally used to describe the reaction and the opposition of the Islamic groups to a political order – both national and international that is perceived to be based outside the tenets of Islam. In its positive connotation it could also be used to describe the political ideology, structures and orders, in a polity that declares itself to be based on the tenets of Islam. In either case, the term political Islam denotes the use of both the idiom and the faith of Islam either in opposition to an existing political order, or in support of an existing political order. At a broader level, this term has been used to interpret the opposition to secular, democratic participatory egalitarian, political order, essentially inclusive in character. The opposition to such an order—however utopian it might prove in reality—is essentially based on the clash of a universalistic worldview as against an 'Islamic worldview' defined in terms of faith, excluding the non-Islamic components. Some of the recent studies[1] have used the term political Islam and Islamic fundamentalism in an interchangeable manner both simplifying as well as complicating the implications of the term. Its interpretations tend to be a country specific in specific historical circumstances, as well as international when situated in a global context.

Irrespective of the differing interpretations of the term, the origins of political Islam could be traced to the reaction of certain sections of Muslims to the colonial rule in the sub-continent. During the 1920s and 1930s there were three major political currents among the Muslims in the Indian subcontinent. One was represented by Jamait-ul-Ulema-e-

Hind - an organization of the traditional Ulema belonging to the noted Islamic seminary located at Deoband – a school that was in agreement with the principles and ideology of the Indian National Congress which played a predominant role in India's national movement for independence. The second shade of political Islam in South Asia was represented by the Muslim League that believed in and pursued the two-nation theory. The third school established by Maulana Abul Ala Maududi who articulated his philosophy of political Islam through Jamaat-e-Islami, which was founded in Lahore on 26 August 1941. While the other two movements remained content with incorporating some part of Islam or some objectives accepted by all Muslims, the objective of the Jamaat was to promote Islam in its totality. He professed that the Jamaat would adapt the same system of organization as adopted by the Prophet and that it would not restrict its activities to South Asia alone, but would appeal to the Muslims all over the world. [2]

It was in the teachings of Maududi and the activities of the Jamaat that the schism between the objectives of a modern territorial state and the appeals of a faith-based 'Umma' transcending national borders, became evident. This incongruity between the tenets of true faith as perceived by specific schools and the imperatives of a secular universalism has assumed different forms, and types of conflict resulting in continuing discourses between the legitimacy of the primordial and the limits of the universal. Following the dialectical concept of history, Maududi puts Islam against all that is non-Islamic. The struggle between the two must inevitably culminate in an Islamic revolution and the creation of an Islamic state, which will initiate in society large-scale reforms leading to a utopian Islamic order.

The irony of this approach, as also of that adopted by the later voices of Islamic fundamentalism, is that while it acknowledges the universal nature of Islam transcending states and borders, and striving for a 'Dar-ul-Islam', it denies the same universalism to the larger humanity outside the Islamic world. Its inclusions and exclusions are determined by an interpretation of faith that is imposed as the only correct interpretation. This doctrinaire rigidity encourages the dogma of intolerance and denial of rationality, which is the heritage of all mankind and not just of Muslims alone. While this interpretation suffocates a creed that itself was a liberating force in history, to an existence at the margins of enlightenment, at the political level it rationalizes 'a million mutinies' in a wider world struggling for order, welfare, legitimacy and democracy.

Parallel to this development the end of the Second World War and desalinization in most of the Third World left much of the Islamic world, with the notable exception of Turkey, untouched by the surge of new ideas. Political Islam as first articulated by Maududi found base, support and followers in societies and states left untouched by both the revolutionary changes sweeping across Europe, and the movements for democracy and self-rule motivating the elite in the Third World. Political Islam filled in the intellectual and the ideological vacuum and assumed the role that ideology had played in the evolutionary upheavals that changed the political contours of Europe.

However, it would be fallacious to believe that there exists one single brand of political Islam. Its association with Islamic fundamentalism would have us believe that there exists a universally relevant and globally applicable agenda of Political Islam. For example, Saudi Arabia, Libya, Pakistan and Iran have been called fundamentalist states but this tells us nothing about their nature. Saudi Arabia is a conservative monarchy, Libya a populist socialist state headed by a military dictator - its label says nothing about the state's Islamic character or orientation. Pakistan under Zia ul-Haq embodied a conservative Islam, Islam in Libya is radical and revisionist, clerics dominate in Iran. If political Islam based on Islamic fundamentalism is equated with anti-Americanism and extremism, Libya and Iran have often denounced America while Saudi Arabia and Pakistan have been close allies of the US. After the Iranian revolution of 1978-79 the reassertion of Islam in Muslim personal and public life were referred to as political Islam. It is essentially a result of a global reassertion of Islam after the end of the Cold War that extends from Libya to Malaysia. Though there have been country-specific causes for the reassertion, there have also been identifiable commonalities. These can be listed as failure of secular nationalism in Islamic societies to provide a sense of national identity or prosperity, failure to establish political legitimacy by the ruling elite in the Islamic world, failure to reduce the gap between the rich and the poor, failure to liberate Palestine, to resist Western political and cultural hegemony. In many ways, political Islam can be regarded as the culmination of failed nationalist programmes.[3] Within the Islamic societies a 'rejectionist minority' sought to impose change from the above through holy wars, while many others reaffirmed their faith and worked at the bottom reforming societies and undertaking those tasks where the establishment of state failed to perform.

In such situations the former members of the nationalist movements became the founders of Islamic movements.

They offered a third way –an Islamic alternative to both capitalism and communism and drew highly educated young professional men and women into the movements. This led to the emergence of an alternative elite in several Muslim countries with modern education but self-consciously oriented towards Islam with a commitment to social and political activism. This phenomenon is reflected in the presence and often domination of Islamists in professional associations. Along with this social activism came an enhanced political participation. The surge for democracy that followed the disintegration of Soviet Union was visible not just in Europe but also in Islamic countries like Egypt, Tunisia and Jordan. However the demand for democratization by the parallel Islamist elites was interpreted as acts of violent revolutionaries, lacking popular support by the political elites. Their repression after a success at the polls, as in the case of the Islamic Salvation Front in Algeria, was ignored by the world including the traditional advocates of democracy. For the world the assertion of the Islamists through the ballots was a greater danger than their assertion through the use of bullets.

The fear of fundamentalism, like the fear of Communism led to strange alliances like Tunisia, Algeria and Egypt joining Israel against a regional and international Islamic threat. By the 1980s Islam came to be portrayed as a triple threat-political, civilizational and demographic. The assertion of an 'Islamic identity' as perceived and defined by specific Islamists challenging the political regimes was perceived as a political threat. The reaction and the remarks of the intellectuals from the West like Raymond Aron's warning of an Islamic revolutionary wave generated by the 'fanaticism of the prophet', Krauthemer's assertion that the 'fundamentalist Koran waving Khomenism' signified 'no less than a clash of civilizations...an irrational reaction of an ancient rival against our Judaeo-Christian heritage'[4] represents the perception of Islam as a civilizational threat. The sheer increase in numbers and growth of Muslim population in Europe has made Islam the second largest religion in Germany and France and the third largest in Britain and the US representing the demographic threat.

Though the years preceding the 11 September attack on US saw several analyses of the likely shape, character, range, and reach of political Islam as evident in the discussion above, it is unfortunate that terrorism, particularly after 11 September has somehow come to be associated with political Islam and Islamic fundamentalism. It has been a part of all civil societies throughout history as a form of civic protest and has been justified by the ideologues as a valid mode of protest in societies where the instruments of redressal of social and political grievances do not exist. The form and substance of terrorism change according to the nature of societies in which it emerges. However, in recent times, there has been a tendency to essentialize it, leading to a blurring of distinction between kinds of terrorism and kinds of violence. While terrorism is rooted in the ideology of violence as a mode of political and social coercion, all violence is not terroristic. Precisely for this reason there has been no agreement on an acceptable definition of terrorism, and what and who determines legitimate violence. Is violence of any kind legitimate at all? Do we have alternatives to violence as a mode of protest, as a mode of social and political change? What about other forms of violence like wars, environmental damage, communal killings, genetic mutilation and annihilation?

However as terrorism and Islam have come to be seen as synonymous, it is time that we reflect on this sad and tragic development of our times. While the most crucial requirement is to make a distinction between Islam and terrorism, equally crucial is the need for the Islamic people to reassess their perceptions of the essence of a faith that has 1/5th of humanity as its followers. Regarding the distinction between Islam and terrorism, it must be remembered that it is the extremism in Islam that constitutes the fertile grounds for terrorism, and not Islam per se. The extremist, fundamentalist Islam also described as political Islam is generally based on the following dictums:

1. A religious interpretation of world history, which separates the Islamists from the rest of the world.

2. A total rejection of the existing world order from the positions of negating it and considering it as a world of infidels and atheism with a strong belief in the struggle to change it.

3. A reversal of the historical evolution back to the era of Islamic state – a return to the Caliphate pattern of the Islamic state.

4. A total denial of the basic rights of women.

5. A cancelling out of the rights of the believers of other religions and foreigners.

6. A rejection of common universal human values.

7. Antagonism towards science, secularism and enlightenment. The vertical growth and horizontal expansion of Islamic extremisms has been attributed by a Somali scholar, Haji Omer[1] to three main factors:

a. The dilemma of backwardness under which a vast majority of Muslim populations live in extreme poverty, destitution, ignorance and disease, leading to deep divisions between rich and poor, within the Islamic world as well as the international level.

b. The prevalence of military, totalitarian and autocratic systems in the entire Arab world and a total absence of democracy and human rights not only on the economic and political level but also in the family sphere. Rigidly patriarchal traditions still constitute the basic value system that generate the way of thinking which encourages antagonism and rebellion, unemployment, inhibition, suppression and frustration radicalize young generations. This creates circumstances in which there is no gleam of hope for change and reformation as an alternative to the status quo in the Arab and Islamic worlds.[6]

c. Added to these has been the negative influence of petrodollars within the Islamic world.

Bin Laden and Al-Qaeda do not represent an isolated cult like Branch Davidians on Aum Shinrikyo; they represent a culture shaped by the factors discussed above and culminate in the distrust and hatred of the West. Though the Islamic countries – equally wary of the Bin Laden phenomenon have publicly displayed their support for the US action against terrorism, the public mood does not totally hide the admiration for Bin Laden. If Paul Johnson argues that Islam is intrinsically an intolerant religion, Joseph Espisito traces the humanitarian foundations of Islam. However the many exercises in search for 'true-Islam' will be futile, for every religion is compatible with the best and the worst of humankind. From the crusades of the 11th century to Turkish expansion of the 15th century up to the colonial era, Islam, and the West have often battled militarily. But despite these military confrontations there have been spells of Christian Islamic and Jewish-Islamic peace and harmony.

It was during the decades of decolonization and Cold War, with the emergence of Nasser in Egypt, the Arab world hoped for democracy and modernity. But the efforts to modernize failed. The choice of socialism by some Arab countries produced stagnation. The Arab Republics, to quote Fareed Zakaria, "calcified into dictatorship".[7] The dreams of Pan Arabism could not withstand the articulation of different national interests. The humiliating defeat of the Arabs by Israel in 1967 and 1973 wounded the Arab psyche and the Iraqi invasion of Kuwait in 1990 destroyed the remnants of the Arab idea. The entire denouement was also accompanied by a regression in intellectual life – for example, Egypt, rated for higher 'literacy' among her neighbours, produces 375 books every year compared to Israel's 4000 books per year. Within a span of 30 years, Iraq once considered as the most modern and secular among the Arab countries with women working, artists thriving and journalists writing – lapsed into a 'squalid play pen for Saddam Hussein's megalomania'. Lebanon, with a diverse cosmopolitan society has become a zone of war and terror. Almost every Arab country today is less free than it was 30 years ago. This failure of the Arab states becomes more humiliating in compared with the achievements of Israel, located in the same region with a modern society, high technology and a functioning democracy. Poverty and wealth both produced failure in the Arab world. The petroleum money was expected to bring a substantial change in the Arab world but this produced a new class of globe trotting-rich Arabs, who are despised within the Arab world. This frustration, bitterness and discontent among the Arab youth added to the bulk of Al Qaeda and Bin Laden's supporters.

The intrusion of superficial Western symbols of prosperity and wealth has created an aversion to the West and disillusionment with its attributes. The project of modernity and its different paths like socialism, secularism, and nationalism failed drastically in the Arab context. The essence of enlightenment – the critical subjectivity and the inner ingredients of political modernity like free market, political parties, accountability, rule of law and civility – were perceived as difficult and dangerous and were shunned by the rulers. No taxation for the Arabs also means no representation. The impact of globalization has been unsettling for the Arabs for it means a visibility of its attributes, but a denial of its essence in the lives of young people. Fundamentalism and political Islam has shrunken the geographical distances erasing the national boundaries in unison of unreason. Syed Qutb's "Signposts on the Road"[8] thus becomes the response of the fundamentalist to the reach, range and intrusion of globalization.

The Arab world has been described by Fareed Zakaria as a political desert, "with no real political parties, no free press and few pathways of dissent." As a result, mosque becomes the centre for political discussions. From politics to social services to medical assistance, the fundamentalist groups provide an alternative to state inaction and legitimacy as these activities are rooted in the tenets of faith – Islam and not in the legislation of a modern state. Societies so broken add a dangerous dimension to the use of education and technology as was evident in the background of the identified terrorists after 9/11.

If the intellectuals in Iran protested against "westoxification," the moderate monarchies in the Persian Gulf and Saudi Arabia indulged in a more deadly game of funding religious schools as a defence against what was perceived as Westernization. Nurtured on the puritanical exclusivistic Wahabi brand of Islam, the madrassas funded by Saudi Arabia churned out tens of thousands of half-educated, fanatic Muslims who view the modern world and non-Muslims with great suspicion, hatred and antagonism. The total failure of the political institutions in the Arab world has been the major cause of the rise of fundamentalism there. Through the instrumentality of religious linkages, this fundamentalism gets transported to all areas of the world where there exist substantial sections of Muslim population. In this destructive and dangerous process the elite and the moderate Muslims make a conscious choice of silence. When Islam is being hijacked by those, who kill, maim, destroy and deny human rights, by petty theocrats and religious commissars, the revolt of the intellectuals remains stifled within the confines of conscience lest they are subjected to the treatment meted out to Salman Rushdie. If Muslims do not take it upon themselves to stop their religion from falling prey to medievalists, no action from the outsiders can save them.

This entire process of the cultivation and nurturing of an exclusionist, narrow identity, limited to specific interpretation of Islam as articulated by the self-proclaimed clerics has resulted in the ghettoiation of Muslims as a community. It should be a matter of serious concern for all

Muslim intellectuals in particular, and the enlightened intelligentsia in general, to ponder over the fate of a faith that had attained a global reach at one point in history, to be reduced to the convenience of self-proclaimed mullahs engineering instant "Jihads". To attribute the decline of Islam and Islamic societies to the machinations of the west would be to ignore the fact that Islam was already in decline by the time of the Renaissance and Reformation, because of its inability to reconcile a theoretically conceived unity and a historically generated diversity. The absence of a revolutionary fervour that changed the societies in Europe and prepared the ground for the rise of the modern nation-state missed the agenda of Islam. Within the Islamic world, colonialism had led to a consolidation of existing feudal order to ensure dependency on Europe, which led to the rise of the states with no scope for democratic reform or change. In the absence of any secular ideology, the desire for change and reform found expression only in the interpretation of Islam to make it consistent with democracy, socialism and revolution. However, the Cold War thwarted this revolutionary impulse by turning political Islam against Marxism.

The Western powers found it expedient to use Islam against socialist movements to ensure a continuous supply of oil and a continued hegemony of the West. The Western world found it expedient to support the ruling elite of the Islamic world, frustrating the popular political aspirations. Added to this the creation of Israel and the military occupation of the Muslim lands remain a visible humiliating symbol of the hegemony of the West. The failure of West to find a solution to the problems of the Middle East creates conditions for large-scale discontent among the Muslim population. The symbolic and the real presence of the West within the region adds to the fervour of Jihad – a Jihad not against their own rulers who deny them human rights, accountable democracies, fruits of multi-culturalism and lull them into the acceptance of status quo through a veneer of material prosperity – but against the Western powers and their visible symbols of material prosperity and political domination. This accumulated and growing discontent has been the source of great social and political turbulence in the Islamic societies all over the world. It has, however, local, national and international configurations depending upon the interpretations given to it the local Ulema. Over and above all these, the sheer irrationality of the Ulemas who have declared the 21st century to be the Islamic century – just because Islamists could attack the Twin Towers – testifies to the vast chasm that exists between the international political reality and the misplaced utopia of the Mullahs obsessed with the indispensability and validity of their stance.

While it is natural to associate Islam with its many political trajectories, it will be erroneous to treat Islam and Islamic societies as terroristic. It will be more appropriate to strengthen the forces of change and reform that are showing signs of emergence in the Islamic world. They must create conditions in which Islam becomes self-reflective and self-critical to see its own diversity and the diversity of the world it inhabits. It must come out of its own binary to embrace plurality to ensure the emergence of democratic peace. Both crusade and Jihad should mean the end of inequalities that keep one-fifth of mankind trapped in uncritical and an inadequately interpreted faith.

Notes

1. See Bassam Tibi, *The Challenge of Fundamentalism: Political Islam and the New World Disorder* (Berkeley: University of California Press), 1998.
2. See Kalim Bahadur, "Political Islam", *Economic & Political Weekly*, vol. 37, no. 4, 26 January- 2 February 2002, p.306.
3. Joseph Esposito, "Political Islam: Beyond the Green Menace", *Current History*, January 1994, downloaded at htpp://www.arches.uga.edu/~godlas/espo.html
4. *Ibid.*
5. H.Haji Omer,"'Political Islam' and the War on Terrorism in Somalia", http:/www.waltainfo.com/Conflict/Articles/2002/January/article4.html.
6. *Ibid.*
7. Fareed Zakaria, "The Roots of Islamic Rage and What Can Be Done About It", *Newsweek*, 15 October 2001, p.17.
8. *Ibid.*

Tackling Terrorism : Fight Disease Not Just the Symptoms

Mohd. Moazzam Ali

Although age-old, evolving from the religious origins of the Jewish Zealots' Sicarii revolt against the Romans (66-70 A.D) to the increasingly secular ones after the French Revolution, terrorism happened to hog the headlines in the late 1960s. It was the sensational Palestinian Black September organization's hostage taking of Israeli athletes in 1972 at Munich Olympic games that traumatized the world. Many hijackings, kidnappings, seizure of embassies, hostage-takings, etc. were to follow. However, the overall attention paid to it was meagre and ephemeral. But the ensuing decades witnessed a phenomenal increase in the incidence of terrorism.

Terrorism today stands out as a hydra-headed monster on an unencumbered global prowl. The number of innocent victims it has claimed on its numerous visitations is already beyond the tolerable limits. We cannot possibly characterize our epoch as civilized if this hideous leviathan persists in its meanderings around with impunity. It is a matter of grave international concern that of the phenomenon of terrorism going global is greatly facilitated by the ever-growing sophistication in technology, modes of transport and communication, miniaturization of weapons and, in many cases, its state sponsorship etc.[1]

While a fool-proof elimination of this age-old phenomenon in its multifarious new forms may not be possible, its incidence could certainly be greatly minimized with the help of an in-depth, sophisticated understanding of the phenomenon. The extant responses to combat terrorism are too narrow and sectarian (for example, the obsession with a single individual Osama bin Laden and his organization Al Qaeda, the so-called "rogue states" etc), much hyped, sensationalized and tendentious, partisan and partial, shallow and superficial, diversionary and misleading (associating Islam and Muslims alone with terrorism, although the Irish, Basque separatists, Tamils of Sri Lanka and also the Oklahoma city bomber Timothy McVeigh culprit of the Oklahama bombing and the narco-terrorists of Latin America are not Muslims at all), ad hoc and expedient (ignoring the need for an in-depth and long-term approach), glossing over the past (not long ago, the Soviet, US, UK, China and many other states were involved in the game of state-aided terrorism in varying degrees and forms)[2], bulldozing the masses to insensitivity and submission with regard to state tyranny and violence in the name of combating terrorism, (like the draconian laws, police repressions, arbitrary arrests, violations of legal norms and human rights, etc.), seeks to fight just the symptoms and not the disease.

Instead of sensationalizing terrorism, it may help to recognize that any act of violence is not terrorism and that anyone indulging in violence is not a terrorist. Terrorism is not just insensate violence or it is a random act impulsively and senselessly attempted. It is an act well-planned and often executed with deadly accuracy. It is a secretive, conspiratorial act symptomatic of a deeper malaise or problem. Terrorism is not an aimless act. It sets for itself certain objectives (clear enough and sensible for the perpetrators of terrorist acts at least). A terrorist terrorizes for a purpose. It is not a spontaneous and unconscious act but well-calculated and calibrated one. Terrorism is also believed to be "a tactic of the powerless against the powerful."[3] A Palestinian, a Kurd, an Irish man, a Basque activist, a Khalistani, a Kashmiri, an LTTE member, looks at it that way. A failed fighter earns the opprobrious label of a terrorist and a successful one wins the apotheosis of a liberator. Terrorism does not take place in vacuum but has underlying causes, reasons and contexts. It can be resorted to by an individual, group, organization, cult, sects, ethnic and national group, dispossessed, deprived, exploited. Both secular and religious groups may take recourse to terrorism. Terrorism may be resorted to for personal or group gain or to draw individual, local, national and international attention. Terrorism may be resorted to in the name of a cause however ill-defined and misunderstood by others. It could be a response of desperado or desperadoes faced with great odds, too powerful for a perceived or real enemy or a high degree of persecution. A minority faced with persistently high degree of repression, harassment and humiliation from a very powerful, impervious majority could take recourse to terrorism. Terrorism may represent a very high degree of alienation suffered by an individual, group, sect, etc. who feel discarded, humiliated, ignored or marginalized. Terrorism may also represent a high level of frustration and anger and hence a brutal revenge response in the form of a terrorist acts. Given a critical situation, any individual or group, when pushed to the wall, has the potential to take recourse to terrorism. Hence, blaming terrorism on a particular religion, ideology, mental frame of mind is misleading. Terrorism is basically a mundane, this-worldly, phenomenon espousing mundane, this-worldly, causes. Further, viewing a terrorist, self-righteously, only as a misguided fanatic or fundamentalist is not often a rewarding exercise.

Merely countering or condemning terrorism is only half a battle won. To eliminate terrorism, one has not only to bring the terrorist to book but also endeavour to eliminate the causes that led to that terrorist act as well. Fighting only the symptoms (the acts of terrorism) and not the disease (the real causes that breed terrorism) is a vain, unproductive, wasteful exercise, also an ineffective and inconclusive battle. Mere blame-game is no good either. The ISI may be blamed for everything and real causes for terrorist acts may not be ascertained. Such an approach can be dangerous too, since it may make the fight against terrorists or terrorism persistent, permanent and never-ending. It may end up fostering permanent violence, a kind of perpetual war, a war without end or at least a permanent war-like situation. From this point of view, the so-called 'war against terror' or 'international war against terrorism' may end up robbing the world of peace and perpetuate a war-like situation. It may also condone an elongated spell of state terrorism bulldozing people into insensitivity and submission.

A terrorist is a fugitive. In a world of sovereign states and with well-protected boundaries, he is hard to pin down. Hence, well-defined, face-to-face battles against terrorism are not possible. A terrorist could simply go underground a la Osama and others in Afghanistan. There cannot be total or absolute success ever in completely eliminating terrorism.

What has rendered the situation more complex is the fact that there exists a range of terrorisms: individual terrorism, group terrorism, cult or sect terrorism, ethno-national terrorism, minority-majority terrorism, class terrorism, terrorism of the poor or dispossessed, deprived and exploited, marginalized, alienated group terrorism, narco-terrorism, criminal gang terrorism, ideological, religious, fundamentalist, fanatical terrorism, terrorism of the mentally sick or deranged, state terrorism, politico-economic terrorism, techno-terrorism, info-terrorism, cyber-terrorism, bio-terrorism, eco-terrorism, nuclear terrorism, etc. Terrorism is sometimes broadly classified into, politically motivated terrorism and criminally motivated terrorism.[4] To tackle terrorism, one cannot lump all of them together. An ideal approach would be nuanced and sophisticated requiring each type of terrorism being responded to or tackled differently. Right now the focus is on political terrorism. Even here, all the energy is squandered in fighting just the symptoms. Under the present dispensation, the terrorism of the strong and also the state terrorism are more or less completely ignored.

The difficulties to tackle terrorism are also compounded by the fact that the phenomenon of terrorism has still not lent itself to a precise, universally acceptable definition. The term's usage, and even more frequent abusage, has brought about a situation where, a la socialism, it may be compared to a hat, which has lost its shape because too many people have tried to wear it. Any political opposition today sought to be condemned in terroristic terms. Any hard-core political opponent may be branded as a potential or real terrorist or at least having links with some terrorist group inside or outside the country. Linking of political opponents to underworld terrorist groups is also not uncommon. Arbitrary arrests without appropriate trial, torture, extradition and even death in the name of combating terrorism are frequently reported. Today, a situation has come to pass where any resistance to the powers that any struggle against injustice, oppression, exploitation, imperialism, etc. could be called a terrorist act and the same is sought to be brutally suppressed in the name of terrorism. Terrorism has begun to serve as an alibi to resort to massive crackdowns, political interventions with a view to bulldoze opponents into silence and submission, to the passage of Draconian laws, to the circumvention of the legal procedures, etc.

Linking terrorism to a particular religion has brought about a situation where unfounded prejudices have begun to take root. These prejudices are senselessly applied without compunction as is done in the 15-member EU- countries with regard to Muslims. This has been openly condemned by the EUMC Director, Mr. Beate Winkler.[5] In India, Muslims, for long, have been the victims of hate campaigns, riots and various other prejudices besides the state-sponsored terrorism in Gujarat since 28 February 2002. The recent crackdown on Muslim madrasas represents the same prejudice.[6]

A good deal of misuse of the term terrorism could be avoided if the term could be accorded a cogent, comprehensive, universally acceptable definition. Attempts made in this direction have not borne fruit. *The Encyclopedia of Social Sciences* sought to define the term terrorism in terms of an organized group or party, which seeks to achieve its avowed aims chiefly through systematic use of violence.[7] But the question of the nature of aims is extremely important. It cannot be talked of in a detached way. The first effort by the UN to define terrorism was made on 24 October 1970, when the General Assembly adopted the Declaration that stated: "every state has the duty to refrain from organizing, assisting or participating in acts of civil strife or terrorist acts in another state..." But the same Declaration also enjoined: "Every state has the duty to refrain from any forcible action which deprives people ......of their right to self-determination and freedom and independence."[8] The UN was always torn between proposing anti-terrorist measures and upholding the right to self-determination. In 1973, the UN established an ad hoc committee on International Terrorism which stated that each instance of insurgency was not an act of terrorism: "...the inalienable right to self-determination and independence of all peoples under colonial and racist regimes and other forces of alien domination.........the struggle of national liberation movements" etc. are granted under the "UN Charter and relevant resolutions of the UN." In 1974, the UN General Assembly sought to forbid sending of armed bands, groups, irregulars and mercenaries of one state to another one. But in the same Article-3, the UN upheld the right to self-determination, freedom, independence, etc. On 9 December 1985, the UN General Assembly again made an attempt at defining terrorism but concentrated more on crime oriented terrorism such as hijacking, hostage-taking, etc.[9] In an unprecedented move, the UN Security Council, in place of a definition, voted 15-0 dramatically on 28 September 2001, in favour of a US introduced Resolution -1373 under Chapter-7 (mandatory for all the 190 members) that enjoins members of the UN to deal sternly with terrorists. The financing of terrorism was declared a criminal offence. The assets of the terrorists were to be frozen. As a mark of protest, the 57-member Organization of Islamic Conference remained silent on Resolution -1337 while supporting the Security Council's other Resolutions-1267, 1333 and 1368. The British Ambassador, commenting on who is and who is not a terrorist, made a strange remark: "For most of the time, if something looks like a terrorist and makes noise like a terrorist, it's a terrorist."[10] The amazing, unprecedented alacrity with which the Resolution -1337 was adopted was indicated by the fact that the drafting, debating and passing of the Resolution was done on the same day to ensure that the matter was clinched before the UN General Assembly commenced its specially scheduled debate on defining the term terrorism on 1 October 2001. The Assembly, as expected, failed to agree on a definition of the term terrorism. The views expressed were too divergent to be accommodated in a concise definition.

Before 11 September attacks, many academics attempted to define terrorism but inadequacies persisted. Walter Laqueur maintains that, "no definition of terrorism can possibly cover all the varieties of terrorism that have appeared throughout history." [11] One nation's terrorism is another one's liberation struggle. Any anti-establishment struggle can be termed as terrorist. However, Laqueur identifies certain features, which are important. He writes: (1) terrorism is a new, unprecedented phenomenon. For this reason its antecedents (if any) are of little interest, (2) terrorism is one of the most important and dangerous problems facing mankind today, (3) terrorism is a response to injustice; if there were no political and social justices, there would be no terrorism. (A point which is ignored today at our own peril), (4) the only means of reducing the likelihood of terrorism is a reduction of the grievances, stresses and frustrations underlying it, (an extremely valuable point), (5) terrorists are fanatical believers driven to despair by intolerable conditions: they are poor and their inspiration is deeply ideological, (6) terrorism can occur anywhere.[12] May we add that terrorism may be the response of the underdog against the oppressor, although the reverse could also be true as Noam Chomsky points out.[13] It could also be looked upon as a low-intensity conflict.[14]

For all these features, we still fall far short of an agreeable definition, although attempts for it are continuously made. On 1 April 2002, a three-day conference of the foreign ministers of the Organization of Islamic Conference (OIC) began in Kuala Lumpur. While condemning the linkage of Islam and Muslims to terrorism, the Conference failed to produce a consensus definition of the term terrorism. Prime Minister of Malaysia, Mahathir Mohd, called upon the UN to define terrorism because condemning terrorism without defining it would be something bizarre.[15] Many ministers at the Conference insisted on an acceptable definition of terrorism that differentiated between legitimate national liberation struggles and acts of terrorism. The OIC Declaration rejected "any attempt to link terrorism to the struggle of the Palestinians..." The Declaration also rejected, any unilateral action taken against any Islamic country under the pretext of combating international terrorism, as this will undermine global cooperation against terrorism." However, the Declaration, while condemning all forms of terrorism, including the state terrorism, maintained, "we reject any attempt to link Islam and Muslims to terrorism as terrorism has no association with religion, civilization or nationality." "We reiterate", the Declaration said, "that preventive action taken to combat terrorism should not result in ethnic or religious profiling of the targeting of a particular community." The Declaration recommended the removal of the root causes breeding terrorism, which included, "foreign occupation, injustice and exclusion."[16] On 20 May 2002, the security ministers of the 10-member ASEAN deliberated at a two-day conference on the regional counter terrorism measures. Here too, Malaysia insisted on working out an agreeable definition of the term terrorism. But the Singaporean Home Minister, Mr. Wong Kan Seng, downplayed the attempt saying that the job of defining terrorism should better be left to the bodies like the UN. He tated that "Even without a definition, I think we all know who are the ones who commit terrorist acts." But the Malaysian Deputy Prime Minister, Abdullah Ahmad Badawi observed that it was a "great irony" that the world cannot define terrorism. "We all know it exists and we are all engaged in a fight against it...But we will not commit to a definition of what it is."[17] However, the joint communiqué of the ASEAN meet agreed to "counter, prevent and suppress all forms of terrorist acts" while insisting on eradicating the root causes breeding terrorism.[18] On 6 May 2002, at a meeting of Religious Affairs Ministers of the OIC, Saudi Arabia approved suicide bombing while Malaysia differed.[19]

While the difficulties in defining terrorism have multiplied, the US has succeeded in mobilizing all the important international organizations to agree on counter-terrorist measures. The ASEAN Heads of State had already agreed on counter-terrorist co-operation in November 2001. On 7 May 2002, Malaysia, Indonesia and the Philippines signed a tripartite pact (open to other 10-member ASEAN grouping) to cooperate against terrorism.[20] On 1 August 2002, the US and ASEAN states signed a joint declaration for Cooperation to Combat International Terrorism. On the other hand, the 19-member NATO chalked out a plan to combat terrorism into which Russia is fully integrated. At a meeting in St. Petersburg on 7 June 2002, the Shanghai group of six signed the Charter of Shanghai Cooperation Organization. That made the group (Russia, China, Kazakhstan, Uzbekistan, Kyrghistan, and Tajikistan) a full-fledged international body. The three principal tasks outlined were: regional security, economic and humanitarian cooperation and the fight against terrorism and separatism (which is declared to be the priority task). "The struggle against terrorism must be conducted on the basis of norms and principles of international law, it must not be identified with the struggle against any religion, countries or nationalities. It must be free from bias and "double standards." A regional anti-terrorist structure is also to be set up."[21] The 16-member Conference on Interaction and Confidence-building Measures (CICA) adopted a 35-point Almaty Act on 4 June 2002, with a thrust on combating international terrorism.[22] The US President, George Bush, on his part, announced, on 6 June 2002, that the US which "is leading the civilized world in a titanic struggle against terror" would establish a new agency called the Cabinet Agency for Homeland Security with a budget of some $ 37 billion and a work force of 170,000 employees.[23] Further, he noted that "America will not forget the lives that were taken or the justice that is required. Every terrorist must be made to live like an international fugitive. He should have no place to sleep and no government to hide behind." [24] It still appears unlikely.

Virtually all countries and international organizations of the world are by now already roped in for what Bush called the titanic war against terrorism. The US Secretary of Defence, Donald Rumsfield told a press conference on 22

June 2002, that over 180 countries either offered or actually helped the US in fighting terrorism. A super-power backed by the international coalition of countries is pitted primarily against just one individual, Osama bin Laden and his organization Al Qaeda. The US remains in jitters, unnervingly fearful of fresh bouts of terrorism. Every other issue is pushed into the background. However, nothing is done to stop the ongoing bloody Israeli incursions into the Palestinian areas—one of the root causes of terrorism. Are the US-Israel combine, under paranoiac siege mentality slapping essentially their fight or agenda (i.e. fighting terrorism) on the world? Other countries are not so direly affected. After all, it is widely acknowledged that most of the terrorist attacks target either the US[25] or Israel. From this point of view, the response appears disproportionately on the high side. Terrorism is being fought on the wrong lines relying only on massive use of force and violence that might incite more terrorist attacks. Terrorism is sought to be countered only through force and counter-violence. This may lead to more acts of terrorism and violence. We may all end up in a hapless situation where terrorism and counter terrorism will perennially feed on each other.

This kind of barren, counterproductive approach will never eliminate terrorism. Rather, it will perpetuate terrorism as is evident from the terrorist attack on the US Consulate in Karachi on 14 June 2002. The point bears repetition that only symptoms are sought to be fought and not the disease (i.e. the root causes that serve as breeding grounds for terrorism). An entirely West-centric not global centric approach is followed. Ad hocism reigns supreme and no long-term universally agreeable perspective is sought to be evolved. Double standards galore. In the name of fighting terrorism, other agendas like settling scores with political and other opponents or realizing covertly the foreign policy objectives, domination of oil and other resource-rich areas and global markets is sought. Terrorism is being used as an alibi for imperialism. Norms, humanitarian principles and considerations are ignored. A particular religious group is sought to be targeted. Using terrorism as an alibi, an environment is sought to be created in which any opposition to the Western agenda is construed in terrorist terms. The world is sought to be bulldozed into embracing largely an American-Israeli agenda at the expense of the real problems of poverty, illiteracy, health, employment, education, environment, inequalities, etc. An ominous, war-like situation is sought to be perpetuated. In the name of terrorism, the Western agenda of mastery over global resources and markets is sought to be pushed. It is not realized that such massive sensationalization, paranoia, over-reaction accompanied with colossal expenditure and use of force is not required to fight some stray acts of terrorism primarily from a small band of terrorists. The scenarios of civilizational or cultural or religious wars, the fears of bio-terrorism like the use of weapons of mass destruction, nuclear terrorism, the missile attacks from the so-called rogue states are all highly exaggerated and misplaced. In the name of countering terrorism, Draconian laws are pushed through without adequate political and social debate, imperiling human rights, legal and democratic norms and procedures. It is not seriously examined why certain individuals or groups are willing to sacrifice their lives. The current approach is highly expensive, senseless, impractical, dangerous and counterproductive. The US, acting as a global cop, will have to police too many areas, overextend itself and become unpopular. *The Los Angeles Times* reported that a secret Pentagon report to Congress had identified seven centres against which the US was planning to use nuclear weapons. They were: Russia, China, Iran, Iraq, Libya, North Korea and Syria. The Russians were prompt in demanding an explanation from the US.[26] If history is any guide, no country has been able to fight on too many fronts. This kind of overextending could lead to the undoing of any power a la Paul Kennedy's thesis outlined in his well-known book entitled *The Rise and Fall of Great Powers*. The sooner it is realized, the better it is for everyone.

To tackle terrorism the extant sensationalism and paranoia has to be avoided. What is required is to overcome definitional deficiencies and at least identify certain main components of a definition of the term terrorism, which are universally acceptable. The different kinds of terrorism should not be lumped together but differentiated with a view to tackle each one of them separately and effectively. Over-concentration on only one or two kinds of terrorism would be myopic. The fight against terrorism calls for a very nuanced and sophisticated approach. Merely countering an act of terrorism is not enough. The root cause or causes of acts of terrorism need to be gone into and eliminated or ameliorated. The issues or areas that give fillip to or create a breeding ground for terrorism need to be identified and steps initiated to eliminate them expeditiously. Linking terrorism to religions, cultures, civilizations is both fatuous and mischievous and needs to be avoided. For acts of terrorism, only the terrorist or terrorists involved need to be dealt with and not a whole area or a people.[27] The loss of innocent lives need be treated on an equal basis. American lives are as precious as the lives of the people elsewhere. The blame-game should not be directed only against the non-Western areas.

Notes

1. It is well-known that the state-sponsored terrorism has a long history. States provide weapons, training, passports, finances, transport, sanctuary or asylum to further a proxy war to achieve their foreign policy objectives at a cost much cheaper than a full-fledged war. See Charles W. Kegley Jr and Eugene R. Wittkopf, *World Politics-Trends and Transformation* (New York: St. Martin's Press, 1995), p. 464. Many states, including the former Soviet Union, Syria, Iraq, Iran, Libya, Pakistan, etc. have been accused of state terrorism. The US was blamed for sponsoring terrorist activities in Vietnam, Chile, El Salvador, Nicaragua, Afghanistan and elsewhere. See *ibid*. The US air strikes against Libya in 1986 and against Sudan and Osama's camps in Pakistan were termed as "state terrorism." See "History of USA's State Terrorism" (containing a list of year-wise terrorist activities of the US around the world), in Prabhat Patnaik (ed), *No To Terrorism To War* (New Delhi: CPI (M) Publication, 2001), pp. 49-56.

2. Taliban and Osama were the CIA creations who turned against their own masters just as Bhindranwale had turned against Indira Gandhi. Chomsky writes that Bin Laden's men were brought together in the 1980s by the CIA. "The idea was to try to harass the Russians...." Some one lakh "best killers they could find" were brought together from diverse countries. Chomsky also writes that the Philippnes' conquest caused the death of 100,000 Filipinos. See Noam Chomsky, "The New War Against Terror" in Patnaik (ed), n. 1, p. 18. "For hundreds of years, Europe has

been casually slaughtering people all over the world. That's how they conquered the world. Congo didn't attack Belgium, India didn't attack England, Algeria didn't attack France. See William J. Pomeroy, *American Neo-Colonialism—Its Emergence in the Philippines and Asia*, (New York: International Publications, 1970), p. 13. The Nicaragua war left "tens of thousands of people dead, the country ruined ......Nicaragua tried all (international legal) measures. They don't work in a world that is ruled by force." *Ibid.*, p.14. During the Reagan years alone US/UK backed South African attacks against the neighbouring countries killed about one and a half million people and left $ 60 billion in damage and countries destroyed. *Ibid.*, p. 15. For the Soviet involvement in state sponsorship of terrorism, see Walter Laqueur, *The Age of Terrorism* (Boston: Little, Brown, 1987), pp. 270-280, Michael Stohl (ed), *The Politics of Terrorism* (New York:Marcel Dekkar Inc, 1983), pp.233-235, Leonard Weinberg and Paul B. Davies, *Introduction to Political Terrorism* (New York: McGraw-Hill, 1989), pp. 41-64 and 145, for China's involvement in terrorism (both internal and external) see S.K. Ghosh, *Terrorism : World Under Siege* (New Delhi: APH Publishing Corp, 1995), pp. 7-8; China's involvement in Vietnam, Cambodia, and elsewhere in ASEAN area is well-known.

3. See Kegley Jr and Eugene n.1, p.462.

4. See Ghosh, n.2, p. 16.

5. The EUMC (European Monitering Centre on Racism and Xenophobia) Report 2002 states that physical and verbal abuse against Muslims in the EU countries is

on the rise since 11 September 2001. Headscarves worn by Muslim women and the turbans the Sikhs wear have come under attack. Numerous attacks against mosques have been reported. The EUMC Director, Beate Winkler observed on 24 May 2002, that, "An atmosphere has been created in which Muslims have to justify themselves that they are not terrorists." See *The Hindu*, 25 May 2002, p. 15. The situation obtaining in the US is no different.

6. See *The Hindu*, 19 May 2002, p. 10 and *The Hindu*, 18 June 2002, p.1.

7. Cited in Ghosh, n. 2, p. 4.

8. *Ibid.*

9. For details regarding the UN attempts at defining terrorism, see *ibid.*, pp.4-6.

10. See *The Hindu*, 30 September 2001, p. 1 and 29 September, p. 15. This was a strange comment. Apprehensions about the manner and speed with which the Security Council passed the resolution remained.

11. See Laqueur, n. 2, p. 11.

12. See Walter Laqueur, *Terrorism* (London: Little Brown, 1978), pp. 15-16. For the elaboration of some of the features of terrorism, see *ibid.*, pp. 264-273. See also Ted Robert Gurr, "Some Political Characteristics of Political Terrorism in the 1960s" in Stohl, n.2, pp. 23-45.

13. Noam Chomsky writes, "it is very serious analytical error to say, as is commonly done, that terrorism is the weapon of the weak. Like other means of violence, it is

primarily a weapon of the strong, overwhelmingly, in fact. It is held to be a weapon of the weak because the strong also control the doctrinal system and their terror doesn't count as terror." See Chomsky, n.2, p. 15.

14. See Weinberg and Paul, n. 2, pp. 152-53.

15. Argued Prime Minister Mahathir Mohammad: "Muslims everywhere must condemn terrorism once it is clearly defined. Terrorizing people is not the way of Islam. Certainly, killing people is not Islamic." We must object strongly to the linking of Muslims with terror just because a few Muslims have resorted to acts of terror. We must point out that Christians, Buddhists, Hindus, Jews and others are equally guilty of terrorism. Terrorists must be identified by their acts and nothing else." The 11 September attacks were an "unmitigated disaster" for Muslims all over the world. "Our image which had not been good, has been made worse. It does not help that we are weak and disunited. Unless we are able to turn the present worldwide anger over the terrorist attack of 11 September into a real campaign against all terrorists irrespective of their religious faiths, we are going to find that Muslim bashing will be heightened." See *The Hindu*, 2 April 2002, p. 14.

16. The Declaration mentioned: "We emphasize the importance of addressing the root causes of international terrorism, convinced that the environment that breeds terrorism, including foreign occupation, injustice and exclusion, is allowed to thrive." See *The Hindu*, 4 April 2002, p.14.

17. See *The Hindu*, 21 May 2002, p. 14. However, at the end of the conference, Mr.Abdullah relented, "The

issue is that we should not be spending all our time trying to argue who is a terrorist and what is terrorism so much so that we have no time to talk about what we should be doing together (to tackle the issue)". See *The Hindu*, 22 May 2002, p. 14

18. See *The Hindu*, 22 May 2002, p. 16.

19. Malaysian Deputy Prime Minister, Abdullah Ahmad Badawi, maintained that the holy war couldn't be won with violence and suicide bombers, which achieved nothing except earning for the Palestinians the epithets of terrorists. Building strong economies was more important for fighting against injustice than suicide bombings. Muslims should not "allow Islam to be hijacked by those who have a flawed understanding of our faith and rally under the banner of militancy." The idea that Jihad means carrying out militant attacks needed to be dropped. Jihad must "not be pursued with guns and bombs" but should be translated into actions that would help to lift Muslims "from the throes of poverty." The Saudi Minister for Islam, Sheik Salleh Abdul Aziz, however, asserted: "The suicide bombings were permitted" and that "the victims are considered to have died martyrs' death." See *The Hindu*, 7 May 2002, p. 14.

20. See *The Hindu*, 8 May 2002, p. 15.

21. See *The Hindu*, 7 June 2002, p. 14.

22. See *The Hindu*, 5 June 2002, p.1 and 8 June 2002, p. 14.

23. See *The Hindu*, 8 June 2002, p. 14.

24. See *The Times of India*, 13 March 2002, p. 10.

25. Laqueur writes that, "most of the victims of terrorism are American." See Laqueur, n. 1, p. 8.

26. See Gosh, n. 2, p. 14.

27. The figure of 7000 is given by Lisa Beyer in *Time*, 1 October 2001, p. 43. See also Chomsky, n.2, p. 21.

Section-III: Bio-Terrorism

Biological Warfare, Bio–Terrorism, The World and Us

Pushpa M. Bhargava

When the history of the second half of the 20th century is written, the following will, no doubt, find a place of 'honour' in the list of follies and misconceptions of mankind during this period:

a.) that affluence and prosperity of the kind the US has experienced would make a country invincible and that arms would win wars.

b.) that exploitation and injustice – international or intra-national – can be sustained by power;

c.) that a power-wielding government or nation can keep on pushing people fighting for justice and basic human rights, against the wall, without their reacting unethically and unreasonably and seeking unholy alliances such as those with religious fundamentalist groups;

d.) that marriages of convenience in the economic and political fields can be made to work for long;

e.) that religious fundamentalism is a creation of fundamentalists and not of unethical, and unfair governments; and

f.) that one would engage in massive biological warfare or bio-terrorism is in the domain of fiction.

Given these follies and misconceptions which led to

the first major conflict after the Second World War – the Palestinian problem – and then to many others such as Suez, Vietnam, Ireland, the Middle East (Iran-Iraq-Kuwait), Argentina, Sri Lanka, Soviet Union, South Africa, Western Africa, Central Europe, North-Eastern India and Kashmir, the emergence of guerrilla warfare and of terrorism was inevitable. Was there, indeed, any other choice for the deprived and the unprivileged but to depend on ones wits?

The fundamentalists that have always been around saw in this situation a marvellous opportunity to propagate their cause, and alliances were easily struck. For those deprived of any other identity, religion gave them one. And the dependence of the economy of the "great" nations on arms, made it imperative for them to create conflicts so that they could sell arms, often to both sides. Pretexts such as the fight against communism or capitalism, were easily found.

Given the lack of ability and of desire around the world to get to the root of the problem and not seek merely ad hoc solutions, it was clear to many of us a decade ago that bio-terrorism and biological warfare would soon be upon us.

Therefore, when, during the Iraq-Kuwait conflict from 16 January to 20 February 1991, Saddam Hussein said that he had the final weapon, several of us had predicted that what he was referring to were biological weapons such as botulin or anthrax spores which could be put on a Scud war head, even though Iraq had initially denied that it had a biological warfare programme.

On 31 May 1991, a distinguished American scientist, Mathew Meselson (the author of the famous Meselson–Stahl experiment that established the double-stranded structure of DNA, and a member of the US National Academy of Sciences) and I were invited to address the ambassadors in Geneva, at Chateau de Bossey on lake Geneva under the auspices of a residential conference on biological weapons. During my talk that evening, I mentioned my surmise about Saddam Hussein having biological weapons. Immediately after the meeting, the organizers introduced me to two German gentlemen who had set up the biological weapons factories in Iraq! These were the factories unearthed later on by the CIA. In fact, later, Iraq declared it had 157 aerial bombs and 25 warheads with botulin, anthrax spores and aflatoxin, the first two of which are the most fatal biological weapons known. An area of 18 sq. kms which had been fenced and which Iraq maintained, was for making single cell protein, essentially housed facilities for making biological weapons. In 1995 it was discovered that Iraq had imported 40 tons of bacterial growth media in the 1980s.

When on the night of the 7 October this year, while watching the CNN channel, we learnt that the United States had started bombing of Afghanistan, I told my wife that this would now be the beginning of biological warfare. The argument was simple. The suicide-bomber attacks on the United States would have never been made if those who were responsible for it did not have a follow up strategy, and there couldn't be a better strategy than to be prepared for engaging in bio-terrorism.

Biological weapons have been often called the "poor man's atom bomb". The material, equipment and infrastructure required to make them is easily available and inexpensive. There is no dearth of microbiologists around the world who could do it all, especially as all the required information is in the public domain. Biological weapons are easy to store, easy to deliver and extremely effective. They can be used either for an immediate effect – that is within a few days – or for an effect which would be felt after a long time; you could target a country today and have its effect felt a year later. They are, therefore, ideal agents for both overt and covert warfare.

According to an excellent report of the Office of Technology Assessment of the US, a single warhead of anthrax spores landing in Washington on a day of moderate wind, could kill up to 100,000 people, which is more than a Hiroshima-sized atom bomb would, with the additional advantage that property would not be affected. And less than half a kilogram of botulin put in the water supplies around the world could theoretically kill half the world population in a few days. Further biological weapons can be used to target individuals as well as large groups or whole populations. Biological warfare agents can also be used to harm animals and plants as well. They can, therefore, destroy a country's agriculture. True, the extent of their deleterious effects would depend on several factors such as wind direction, weather, temperature and humidity, but the ease of their production and delivery and their efficacy under optimal conditions would more than compensate the disadvantages.

II

Except US the Rest of the World has been Aware

In view of my concern about and awareness of biological weapons over the last nearly two decades, and with the increasing fear that I have had on that account during this period, as soon as I awoke on the 8 October morning, I called up my esteemed friend, A.P.J.Abdul Kalam, the then Principal Scientific Adviser to the Government of India (the present President of India), suggesting that he may consider looking into this matter on an urgent basis. The same day I issued a press note through PTI in which I said, "I am extremely worried at the possibility of the use of biological weapons such as anthrax or the intestinal toxin, botulin, by Osama bin Laden and the Taliban, specially in selected countries such as the USA, Great Britain and India." I added, "Even a limited use of biological weapons could change the face of the present war." This was before the discovery of the first use of anthrax in the United States, the same night. On the 9 October morning, I formally wrote a letter to Dr. Kalam.

Just after the Kuwait-Iraq war, I had also spoken to V.S. Arunachalam, the then Scientific Adviser to the Minister for Defence that we needed to work out a national strategy in respect of biological weapons. I doubt if any such strategy was actually worked out, though I was invited to visit the DRDO Laboratory in Gwalior, which has been concerned with this area.

On 18 September 1995, I had brought to the notice of Dr. G. Satyavati, the then Director-General of the Indian Council of Medical Research, a proposal of the Federation of American Scientists in respect of a global programme to monitor emerging diseases. This would have involved setting up an organization like the Centre for Disease Control in the United States which has played an extremely important role in shaping modern medicine and medical and health care; it was at the initiative of this Centre that the causative agent of AIDS was identified. And it is this Centre, which is today playing a key role in analyzing what may be the agents of bio-terrorism in the United States today.

I wonder why no action was taken by the Indian Council of Medical Research on my letter, a copy of which was also sent to Shri A.P.B.N. Sarma, Principal Secretary, Health, Government of Andhra Pradesh. I did all the above even though I was fairly certain that nothing would be done as, in our country, we are not used to doing the right things at the right time; generally, we just don't do them at all! I was also aware of the culture of our Government – both the political and the bureaucratic wings – that what they don't know is not worth knowing. Our governments everywhere, with a few notable exception, (Andhra Pradesh to which I belong is certainly no exception) may be amongst the most unprofessional and the least socially concerned anywhere in the world – besides being, of course, among the most corrupt. As we shall see later, we may be on the verge of paying an extremely heavy penalty on this account.

Thus, biological warfare, which is now upon us in the garb of bio-terrorism, is something that was predicted by thinking people around the world –the kind of people that governments like ours want to keep miles away.

The whole world, except us, seems to have been concerned about biological weapons in the last two decades. This is yet another example of the social insensitivity of our scientists and technological insensitivity of our politicians.

What has been particularly worrying is the inevitable alliance between terrorism and biological weapons. R.A. Zilinskas, in an article in "Perspectives in Biology and Medicine" in 1990, lists 153 organizations that were designated as "terrorist" by the government of the country in which they were active or by the US in early 1990. The countries in which these organizations functioned were: Algeria, Argentina, Bangladesh, Belgium, Bolivia, Chile, Columbia, Equador, Egypt, El Salvador, France, Germany, Greece, Guatemala, Honduras, India, Italy, Middle and Near East, Morocco, China, Peru, Philippines, Portugal, Puerto Rico, Spain, South Africa, Sri Lanka, Tibet, Tunisia, Turkey, UK, Venezuela and Yugoslavia. The linkage of terrorism with biological weapons is very well articulated in the above article, which makes the point that there are a large number of ways in which biological weapons could be used by terrorists. For example, the article says, "an easily accomplished attack could take place as follows. Terrorists armed with 20-ml syringes equipped with 26-guage needles and filled with the bacteria or toxin-containing solution could, in a short time, inject a large number of cereal boxes, baby-food jars and other containers. The minute hole would not be noticed by most consumers, and the incubation time or the time of reaction will allow the perpetrators to make their escape before the first symptom of illness appeared."

Even though India has been for a long time one of the countries with the highest risk of being attacked by biological weapons, we have no national forum at which matters relating to biological warfare or biological weapons could be discussed. This is in striking contrast to the situation elsewhere, such as in the US where a large number of organizations with highly qualified and responsible individuals as members, have been looking at the question of biological weapons in depth over the last decade and a half. Some of these organizations are the Federation of American Scientists, which has more than half of the US Nobel Prize winners as members, Human Rights Watch, and

Council for Responsible Genetics. Joshua Lederberg, the Nobel Prize-winning American geneticist, is amongst the leading scientists concerned with biological weapons in the US. Contrast this with the situation in our country. Not even one of our six national scientific academies including the National Academy of Medical Sciences and the National Academy of Agriculture, on which our government spends so much money has so far expressed any concern in this regard.

India is a signatory to the Biological Weapons Convention of 1972. By 1 April 1991, 112 parties had joined this "Convention on the Prohibition of the Development, Production and Stock-piling of Bacteriological (biological) and Toxin Weapons and on their Destruction." I had the pleasure of being the member of a small, high power committee appointed by the United Nations Institute of Disarmament Research to work out a document for the Third Review Conference on the Biological Weapons Convention held in Geneva in 1991. India has not, so far, taken this Convention seriously and derived optimal benefit from being a signatory to it For example, I doubt if we have ever sent a strong delegation to the Review Conferences on the Convention held every five years after 1972. The Fifth Review Conference is scheduled to be held towards the end of this year in Geneva. As of today, 143 countries have signed the above convention.

III

The Biological Weapons: The Old and the New

Elsewhere in this article, I have provided two tables listing "living" and "non-living" agents that could be used as biological weapons; some of these are easily accessible or easy to procure and could be used for mass destruction, while others are likely to have only restricted use – for example, temporary incapacitation. In the "living" group, the biological warfare agent of choice would be anthrax and in the "non-living" group, botulin which is the most deadly material so far known to mankind. In 1990, I did a literature survey of papers published on botulin and found that most of the work on it was done after 1974. Between 1974 and 1990, over 40 papers were published on botulin, mostly from the USSR with a sprinkling from Poland, China, Japan, Italy, Germany and the US; this was also the period during which terrorism came of age.

Unfortunately, advances in modern biology have opened up avenues for making designer biological weapons, which, for example, would exploit genetic or ethnic differences and then affect only particular groups.[1]

For example, it has been reported that in the US, those who are above 50 have a depleted immune response. They would thus be far more susceptible to small doses of certain toxic antigen (living organisms or chemicals), which would have no effect on the adult Indian population. Release of these antigens in the environment in an appropriate manner could cause at least temporary disability amongst the Americans over 50, while not affecting Indians. Indeed, when it comes to developing and using biological weapons it is essentially a battle of wits – something in which, perhaps, the deprived section of the world has an advantage, as they have been in any case living by their wits!

Those who have commented on the possibility of designer biological weapons being very real, include Craig Venter, one of the individuals who sequenced the human genome independently of the international project. Australian genetic engineers unknowingly created a mouse virus that killed every one of its victims by wrecking their immune system.[2] There would be, as of today, no defence against such a human virus, which would be easy to create and mass-produce. The fear that biological materials used by well-meaning research scientists could be turned into biological weapons if acquired by terrorists is very real.

Unfortunately, there is a tendency to believe that biological weapons have never been used. This is just not true. Before the collapse of their empire in 606 BC, the Assyrians used an ingenious method of poisoning their enemy. Rye was widely used at that time and in that region both as a cereal for human consumption and as forage crop. It is however, liable to attack by a poisonous fungus, *Claviceps purpurea,* which grows in place of the grain and forms a horny mass called ergot. The Assyrians used this rye-ergot to poison their enemy. Eating rye bread contaminated with ergot can cause gangrene, abortion and hallucinations.

The ancient Romans threw carrions into wells to poison the drinking water of their adversaries. In 1347, the Tartars catapulted the bodies of bubonic-plague victims over the city walls of Kaffa, a Black Sea port that served as a gateway to the silk trade route – a manoeuvre that worked. In 1942, the Soviets infected the German occupation troops with the Tularemia–causing agent, which eventually led to more that 100,000 cases of the disease on both sides. Between 1936 and 1945, the Japanese Military Unit-731 experimented with biological weapons on the Chinese at PingFan in Manchuria, killing thousands of prisoners of war with agents like anthrax, cholera, plague and dysentery. The Japanese also released plague on the Chinese civilian population of

Chekiang province on several occasions by dropping from aeroplanes fleas fed on infected rats. In fact, according to a recent report, China was plagued by diseases from Japan's biological weapons (typhus, bubonic plague, cholera and anthrax) between 1940 and 1950.[3] In 1978, Soviet intelligence agents used ricin (see Table 2) to murder Georgi Markov a defector from Bulgaria. In 1979, an accidental release of anthrax from the Soviet bioweapons facility in Sverdlovsk killed some 100 people and much livestock. In 1984, Salmonella was released by the cult followers of Bhagwan Rajneesh in salad bars in four restaurants in the Dalles in Oregon in the US, which made 750 people ill; the objective was, apparently, to keep voters from the polls to influence a local election! And between 1990 and 1995, the Japanese cult, Aum Shinrikyo, made several unsuccessful attempts to use biological weapons including botulin.

In spite of their being signatories to the Biological Weapons Convention, at least Great Britain, the United States, the erstwhile Soviet Union and now Russia, Canada, Germany, South Africa, Japan, Iraq, Iran, Syria and North Korea have had extensive biological weapons development and testing programmes – in some cases for at least 80 years, Biological weapons must, therefore, be regarded as amongst the oldest weapons in human history: what has perhaps limited their use are the possible repercussions on the user itself. As means of their containment are worked out, their use in preference to all other weapons is bound to become more likely, unless the root causes of conflict are eradicated.

A well-documented example of testing a prototype anthrax bomb would be that recently uncovered by Brian Balmer of the famed University College of London. It is now established that Britain tested the bomb on the Gruinard

Island in Scotland in 1942, leading to an outbreak of anthrax in sheep and other animals, not only on the island but also on the mainland in 1942 and 1943. The island is till today believed to be out of bounds. There are, indeed, many documented cases of plans, which had reached an advanced stage, to use biological weapons through bombers and missiles – for example, in the military history of Britain and Iraq in the last century.

It is well known that at least the US, Iraq and the Soviet Union have been actually stockpiling biological weapons. According to a report, one of the world's largest stocks of anthrax spores is on the Vozrozhdeniye island in the middle of the Aral Sea; it is at the moment unguarded.[4] The world's biggest biological weapons factory, it now appears, was in Stepnogorst in Kazakhstan. Although this facility has been dismantled, it is feared that the knowledge developed in this facility may be now available with criminals to mount attacks against which the world may be totally defenceless. It appears that South Africa's notorious "Doctor Death" who ran the biological warfare programme of the South African Government during apartheid, had his lessons on biological weapons from Saddam Hussein. He (real name, Wouterbasson) even learnt how to use biological warfare agents to kill opposition guerillas.

What has, however, been most perturbing is a very recent rejection by the United States of the proposed protocol for bioweapons inspection and verification, which would strengthen the Biological Weapons Convention and Treaty. This protocol would allow monitoring and verifying the compliance required by the Convention.

IV

The Indian Situation

Finally, as regards the situation in India, my fears of the 7 October 2001 have come true. Bio-terrorism is upon us and is likely to continue even if the US-Afghan war comes to an end. What has been particularly amazing and extremely worrying is the flouting of ignorance about biological weapons on the part of the governmental authorities as well as individuals in positions of authority who have spoken. Before I give examples, let us look at what the real situation in the country is.

As of today, we have no place where information on biological weapons has been documented, classified and could be made available to any one wanting it. We have no inventory of experts who, for example, have an in-depth knowledge of microbiology and molecular biology and of biological warfare (what is documented and what is not documented–that is information obtained through international connections), and who are socially responsible and politically savvy. We have no organization like the Centre for Disease Control in the United States to which suspected cases of victims of an attack by biological weapons could be referred to for quick analysis. We have not taken any steps to guard our airspace or water supply systems. (What prevents the bio-terrorists from spraying a biological warfare agent such as botulin in our water reservoirs instead of a pesticide, from the air?) We have produced no reliable publicity material such as pamphlets, to educate our people. We have not made appropriate announcements that we should have on television and radio – announcements that would contain authentic and useful information presented in a user-friendly way.

I wonder how many of our physicians would know how to diagnose symptoms of Anthrax, Brucellosis, Glanders, Q fever, Rocky Mountain Spotted Fever, Tularemia, and the various haemorrhagic fevers, or symptoms of toxicity due to Botulin, Epsilon Toxin or Ricin, in real time – that is before the person has succumbed to the disease. For example, in the case of pulmonary anthrax caused by inhalation of the anthrax spores (the "white powder"), which can be treated by ciprofloxacin, the diagnosis must be done within a day or two for the drug to be effective. As the early symptoms resemble that of flu or influenza, the patient is unlikely to report to the doctor in the above "window" period. And how many of our government hospitals or health centres have stocks of ciprofloxacin (an expensive drug) to dispense to individuals suspected to be infected with anthrax, who would need 120 tablets of 500 mg each of this drug for the full course? The cost of the 120 tablets would be about Rs.1,100, fortunately much lower that $650 or so in the US.

How many of our places have the ability to identify spores of anthrax – just one biological warfare agent – in real time, with minimum delay? The fact is that not one of our organizations – be it in the defence, science or health sector – has been so far set up to identify quickly, using modern technology, the various likely agents of biological warfare, specially those that have been weaponized. An honest institution such as the CCMB at Hyderabad, which has otherwise world-class facilities, has stated its inability to identify anthrax spores as of now. For such an identification, the lab would need an appropriate and dedicated containment facility (preferably of P-3 standard); facilities for doing molecular biological work such as isolation and sequencing of DNA and the synthesis of oligodeoxyribonucleotides as primers; access to molecular biological data bases, high-quality microbiological and animal house facilities; trained and experienced molecular biologists and microbiologists with state-of-the-art knowledge in the field; and control human anthrax material. The only institute in the country today which would come close to having all these facilities for identification of anthrax and, possibly, a few other (but surely not all) agents of biological warfare, is the ICMR's National Institute of Communicable Diseases (NICD). One of their assets is that they have, for use as controls, two isolates of Bacillus anthrax from humans who were affected with this organism in Bangalore and Calcutta a year or two ago; these infections were cattle-derived. They also have one cattle-derived anthrax culture.

The NICD has a high-quality P2 but not a P3 containment facility. It follows standards set up by WHO for unweaponized *Bacillus anthracus*. Weaponized *Bacillus anthracus* may be, for example, coated with bentonite; this may require different pre-treatment, growth media and processing for amplification of DNA by PCR. It is, therefore, likely that the actual number of anthrax-positive case in the country may be far more than sent to and confirmed by the NICD.

We should not forget how long it took us to identify the causative organism of Surat's recent problem and till today. In fact, we cannot say with confidence if it was as epidemic of plague due to natural causes or a covert act of some kind of biological warfare. If, today, a thousand people die of anthrax in a thousand villages spread across the length and breadth of the country, that have little or no access to modern medicines, over four weeks, our health ministers will surely keep on saying that we have had no case of anthrax. Our government's concern for reliable epidemiology has been so far as real as their concern for routing out corruption.

And how many of our laboratories have the capacity to distinguish between different strains of anthrax and determine if they are genetically engineered or are high toxin-producing strains? Thus if we find anthrax spores in postal envelopes in ten different places in India, which laboratory in the country today can tell us in a short time whether or not they are the same strain ? The few laboratories that have the capacity to do so are simply not equipped for this work. It is again being established that foresight and precaution are not in the dictionary of our politicians and bureaucrats, including scientist-bureaucrats. The matter is made worse by their propensity to lie and to mislead the people. Look at some of the statements that have been made by them, as reported in various newspapers.

New Delhi, 9 October 2001: After an emergency meeting, top WHO specialists agreed unanimously that "there was no need to panic as India was adequately prepared to handle any eventuality of germ warfare". The Communicable Diseases Director, Dr. Vijay Kumar, said that it is a myth that germ warfare can kill entire populations within a few days. "It is not easy to spread enough germs to infect a whole town," said Dr. Kumar. What about a privately rented small aircraft spraying 100 kilograms of weaponised anthrax spores on a crowded city (that is, spores of the right strain of anthrax which are in a physical state that they can stay suspended in air and move with a breeze or wind, for sustained period)? And what about someone putting a few hundred grams of botulin in the municipal water supply system of one of our cities or towns?

New Delhi, 10 October 2001: Dr. A. K. Agarwal said that "vaccines (for anthrax) were available to prevent it." Where are those vaccines? Where are they available? Dr. Agarwal is obviously not aware that the anthrax vaccine for humans is not readily available, now is it foolproof or totally safe. The gulf war syndrome with which many in the American Defence Services suffered, has been partly attributed to the anthrax vaccine they received as a precautionary measure against the anthrax attack by Saddam Hussein.

New Delhi, 12 October 2001: According to Subhash C. Arya, of the Centre for Logistical Research and Innovation, "Why should a terrorist unleash a weapon that is known to be curable or has an antidote?" (Answer: because by the time you are likely to find it all out, the person would be dead.)

New Delhi, 12 October 2001: Dr. K. K. Datta, Director, NICD, probably the best equipped and the most experienced lab in the country to identify organisms such as Bacillus anthracus that causes anthrax, said, "Our labs have the ability to respond fast, get to any affected area quickly. Depending on the vaccine needed, we can go into mass production." Have we ever known our government to respond in real time? And surely, Dr. Datta would know how much time it would take to produce a vaccine that we have never produced!

Chennai, 12 October 2001: In this report emanating

from the Madras Veterinary College, it was obviously not recognized that cattle anthrax is not what we are talking about, and that anthrax acquired through an act of bio-terrorism is not the same thing as cattle anthrax. Thus, the title of this report, "No cause for panic", is misleading. This confusion about cattle anthrax and anthrax acquired through an act of bio-terrorism is reflected in many statements, including that of Tishya Chatterjee, Member Secretary of the A. P. Pollution Control Board[5] and of Andhra Pradesh's Chief Minister, N. Chandrababu Naidu.[6]

Hyderabad, 13 October 2001: Dr. Lakshmi Rajyam, Addl. Director, Communicable Diseases, Government of Andhra Pradesh, said, referring to anthrax that "it is contagious and spreads from one person to another through secretions". The only good thing about anthrax is that it is not a contagious or easily communicable disease!

Hyderabad, 18 October 2001: Keeti V. Shah, of the United States said that, "there have been no authentic reports from any part of the world till date on the use of germ-warfare." He added, "I haven't come across any country which was hit by germ-warfare. There are reports that some countries do have such mass destruction germ-weapons but there is no evidence to prove the same." Could there be any more naïve statements?

Hyderabad, 16 October 2001: The Health Minister, Dr. S. Aruna, of Andhra Pradesh, appealed to people not to panic about anthrax as her department was taking measures to tackle this situation. What measures?

Nandyal, 18 October 2001: The Health Minister, Dr. S. Aruna, said her State (Andhra Pradesh) "was fully geared to prevent the dreaded anthrax bacteria and that there was no need to panic." I would like to know what the Health Minister will do if there are a thousand envelopes received in Hyderabad within a week, all looking different, mailed from different places, all with plausible but with wrong addresses, with white powder, half of which are anthrax: something which is not outside the realm of possibility?

Hyderabad, 26 October 2001: According to city-based homeopath, Dr. K. Mukherjee, "anthrax is not something that has no cure and cannot be prevented." To prevent and cure anthrax all that you need to do is to "take Anthraxinum 200, four pills (morning) for seven consecutive days along with Ipecae 30, four pills in the afternoon for 10 consecutive days." Our enemies should reward him!

The New Indian Express of 19 October 2001 published interviews with four citizens of Hyderabad: they seem to be totally unconcerned about the possibility of anthrax invading Hyderabad. One of the arguments was that "India has no enemies like the United States has!"

Pharmabiz of 25 October 2001 quotes Dr. Rajasambandan, Director of Medical Education, Government of Tamil Nadu, as saying that antidotes to bioweapons can be synthesized and stocked "within a few days"; these antidotes would include "vaccine and sera". The price for such scientific absurdities that underplay the real threat can be extremely high.

According to a report in *Deccan Chronicle* of 24 October 2001, the Chief Minister of Andhra Pradesh has said that the tainted firm Bharat Biotech, vaccine samples of which have been found to be lacking in potency by the

Government's Central Research Institute, Kasauli, is "well-equipped" to handle the anthrax crisis, something that even a lab like the CCMB has said it is not equipped to do. Apart from this, the Government of Andhra Pradesh has also appointed the Hyderabad-based Institute of Preventive Medicine which has no containment or molecular biological facilities whatsoever, as the State-level nodal agency for dealing with anthrax cases.[7] Amusingly, the State has a high-power Medical and Health Advisory Council, which has so far not been consulted on the issue. Fools walk merrily where wise men dread to tread! Ignorance may be bliss for politicians and bureaucrats but it could be a disaster for the people.

In an advertisement in national newspapers on 22 October 2001, the Government of India said, "so far, there has not been a single case in India of a postal article having been found to contain anthrax."[8] Even at that time, the chances that this statement was true, were extremely small; it was likely to be merely a reflection of our inability to detect and identify anthrax. Today, we know that this statement is not true. Bio-terrorism has come to stay and our lives will never be the same again. The sooner we realize this, the better it would be for us. The government must learn that in such matters, transparency is the best policy.

We must also realize that, as of today, there is no foolproof way to fight bio-terrorism except, perhaps, by removing the causes of worldwide inequities and injustices, stopping the arms race and reducing expenditure on agents of war. Till then we can only ameliorate this situation. How may we do that?

V

What May We Do?

I suggest the following concrete steps to take care to the extent possible, not only the immediate problem but also the future problems in respect of bio-terrorism, keeping in mind that after 11 September and then 7 October the world has changed for ever, that the threat of biological weapons is no longer just a threat, and that it may cost us very dearly if we are not prepared to deal with it.

1. The government should set up a high-power national committee to devise, implement and monitor our policy in regard to biological warfare, under the chairmanship of Dr. A.P.J. Abdul Kalam. The committee should be serviced by the Defence Ministry and should have appropriate, carefully and purposefully related defence experts, media people, experts from six ICMR, CSIR and DBT laboratories, (CCMB at Hyderabad, IMT at Chandigarh, IICB at Kolkata, and NICD, NII and CBT at Delhi), scientists from the private sector who have in-depth knowledge of concerned fields and of biological warfare, and representatives of the Ministry of External Affairs, the Ministry of Home Affairs, the Indian Council of Medical Research, and the Directorate-General of Medical and Health Services.

2. A centre should be set up jointly by the Department of Science and Technology and DRDO, which would collect information on biological weapons, collate and document it appropriately, and make it available to anyone wanting it. As I said on many occasions, the best way to contain biological warfare if not to eliminate

it, would be to have as well-informed a public as possible.

3. A carefully selected, knowledgeable and concerned small group (which should include medical doctors, pathologists, and experts in molecular biology and micro biology, with knowledge of biological warfare and its various implications) should have a dialogue with the Centre for Disease Control in Atlanta in respect of the mechanism that they have been using to identify and handle biological warfare agents.

4. Laboratories, which could be equipped with the latest technology and information for handling and identifying agents of biological warfare, should be identified. I dare say that, with the possible exception of the National Institute of Communicable Diseases and the Centre for Biotechnology (CBT, some of the staff members of which have done some excellent original work on Bacillus anthracus which could lead to the development of a vaccine for anthrax), both at Delhi. None of the other laboratories in the country has any experience of even handling the organism that causes human anthrax.

5. A long-term publicity programme, using appropriate publicity material, pamphlets, posters, advertisements in the press, the radio and the television, for various categories of people including those in the villages, should be worked out.

6. A strategy should be devised to make medicines or vaccines, wherever known to be effective, available as and when required, in real time.

7. Information on biological weapons should be introduced in our medical curriculum. There should be a continuing medical education programme on the effects of biological weapons.

8. A machinery should be set up to ensure that programmes don't remain on paper but they are actually implemented. Biological warfare is a matter of national concern and should fall outside the purview of political expediency and personal egos.

9. To prevent delivery of active biological agents through the post, two steps (amongst other possible ones) could be considered. Organizations like ECIL should be encouraged to develop at the earliest, machines that would detect powder in postal articles and then separate them automatically. If all mail is routed through 20-30 centres, the powder-containing letters could be radiation sterilized using machines (such as ISOMED) that the Department of Atomic Energy (DAE) has already developed. Studies in regard to the radiation dosage requirements for the killing of anthrax spores could be commenced straightaway by DAE in collaboration with NICD.

10. Work towards development of quick detection kits for agents of biological warfare listed in Tables 1 and 2 should be started in appropriate labs and supported on a war footing.

If you ever suspect that you are exposed to anthrax, say through a letter, do not wait to obtain a report on the powder. Please see a doctor within 24 hours and then again after 24 hours. The doctor should look for any skin condition or beginning of flue or influenza like symptoms, and prescribe ciprofloxacin (2 tablets of 500 mg per day for 60 days), during which period he must examine and advise you periodically – say every 10 days. An alternative to ciprofloxacin may be doxacyclin.

If you wish to obtain further information on the organism that causes anthrax, the disease itself, and the use of anthrax as an agent of biological warfare, you could log on to the following sites on the Web:

- www.mywebmd.com / content / article / 4058.322
- www.washingtonpost.com / wp-dyn / nation / specials / attacked / bioterrorism /
- www.emedicine.com / emerg / topic864.htm
- www.usmilitary.about.com / library / weekly / aa101401a.htm?terms=Anthrax:
- www.cdc.gov / ncidod / dbmd / diseaseinfo / anthrax%5fg.htm:
- www.aomc.org / comdiseases / anthrax.html:
- www.anthrax,ods.mil /
- www.medicalmailbox.com infectious % 5 Fdiseases. htm:
- www.govrnment.about.com / cs / anthrax / index.htm:

Finally, we all – the politicians, the bureaucrats and the citizens – must keep reminding ourselves that anthrax is not the only agent of biological warfare that may be against us. For example, the threat of recurrence of small pox, which we believe has been wiped out from our planet, is real. Ostensibly, we have stocks of small pox virus stored under an international agreement in the US and in Russia. We havc no way of knowing if the terrorist states or groups also have such a stock. If you have the virus, small pox vaccines are easy to produce; so you can protect your own people while leaving the rest of the world vulnerable to the disease. The threat to our environment through even a limited use of agents of biological warfare has so far never been assessed.

Table-1

Pathogenic Microorganisms Produced or Studied as Potential BW Agents

VIRUSES

Disease	Pathogen	Death rate (%) in untreated cases of natural disease*
Influenza Psittacosis	Chlamydia peittaci	10 – 100
Yellow fever	Yellow fever virus Aedes aegypti, carrier)	30 – 50
Dengue fever	Dengue fever virus	0 – 1
Chikungunya	Chikungunya virus	0 – 1
O'nyong-nyong	O'nyong-nyong virus	R-NA
Mayaro	Mayaro virus	R-NA
Ross River	Ross River virus	R-NA
Venezuelan equine encephalitis	Venezuelan equine encephalitis virus	0 – 2
Eastern equine encephalitis	Eastern equine encephalitis virus	50
Western equine encephalitis	Western equine encephalitis virus	0 – 3

Tick-borne encephalitis	Tick-borne encephalitis virus	R-NA
Kyasanor Forest Disease	Kyasanur Forest virus	R-NA
Rift Valley fever	Rift Valley fever virus	0 – 1
Lymphocytic choriomeningitis	LCM virus	R-NA
Argentinan (South American) haemorrhagic fever	Junin and other viruses	5 – 15
Korean haemorrhagic fever	Hantaan virus	R-NA
Lassa fever encephalitis	Lassa fever virus	1 – 50
Sindbis	Sindbis virus	R-NA
Marburg fever	Marburg virus	35
African haemorrhagic fever	Congo Crimean virus	R-NA
Ebola fever	Ebola virus	65 – 80
Small pox	Variola virus	10 – 30

BACTERIA

DISEASE	**PATHOGEN**	**Death rate (%) in untreated cases of natural disease-**
Cholera	Vibrio cholarae	10 – 80
Typhoid	Salmonella typhose	4 – 20
Dysentery	Shigella	2 – 20
Tularemia	Francisella tularensis	20 – 60
Brucellosis	Brucella species	2 – 5
Tetanus	Clostridium tetani	90 – 100

Gas gangrene	Clostridium perfringens	High
Plague	Pasteurella pestis	30 – 100
Anthrax	Bacillus anthracis	95 – 100
Glanders	Antinobacillus mallei	90 – 100
	RICKETTSIA	
Epidemic typhus	Rickettsia prowazakii	10 – 40
Scrub typhus	Rickettsia tsutsugamushi	R-NA
G-fever	Coxiella burnetii	1 – 4
Rocky Mountain spotted fever	Rickettsia rickettsii	10 - 30
	FUNGI (for plants)	
Black stem rust of cereals	Puccinia graminis	3- 90
Rice blast	Pyricularia oryzae	50 – 90

***R-NA** : reliable information is not available

(Agents of biological warfare can be used not only to kill but also to incapacitate for various periods.)

Table- 2

Toxins Produced or Studied as Potential Biological Warfare Agents

Name	**Lethal Dosage (LD_{50})***
Botulin (Clostridium botulinum toxin A) **	0.6
Enterotoxin B from Staphyloccus aureus	—
Saxitoxin (shellfish poison)	200
Cobrotoxin	—
Crotoxin (South American rattle snake toxin)	—
Myotoxin	—
Cardiotoxin	—
Bungarotoxin	—
Aflatoxin	—
Snail conotoxin	—
Scorpion toxins	20000
Ricin (derived from castor beans)	100
Substance P	—
Tetanus toxin	less than 2.5
Trichothecene mycotoxins	highly variable
Shiga toxin (from Shigella dysenteriae or S flexneri)	—
Epsilon toxin (from Clostridium perfringens)	—

* nanogram (10^{-9})/kg estimated to have 50 per cent chance of killing the subject.

** The most potent, easy-to-produce, toxic agent known to mankind. It is an intestinal poison, one kilogram of which could, theoretically kill the entire human population on our planet today.

Notes

1. P.M.Bhargava, *UNIDIR Newsletter*, vol.4, no.2, 1991, pp.6-8 and 26-28. Also see his paper titled "Possible Measures for Increasing Confidence in Biological Weapons Conventions", presented to the above-mentioned working group for preparing a document for the Third Review Conference on Biological Weapons Convention held in 1991.
2. *The New Indian Express*, 12 January 2001.
3. *New Scientist*, 3 February, 2001, p.5.
4. *The Hindu*, 7 October 2001.
5. *Deccan Chronicle*, 17 October 2000.
6. *Ibid.*, 16 October 2001.
7. *The New Indian Express*, 4 November 2001.
8. *Ibid.*, 22 October 2001.

Bio-Terrorism: A Threat To National Security

A. Ravinder Nath

There are certain microorganisms that are practically used as weapons of mass destruction of people. The awareness on bio-terrorism intends to serve the community for preparedness and response from biological weapons threat to international peace and security. At least four diseases – anthrax, botulism, plague and smallpox – are recognized for the most possible causes of bio-terrorism through pathogenic microbiological agents. The knowledge on this topic is likely to address the potential threats of additional and genetically modified microorganisms, which resists the treatment of infection and may be destructive to crops and human survival. The use of anti-crop and anti-animal agents as biological weapons greatly affect the food processing industries, which are the most vulnerable and prone groups for bio-terrorism.

Biological weapons, along with chemical and nuclear weapons are the three systems designated as weapons of mass destruction (WMD). The fear of the unknown and unseen about biological weapons may create silent terror in a populous community. Awareness, education and training are the only defence modes against new and emerging diseases of bio-terrorism. Historical findings reveal that France was the first country, to use bacteria as a biological weapon to thin out the army and disorganize the transport of draft animals for war purposes in the late 1930s and later various states began biological warfare activities as a part of offensive and defensive programmes. The introduction of potato beetle by Germany and France in the 1930s to degrade the food crops of enemies' civilian population has caught special attention on the usage of disease-causing germs as a tool for biological warfare. The disease-causing germs can be weaponised into missile warheads, aerial bombs, on line dispensing drone aircraft and helicopter spray system. Various international agreements and treaties from 1899 to 1972 allowed only partial containment on the usage of biological weapons, but it has not contained the development and proliferation. The biological weapons, pathogenic microorganisms, which release certain poisonous toxins, lethal at very low concentration, are the most potential source of bio-terrorism and are a real threat to the security of public health and international peace.

Some Aspects of Biological Weapons

Most of the biological weapons are disease-causing microorganisms and classified as "class-4" pathogens. It can strike as epidemic for mass destruction of people and spread could take place without any immediate recognition. These are used as tacit tactics to terrorize psychologically or cripple the economy and health of the enemy group or country. They adopt different modes of transmission such as air, water, food and biological vector, which can disseminate easily into a large population.

There is a possibility of spread of unusual strains or variants of pathogenic microorganisms, which fails to respond to standard therapy and diagnosis and is likely to cause more damage and toxic effects on public health, as there is no known effective treatment to employ on genetically mutant pathogens.

The threat of intentional use or accidental release of these are far more frightening than chemical weapons for which definite antidotes and counter measures are available to control the epidemics. It can spread through different routes of exposure such as inhalation, absorption, ingestion and open wound or injection.

Microbiology of Biological Weapons

The microorganisms are broadly classified into two types based on their cell structure.

1. Prokaryotes: Example: Bacteria and Virus
2. Eukaryotes: Example: Fungi and Protozoa

The common hosts that can carry these microorganisms and can spread the diseases are insects, birds, animals and plants.

The research on enhancing the virulence of pathogenic microorganisms would result in the production of mutant varieties of very high virulence different from that of the known.

Hence the known immunizing agent would be ineffective against the newly developed variety likely to cause more threat to the health.

Some Potential and Typical Examples of Biological Warfare Agents

Anthrax:	*Bacillus anthracis*	Bacteria	Infectious
Botulism:	*Clostridium botulinum*	Bacteria	Infectious
Plague:	*Yersinia pestis*	Bacteria	Contagious
Small Pox:	*Variola sps*	Virus	Contagious

Anthrax

Anthrax has been called perfect germ for bio-terrorism, as some anthrax strains developed as biological weapons are resistant to many drugs. It is an acute infectious disease caused by *Bacillus anthracis,* a spore forming gram + Ve bacteria and is not contagious, only those exposed to release of spores gets infected. It is an animal disease that has been around for tens of thousands of years, acquired through ingestion of contaminated soil. Humans can become infected through skin contact, ingestion or inhalation of *Bacillus anthracis* spores from infected animals or animal products.

During the Second World War the British army experimented with an explosive shell filled with the anthrax spores and it can be delivered easily as an aerosol to spread the disease. These experiments were carried out on the coast of the Scottish Island and the spores persisted in the environment for over 36 years.

Human anthrax can occur in three forms-Pulmonary, Skin and Gastrointestinal and can be transmitted through inhalation, injection and ingestion of contaminated food and air.

Pulmonary Anthrax

Flu-like symptoms observed initially and an interim improvement with an abrupt on set of respiratory failure after 2-4 days of initial symptoms and Hydrodynamic collapse, possibly accompanied by thoracic edema. Observing of Gram +Ve bacilli on blood culture in the first 2-3 days of illness. The incubation period is 2-60 days and the mortality rate is very high despite antibiotic treatment, if it is initiated after the onset of respiratory symptoms.

Skin Anthrax

A rash is seen on the head, forearms or hands and also causes localized itching, followed by popular lesion that turns vesicular and within 2-6 days develops into a depressed black eschar. The incubation period is 1-7 days following cutaneous exposure and usually non-fatal, if treated with antibiotics.

Gatro-intestinal Anthrax

Abdominal pain, nausea, vomiting, fever and blood motions occur following ingestion of contaminated food, usually meat. Observing of Gram +Ve bacilli on blood culture in the first 2-3 days of illness is the indication of gastro intestinal anthrax infection. The incubation period for this form of disease is 1-7 days following ingestion and usually, fatal after progression to toxemia and sepsis.

It is not easy to grow deadly anthrax and it is even harder to make it into a weapon. The spores have to be turned into a microscopically fine powder, which is not a simple trick, the isolation of spores in its pure form involves tedious downstream processing techniques. It needs a conducive environment such as temperature, moisture and the wind must be exactly right to contaminate and spread on large population areas. Though it is easy to produce certain biological agents in kitchens, garages, bathtubs and home beer brewery kits, it is difficult to develop virulent varieties, despite the expenditure of money, effort and substantial time.

Botulism

This is another dangerous biological weapon developed from *Clostridium botulinum*, which commonly exists in the form of endo spores and are present in soil and marine sediment throughout the world. This is an anaerobic gram-positive rod bacteria that produces a potent neuro toxin known as botulinum exo-toxin. In humans this toxin inhibits the release of the neuro transmitter acetyl - choline, resulting in a characteristic flaccid paralysis, i.e. muscles do not contract in response to motor neuron activity.

Botulism occurs in two forms as agents of bio-terrorism. One is Food Borne (Gastro-Intestinal form) and the other is the Respiratory form through ingestion and inhalation. The food borne infection is caused owing to improperly canned or preserved food and the respiratory form is spread through air. The food-borne botulism is the most common form of disease in adults and 1/3 of patients may die due to respiratory or cardiac failure within few days of infection and it is not transmitted from person to person. The incubation period for neurological symptoms of food borne botulism begins 12-36 hours after ingestion of contaminated food and release of exo toxin, whereas inhalation botulism begins 24 - 72 hours after aerosol exposure.

The common symptoms of this infection are blurred

vision, difficulty in swallowing and speaking, weakening of jaws, muscles and paralysis of arms followed by respiratory dysfunction and descending weakness in legs.

Plague

Plague is an acute, specific communicable disease caused by the gram -negative bacilli bacteria *Yersinia pestis*. It continues to be a major life-threatening infectious epidemic disease of human beings and animals. It is primarily a disease of rodents and humans are affected incidentally. This is usually transmitted by infected fleas (*Xenophillis cheopis*) and also expected to be air-borne, which can break out into bio-terrorism very easily.

This disease took a heavy toll of life in the early part of the 20th century with an estimated 12.5 human deaths in India alone.

There are two forms of plague, one is Bubonic plague and the other one is Pneumonic plague. The former plague is transmitted to human beings through the bite of an infected rat flea and the latter plague is transmitted from infected person to person through aerosol droplets, which is most fatal and susceptible to all ages and both sexes. The incubation period for Bubonic plague is 2-8 days, whereas for Pneumonic plague, it will be 1-3 days.

The common symptoms of this infection are lymphatic and blood infections resulting in septicemia, fever, cough and chest pain.

Small Pox

This is an extremely serious disease and is the most

probable biological weapon due to its potential to cause severe morbidity in a non-immune population and can be transmitted via the air-borne route. It is caused by the *variola* virus and spreads from person to person and only humans are the hosts for this virus. There is no natural resistance to this viral illness. Since the invention of immunization this disease was eradicated throughout the world, but it is a most potential weapon for bio-terrorism.

This disease afflicted mankind for centuries and at least 300 million people died of small pox, all over the globe in the 20th century. This is three times more than the number of people, who died either directly or indirectly as a result of armed conflicts through wars.

Small pox is transmitted via both large and small respiratory droplets to patients and human transmission is likely from air-borne and droplet exposure, and by contact with skin lesions or secretions. The incubation period for small pox is 7-17 days. The symptoms resemble other acute viral illnesses, such as influenza.

Assessing the Vulnerability

Bio-terrorism is considered to be another easy accessible form of asymmetric warfare adopted by the terrorist forces.

The following four are more vulnerable and potential threats for crippling the economy, creating instability, terrorizing the masses psychologically, causing deaths and ill effects on living systems and can spread through different routes.

1. **Industry:** Chemical, Pharmaceutical and Biotechnology

industries need to maintain the surveillance procedures, frequent monitoring, supervision and workplace management assessments are necessary, even for a possibility of an accidental release of both chemical and bio-hazard materials. For this purpose proper safety and security practices are to be maintained.

2. **Buildings:** The high-rise buildings and densely populated areas are readily prone for attack by terrorists. These are to be designed for proper safety and security measures to prevent from both interior and exterior attack.

3. **Water supplies:** These are other important systems that need attention and vigilance as a probable threat disaster. Especially proper security facilities are to be provided for post-purified drinking water storage facility.

4. **Agriculture:** The food-growing operations are more attractive targets for terrorists, which could present a variety of opportunities to set in motion for outbreak of disease among livestock and crops.

Tackling of Bio-terrorism Threat

Tackling of threat is based on a number of factors, the first and foremost is educating the masses about the strategies and resources available to cope with any kind of eventuality. Secondly, strengthening of emergency response capabilities, identification of hospitals, notifying the affected areas and good communication system. Thirdly, networking of different agencies involved in the community safety and nation's security. Fourthly, understanding of human physiology and enhancing the funding for research on molecular biological studies. Fifthly, evolving an effective management policy.

The response operations include training in laboratory work, rescue operations, vaccination, diagnosis and etiology. Mock exercises and drills help to face the problem easily and pharmaceutical stockpile facilitates to counter any further eventuality.

Conclusion

To meet the exigencies of risk management of bio-terrorism, it may be required to develop awareness among public and media. Education and training should be given to personnel of specific departments such as police, fire, medical, revenue, intelligence and military, involved in safety containment and crisis management. Measures should be taken for prevention of modes of transmission and devising a suitable public health policy. Should establish the databases on chemical and biosafety strategies with appropriate diagnostic and treatment methods. Should develop a core research group for periodic follow up on management strategies in handling the crisis arises out of bio-terrorism and to identify issues of immediate concern by preparing institution-specific response plans.

The advances in biotechnology, information and material sciences may underpin the development of rapid and effective detection and identification devices. Breakthroughs in understanding of human physiology may provide new approaches for improving the immune response to pathogens and molecular biological studies provide role of environmental carcinogens and assist in evaluation of risk effects of human health.

Section-IV: Terrorism in South Asia

The Global Contours of Terrorism: South Asian Predicament

P.V. Rao

Conflict in today's world is hardly confined to state actors. Though the state continues to be the dominant party to a conflict situation, it is one of the several actors, mainly the non-state participants. The state in many conflicts remains one of several combatants and in the ensuing battle to restore order the state has to play different roles including shifting sides from one warring group to another or playing one against another. Warring anti-state groups have successfully gained constituencies, moral and material, far beyond the regional boundaries in the international society. The fragile character of international society itself, erosion of state sovereignty, ubiquity of ethnic movements, rising strength of global NGOs and non-state actors, proliferation of drug-arms network and the revolution in communication technology, among several other factors, have enabled conflicts to gain worldwide attention, rather space.

The distinction between inter-state and intra-state conflict is waning under the cumulative impact of the Web of the above factors. The means and strategies available to dissident movements to resist state authority are far greater today than any other period in the past. An apparent domestic war between the juridical state and its dissident contestant involves a multiplicity of actors both within and outside the conflict zone. The number and range of actors vary from the state, state-within state, militant groups, regional/extra regional powers, international organizations, unorganized groups, irregular forces, Diaspora communities and even underworld mafia. The interplay of such a cross-section of actors, often operating at cross-purposes, makes resolution of conflict an extremely difficult exercise.

What needs to be emphasized, therefore, is the change in the pattern of conflict today, particularly following the end of the Cold War. The change in the zones of conflict, its nature and the actors involved in it has undergone significant transformation. Inter-state wars are replaced mostly by intra-state wars as democratic and ethnonationalist movements gained phenomenal ascendancy in global society. "By the early 1990s, many governments had revaluated their military doctrines in terms of their most likely security threat: ethnic conflict and insurgencies."[1] Small and light weapons illegally procured and proliferated became the primary means of fighting by the rebel sub-nationalist groups so much so in an overwhelming number of current conflicts. In geographical terms, it has been empirically proved that "the density of armed violence and small arms and light weapons is inversely proportional to the distance from the international borders," and in the South Asian context conflicts in this region over the last two decades reveal that "most of them and the availability of small arms have been concentrated in zones close to international borders."[2]

South Asia, over more than two decades, has been a scene of domestic ethnic wars involving the big and small states. More internal conflicts have occurred in recent times than inter-state wars. As against the five regular military-to-military wars in the region since 1947 including the Kargil war, 42 wars of irregular type erupted besides a much larger number of armed conflicts at a lower scale going down to terrorist acts.[3] Such wars have distinguished themselves in their intractability and internationalization. Few regions in the world witnessed the global reach of conflicts with purely domestic content as South Asia. The Khalistan, Kashmir and Tamil separatist movements have thoroughly demonstrated their ability to fight the state power and draw the international attention and support.

A strong state like India and a small island like Sri Lanka as well are unable to find a lasting solution to the current ethnic wars in their societies. In its management of internal conflicts the South Asian state fundamentally faces two elements of global dimension, viz: the internationalization of internal conflict and procurement of arms by militant groups from globally diffused sources. Both the elements are not mutually exclusive but closely interrelated in the sense that political support to a warring ethnic group can also extend war material. Moreover, a state or non-state actor's support to an internal militant group is relatively easy to identify than the sources of arms supplies as there are many illegal agents and channels to transfer the lethal weapons to the militants fighting the state.

The first element, the internationalization of an internal conflict, is the most formidable political factor that the South Asian state has to counter. Extra-regional states and international NGOs are the major actors in the field through whom the ethnic groups, which are challenging the state authority for more autonomy or secession are exerting pressure on the state. To be more specific the Western states like the US, UK, France, Germany and Netherlands and the UN on the one hand, and voluntary bodies like the

Amnesty International, Asia Watch and the European Human Rights Association are the major agencies through which the dissident groups articulate their cause and appeal for action against the state repression.

Human rights violations by the South Asian state over the last two decades have been the most discussed and documented subject by the above bodies. As a matter of fact, it is the human rights paradigm, which has brought into sharp focus the nature and legitimacy of the state in South Asia into global debate as well as pressure. Given the Western understanding and sensitivity to the human rights abuse militant groups were able to muster considerable support to their cause in Europe and America and also subject their state to external pressure for redressal. It is a well-known fact that the National Human Rights Commission in India owes its establishment to the Western pressure during the Punjab and Kashmir secessionist movements. Of no less significant illustration of international pressure on the management of India's internal conflicts is the role of the American Congress in debating and influencing the Administration's aid policy towards India in the context of the alleged repression of civil rights by the security forces in Punjab. The Congress moved the Burton Amendment initiated by the California Congressman Don Burton to stop foreign assistance to India on grounds of violation of human rights in the state of Punjab. Burton was lobbied by the Khalistan Sikh activists living in the US.

What we witness in the prevailing scenario of militancy in the South Asian region is that the sovereignty of the state in defining and exercising its power to control the anti-state movements and their outfits is sought to be externally managed. Hence the state is asked to allow foreign visiting groups into the disturbed areas, permit neutral human rights inquiries, appoint human rights commissions, etc. to address the militant cause.

It is the second element more than the first one, which the South Asian state finds extremely difficult to identify and control. The bare truth is that the widespread and uncontrolled proliferation of illicit arms around the world fuels the ongoing ethnic wars in South Asia. No single state in the region can control such an externally but illegally nourished phenomenon of violence unless there is going to be a regionally coordinated mechanism to combat the lethal sources of support to the terrorist outfits in the region.

Small Arms and Light Weapons

Over the last two decades particularly after the end of the Cold War, there is a free play of lethal weapons in the international society. As Cold War structures and rationale for continued arming of client states disappeared, states declined in their territorial authority, borders became fragile, old states splintered into new nations and arms manufacturers flouted international arms control regimes, acquisition of weapons by unorganized rebel groups and smugglers became an easy task. Light and small arms proliferation has emerged as the most dangerous phenomenon in the global civil society and governments all over the world including the UN are seriously aware of this growing phenomenon but with least controls. Most of these weapons are transferred through illegal means and diverted in a various of ways. As a BASIC (British American Security Information Council) report on light weapons observes:

"Light weapons are transferred illegally in a variety of ways in order to serve many different objectives. Weapons may be diverted from legal channels, stolen from storage facilities, or smuggled across borders. They may be transferred by one state to arm sub-state groups in another, or supplied to parties in a conflict to whom weapons transfers are barred as the result of a UN arms embargo. The weapons are also used by narco-traffickers, criminal syndicates, and private security firms to carry out clandestine activities."[4]

The portability of the light weapons as well as their relative low-cost makes transportation very easy. In sharp contrast to the weapons used in regular wars which are restored to their storage, light weapons are 'recycled' from one conflict zone to another and one warring group to another through various means such as smuggling, concealment, mislabelling, false documentation and illegal money transfers. The illicit trafficking in these weapons, according to a UN report, plays a major role in the violence currently affecting some countries and regions, by supplying the instruments used to destabilize societies and governments, encourage crime, and foster terrorism, drug trafficking, mercenary activity and the violation of human rights.

Afghanistan is a classic example of the spread of light weapons. Arms supplied, procured and captured by the Afghan Mujahideen in their fight against the former Soviet forces flooded into the NWFP area of adjoining Pakistan. It is by now too well known and documented history that a large proportion of arms into this area were supplied by the US through the CIA in its counter offensive against the former Soviet Union. The CIA in turn pipelined an estimated

$6 billion worth arms from its own and other sources through the Pakistan ISI which included the Kalashnikov variants, RPG-7 anti tank weapons, varieties of machine guns, SAMs and explosives. Weapons from sources other than the CIA-supplied included from China, Egypt, South Africa and Israel.[5]

The great arms bazaar that transcends the Pak-Afghan border in the NWFP region is a shopping centre for a varied number of customers who include embargoed states, rebel groups, private armies, drug peddlers and criminal gangsters whose choice of weapons, used by the Punjabi and later Kashmiri militants came from this area.[6] Jasjit Singh notes that the whereabouts of 560 Stinger missiles supplied to the Afghan Mujahideen are unknown, a few were sold to Iran, another 312 reportedly sold in the open market of Landi Kotal in Pakistan in 1993. Historically viewed, if Afghanistan had weighed as crucial element in the strategic calculus of the imperial powers and the security strategies of Cold War adversaries, it is no less important today as the cockpit of deadly insurgencies and exporter of incendiary power.

The recurring internal conflicts in India, mainly Khalistan and then the Kashmir secessionism, were armed by Pakistan with the small and light weapons obtained out of the Afghan supplies. A significant quantity of the CIA supplied weapons were siphoned off by the Pakistan ISI, which diverted most of them to serve its purpose in the western Punjab and Kashmir. Between 1986-92, 26 per cent of the Kalashnikov assault rifles seized from the Khalistan militants were intercepted at the Indo-Pakistan border. Similarly after the secessionist movement erupted in the Kashmir Valley in July 1988 and ever since a large amount of weapons which fall under the small and light weapons categories were captured from the militants which included: rocket launchers; machine guns; AK series; snifer rifles; pistols; grenades; rockets and rocket boosters; mines and explosives.

Even China is no exception to the phenomenon of small arms proliferation. Its proximity to the drug trafficking Golden Triangle, India's north-eastern insurgency zones, open market policies have encouraged the penetration of the drug mafia and its small arms network. In fact, China's Pingyuan City in its south-west province of Yunnan bordering Myanmar and India's NEFA region has reportedly become a 'semi-open arms bazar'.

Besides India, Sri Lanka is another country in South Asia, which suffers from a serious proliferation of illegal weapons procured by the Tamil militants from any available source in the world. It is an established fact that the Tamil groups were trained in several camps in India and were permitted to run their own camps. About thirty-five training camps were run in Tamil Nadu alone apart from those in other states like Uttar Pradesh, Madhya Pradesh, Karnataka and Delhi. Different intelligence agencies of the Indian government chose the militant groups for imparting the armed exercises, the RAW, for instance, groomed the LTTE. TELO was also trained by India and given a large number of arms during the early 1980s mainly as a "lever to bring Jayawardene under control and as a counterweight to the LTTE, which has always been a truculent body, by New Delhi standards."[7] Among all the Indian intelligence agencies it was the RAW, which played a key role by financing and training the militant groups. It also provided material as well as logistical support for acts ranging from the bombing of aircraft to the detonation of bombs in Colombo.

However, despite the full Indian political and military patronage the Tamil rebel groups expanded their activities overseas by cultivating relations with other militant groups and resistance movements. This was despite the Indian intelligence and security agencies' efforts to discourage them from expanding their activities beyond the South Asian region. The LTTE began to procure regularly the weapons and their spares from almost any part of the world with relative ease. Myanmar has been a frequent conduit to smuggle weapons obtained from elsewhere into the island. Denis Perera, a former Chief of the Sri Lankan Army (SLA) informed the author in an interview that the LTTE obtained base facilities on a Burmese island along with five vessels by bribing the Burmese military officers. Subsequently, following Colombo's pressure on the Myanmar government, the Tigers shifted their activities to another island belonging to Thailand. Arms and spare parts were smuggled even through the Colombo Harbour concealed in heavy consignments. Lack of sophisticated surveillance systems for the Lankan navy to patrol the islands coastal waters enabled easy ferrying of arms by the Tigers.

Apart from the familiar Asian sources, NWFP and the Golden Triangle, Tigers obtained SLWs from Ukraine too, a newly emerged ethnic nation anxious to raise revenues through arms disposal. The LTTE could not obtain anti-aircraft guns from India. According to Perera the Sri Lankan Army too bought weapons from Ukraine following the LTTE purchases and the latter reportedly influenced the Ukraine officials to sabotage the SAMs supplied to the Lankan army. Madras Port was also used by the militants to transship external arms supplies. The Madras customs authorities confiscated a huge arms container in April 1985 belonging to the PLOTE, which bought them from a Taiwanese arms dealer. The container was loaded with 1400 rifles of world war model, 300 Sten guns, 5 communication sets, all worth about $300,000. PLOTE's efforts at the highest political level, including Prime Minister Rajiv Gandhi, to obtain its release did not succeed.[8] The IPKF Chief Lt. General Depinder Singh records that in 1987, after the arrival of the IPKF, LTTE imported a consignment of about 700 rifles, ammunition and explosives from Singapore on Illana, a ship procured by it. Illana was later spotted by the Indian Navy in the Rangoon Harbour, and disappeared under suspicion. A second consignment of brand new 25 pistols and other ammunition was confiscated by the IPKF in February 1988.[9]

One of the means of transshipping smuggled arms is to carry them on vessels with false documents and change the flagships according to maritime logistics. The Tigers have mastered this technique by thoroughly exploiting the drug-arms nexus and the loopholes in the international shipping regime. The LTTE owned four vessels-Sun Bird; Golden Bird; Ilyan; Cauline-all registered with a Panama-based shipping front Yarl shipping Co. The international shipping magazine, *Lloyd's List* revealed that eleven ships registered in Panama, Honduras and Liberia transported heroin for the LTTE. The LTTE's connections with Central American countries came to light when M.V. Ahat, a flagship registered in Honduras, apparently cruising from Burma with heavy ammunition was alerted to the Indian coast guard by the British intelligence agency, M-I. The vessel was captured by the coast guard but the Tigers' prominent leader Kittu was killed in the exchange of fire between the Indian coast guard and the militants. *Lloyd's List* mentioned above also revealed that in 1994 the Tigers had smuggled out of Ukraine 50 tons of TNT and 10 tons of RDX.

Africa is another region, which suffers a large-scale spread of illegal weapons. These weapons proliferated rapidly after the end of conflict in Angola and Mozambique. In fact, the major challenge to regime stability and socio-economic reconstruction in Africa today is from the ubiquity of small arms handled by any number of unorganized groups including children. There is not much evidence to suggest the LTTE taking advantage of the vast sources of illicit weapons available in Africa. At least one consignment of arms was procured from South Africa before the advent of the Mandela regime to power. AK 47s was acquired from African countries by obtaining the end user's certificate (EUC).

The Drug Connection

The symbiotic relationship between narcotic trade and arms dealers is too well known. The drug-arms nexus has penetrated into the sinews of international civil society and has been a major source of crime and conflict. Regime changes, conflict situations, insurgent movements and anti-government activities can not be understood without a fuller assessment of the role of drug operators and arms traders in a given situation. 'Narcoterrorism' is a fresh entry into international lexicography, which aptly summarizes the dangerous phenomenon of organized underworld operations conducted by the two closely interwoven criminal sections. With reference to South Asia, the UN report on small arms referred above describes the situation as follows:

> In this region, the production of a trafficking in drugs are directly linked to the proliferation and acquisition of small arms and light weapons. This problem, and illicit trafficking in weapons in general is exacerbated by a lack of either local or international controls of land and maritime borders in certain States of the region.[10]

The role of drug money in fuelling insurgencies in India from neighbouring Pakistan is well recognized. Almost since the beginning of the militancy in the Kashmir Valley there has been enough evidence of the narco-arms nexus supporting the cause of secessionist groups. Independent studies and the J&K former Governor Jagmohan testified the drug traffickers' role in the state's militancy. The Indian Narcotics Control Board reported in the annual report (1993-94) that the seizure of heroin had increased by 150 per cent on the Indo-Pak border while hashish registered a 139 per cent.[11] Drugs were also seized in Rajastan and Gujarat from the Pakistan nationals and the BSF captured drugs and arms from the same source in the Rann of Kutch.[12]

The Tamil groups have thoroughly penetrated into the drug world to augment their armed strength against the Lankan army. The Burmese Island acquired by the Tigers was used to conduct the drug-related arms distribution. The LTTE also offered its vessels to the drug operators. It maintained close links with the Bombay underworld, especially its drug Mafia to raise funds and buy arms. According to the *Sunday* Weekly (6 August 1988), Mudaliar, a Tamil underworld boss, was the key figure in the LTTE's nexus. Arms were reportedly supplied by the Tigers to the Bombay underworld. An interesting feature of the Tigers' drug operations is that it has maintained a close relationship with the Colombo drug mafia, which enjoys enough political patronage on the island. Victor Ivan, a JVP activist-turned-journalist, informed this author that from the north-east heroin is supplied to Colombo big business in return for money, a view confirmed by Denis Perera. Ivan believes that the drug revenue is the LTTE's main source of money.

Apart from the acquisition of arms and drug money, the Tamil movement's greatest source of support is the Tamil Diaspora around the world. The support that the ethnic fraternity extends to their cousins on the island is moral, political and financial. Expatriate Lankan Tamils number between 4,50,000 to 5,00,000 whose contributions by way of donations and extortions are considerable.[13] A Sri Lankan source estimated in 1995 that at least not less than 15 million British pounds came as contributions from Western sources. Tamil refugees in Canada played a prominent role in mobilizing their community in North America to support the Eelam cause by way of propaganda and donations. Tamils elsewhere in other parts of the world including South East Asia, Australia and New Zealand too were mobilized to contribute. Above all, it was in Europe that the Eelam movement worked hard in acquiring a political base for their cause. In fact, the EROS was founded in London by the Marxist intellectual, Ratnasabhapathy. His close relations with other foreign liberation movements made easier early armed training of the cadres.[14] The degree of internationalization of the Tamil cause can be gauged by the fact that as many as 38 quasi-diplomatic offices were located around the world, with an International Secretariat in London.[15] If the Eelam ideology was able to attract greater international attention it was the most sophisticated techniques of the campaign employed by its activities, a sophistication that the Sri Lankan Government could hardly match.

Conclusion

From the above analysis of the role of illicit arms and drug trafficking in South Asia's internal conflicts it is imperative that new paradigms of understanding the ethnic conflict and its resolution, therefore, are needed. Among the most urgent measures required are the controls over the diffusion of the drugs and small arms on the following lines:

1. Strengthening the international legal regime and political will to control the proliferation of illicit arms. The UN is seriously concerned about the issue and recommended measures to be adopted by states which include: containing arms transfers; strengthening national laws and control mechanisms on the possession of arms by civilians; regional cooperation among law enforcing authorities to combat illicit circulation; regional and sub regional moratoriums on transfers and production.

2. Strengthening the regional agreements on controlling and monitoring drug trafficking and arms transfers. The SAARC has already signed Conventions on Terrorism and Drug Trafficking and created Terrorist Offences on Terrorism and Drug Trafficking and created Terrorist Offences Monitoring Desk and Drug Offences Monitoring Desk. Sri Lanka, in fact, strongly appealed to the SAARC partners to make these measures effective.

3. A multilateral regional approach to patrol the shipping of illicit arms and drugs in the Indian Ocean. If the recent International Fleet Review at Bombay is any indication, cooperation in joint naval operations among the South Asian countries on the issue should not be a problem. For the drug arms phenomenon endangers the security of every country in the region and its control is imperative for each of the regional members.

Notes

1. Sthephane G. Neuman, "The Arms Trade, Military As sistance, and Recent Wars: Change and Continuity", *Annals*, vol. 541, September 1995, p.53.
2. Jasjit Singh, (ed), *Light Weapons and International Secu rity* (New Delhi: Pugwash, BASIC, IDSA, 1985), p.56.
3. *Ibid.*, p.52.
4. *Combating Illicit Light Weapons Trafficking: Developments and Opportunities, Report-98.1* (London: British American Security Information Council, January 1998), p.5.
5. Singh (ed), n.2, p.44.
6. Neuman, n.1, p.16.
7. Kumar David and Santasilan Kadirgamar (ed), *Ethnicity, Identify, Conflict and Crisis* (Hong Kong: Arena Press, 1989), p.235.
8. M. Narayana Swamy, *Tigers of Sri Lanka: From Boys to Guerillas* (New Delhi: Konark Publications, 1995), p.28.
9. Depinder Singh, *IPKF in Sri Lanka* (Noida: Trishul Publications, 1991), p.45.

10. UN General Assembly, 52nd session, *General and Complete Disarmament: Small Arms* (New York: UN Publications, August 1997) p.10.
11. Tara Karta, "South Asia: The Narcotics and Weapons Linkage", in Singh (ed), n. 2, p.79.
12. *Ibid.*, p.80.
13. P.R. Chari (ed), *Perspectives on National Security in South Asia, In Search of a New Paradigm* (New Delhi: Manohar, 1999), p.362.
14. David and Santasilan (ed), n.7, p.238.
15. Chari, n. 13, p.369.

Jihad and Cross-Border Terrorism in South Asia

J. Laxmi Narasimha Rao

Presently mankind lives in an age of violence in which terrorism is a phenomenon of extreme and unsettling violence. Although violence and terror have been with human beings since time immemorial, the phenomenon of terrorism has emerged as the greatest threat to individuals, nations and perhaps to the long-term survival of human civilization. It has become a new type of warfare with terrorists or terrorist organizations' accessibility to weapons of unlimited destruction. Now, a few terrorists' organizations are close to the threshold of access to biological, chemical and possibly nuclear weapons that can draw nations into 'total wars'. Thus terrorism demands an urgent response at not only police and military levels but also political, intellectual and civil society levels.

Terrorism seems to have been evolving into an organized international network. Initially it was more of a domestic concern posing threats only to national security. In the post-Cold War period it has emerged as one of the issues of major concerns threatening regional and international security environment. The severity of the lethality has also increased in accordance with the development in technology. In the early years, terrorists used armed revolvers and bombs to open fire either killing or injuring individuals, who in most cases happened to be police or military men or civilians. Once the AK-47 entered the scene, the operation could last only a few seconds but with a greater damage to human life. In the 11 September 2001 incidents, in which not weapons but civilian aircrafts were used, about 5,000 people of various countries lost lives instantly. Subsequently, Anthrax was used to frighten and cause panic among people in distant lands thus raising potential dangers that could arise if biological, chemical and nuclear weapons fell into the hands of individuals or organizations who share hatred and contempt for others.

Nature of Terrorism

The phenomenon of terrorism is so complex and hence, it is difficult to define. Most often it is used as a 'slippery' and 'abused' concept as it is difficult to define and measure it taking into account the short-term and long-term consequences. However, it is easy to feel its impact like love.

Generally, the term 'terrorism' is used indiscriminately, and often applied to a variety of acts of violence. All acts of violence may or may not be politically motivated. Criminals also use violence to obtain ransom and for other forms of private gain. The issue is more complicated when criminals clothe themselves in political slogans of justification. Given the situation different scholars have tried to come to terms with terrorism depending upon their ideological moorings. Yonah Alexander links terrorism with national security. To him "terrorism is the use or threat of violence against random or civilian targets in order to intimidate or create generalized pervasive fear for the purpose of achieving political goals."[1] Paul Wilkinson makes a distinction between political terrorism and other forms of violence. Political terrorism, to Wilkinson, is "the systematic use of murder and destruction, and the threat of murder and destruction in order to terrorize individuals, groups, communities or governments into conceding to the terrorists' political demands."[2] Here, terrorism is more of a psychological warfare in which the target for terrorization is selected, the message conveyed and credibility established by convincing that the threat can actually be carried out. Brian Jenkins defines terrorism as "the threat of violence — or a campaign of violence designed primarily to instil fear — to terrorize — Terrorism is violence for effect — violence aimed at the people watching."[3] In this act, the victim may or may not be the primary target and the amount of violence may be quite disproportionate to the number of people terrorized.[4]

The US government tried to understand the phenomenon of terrorism in a precise and yet comprehensive manner. The Department of State defined it as a "premeditated, politically motivated violence perpetrated against non-combatant targets by sub-national groups or clandestine state agents, usually intended to influence an audience."[5] The term 'non-combatant' is not restricted to civilians, but includes military personnel who are either unarmed or off duty at the time of the attack and the acts of violence are carried out either by individuals or groups or both with support of state for political purposes.

Characteristics of Terrorism

Terrorism has the following characteristics:

1. Terrorism is indiscriminate in its effects. Terrorists may choose a policy aimed at a selective target, yet no one is certain that he/she cannot be victim. It is this kind of violence and unpredictability that the terrorists, hinge on to terrorize society, and strike like lightning.

2. Essentially terrorism is arbitrary and unpredictable as far as its effects are concerned. Highlighting it as a subjective experience, Andreski described terrorism as a kind of tyranny[6] imposed on the victims.

3. Terrorism does not recognize any rules and conventions of war. It refuses to make a distinction between combatants and non-combatants and recognizes no moral constraints and obligations.

Thus terrorism, whatever may be the form, is considered to be the instrument of the weak pretending to be strong before the eyes of the innocent, media and society.

The spectre of terrorism has transformed from a peripheral issue in the 1970s to one of the foremost security challenges in the 1990s. Today the threat has been increasing in scope and lethality. It is no longer a domestic phenomenon for countries, where a few disgruntled elements espousing the cause of the oppressed committing acts of violence against the ruling classes or governments. The saying that terrorists want 'more publicity and not a lot of people dead' applies to the past. Today, by and large, terrorist groups have clear-cut motives and ends and they use violence as an activity distinct from war.

In the contemporary times, terrorism has become a worldwide problem owing due to the revolution in communications, faster movement of people and the support extended by some states or governments to certain political and religious movements. Terrorist groups are also well organized having global networks sharing resources, establishing training facilities, bases and enjoying diplomatic support from some quarters. An international black market for sophisticated weapons provides a central locus for people with similar beliefs to discuss common objectives.

Terrorists are swift in attacking and striking targets anywhere in the world. They acquire more and more lethal and sophisticated weapons. Their increasing activities show that they are crossing national frontiers to carry out their attacks and select their targets at will. The terrorist activities range from hijacking of an aircraft to car bombings, from senseless destruction of property to assassination of political leaders and public figures, from kidnapping of individuals to blasting of commercial buildings. The devices used by terrorists are low-cost, low-risk but high leverage of tools. It is also difficult to combat acts of terrorists because of uncertainty about their origin and threat limits. Terrorism is even more complex and complicated when religion replaces ideological precepts. Religious principles are used to justify the violent acts of terrorism. In other words, throughout the world, especially in the 1990s and after, most terrorist organizations seem to take recourse to religion for justification. Different terrorist groups to carry out their unlawful activities across the boundaries also use religion.

Rise of Religion-fuelled Terrorism

The post-Cold War period has witnessed the rise and phenomenal growth of religion-fuelled terrorism in different parts of the world. The 11 September event has shown that terrorism runs in the veins of radical religious belief. Out of the 100 active terrorist groups, 64 are identified as religiously motivated.[7] Most of these groups operate from South Asia to Central Asia through West Asia and from East Asia to Southeast Asia. Some of the groups extended their operations to Africa, Europe and North America by collaborating with transnational criminal groups of gunrunners, narcotics traffickers and smugglers.

The rise of religion-fuelled terrorism began in the late 1970s with the Islamic Revolution in Iran under the leadership of Ayatollah Khomeni. In the early phase, the Revolution was perceived as a challenge to the preeminent position of the US in the Middle East. Domestically it was considered as a new wave, challenging the Westernization policies of the Shah. But in due course the new regime under the then benign leadership of Khomeni introduced Islamic content into politics. Thereafter polity was Islamized on the basis of the religious tenets of the Koran. Slowly the influence of religion on politics has spread to other societies. Thus there began the expansion of political groups proclaiming the Islamic State, swearing by the Koran alone, calling for jihad and drawing supporters worldwide.

Terrorism fuelled by religion took a new turn with the Soviet intervention in Afghanistan. In its fight against the Soviet Union, Washington not only trained religiously influenced Mujahideen elements but also provided arms, economic aid and gave diplomatic support. During this period, an international Tabligh Jammait Convention was held in Illinois attracting over 6,000 Muslims from different parts of the world.[8] Later on, the Jammait had run training camps for the Mujahideen of Afghanistan.

During the Soviet occupation of Afghanistan, Pakistan collaborated with the US and acted as a frontline state in supplying arms and training to the Mujahideen elements. It also helped the Afghan Islamist groups to launch a holy war against the Soviets. Consequently, Islamabad declared that Islam was in danger and gave a call for jihad. Further,

Pakistani political and military establishment motivated and encouraged the Afghan refugees settled along the Pak-Afghan border to join the holy war.

In due course, both Pakistan and the US jointly provided training to Mujahideen in military camps. These camps attracted Islamic militants from Egypt, Saudi Arabia, Yemen and other countries. Most of the militants from Egypt were either the members or sympathizers of the Egyptian-based Akhwan-Ul-Muslammen[9] (Muslim Brotherhood). Osama bin Laden was one such volunteer to arrive in Afghanistan from Saudi Arabia in the early years in the cause of protecting Islam.

In addition to global and regional developments, the domestic developments in Pakistan also helped the religious elements to raise their head. General Zia ul-Haq, after overthrowing the democratically elected government of Zulfikar Ali Bhutto, transformed the Pakistani polity into an Islamic Republic by a initiating a number of measures. Islam became an official religion. In order to gain legitimacy for his regime, Zia projected himself as a champion of Islam. He also found it politically expedient to use Islam and found an ally in Jamaat-e-Islam, an extremist religious group. Following the Soviet intervention in Afghanistan, Zia emerged as the defender of Islamic faith in the eyes of the Pakistanis. He encouraged Islamist organizations like Janumat-e-Islami and Jamait Ulema e-Islam to set up a chain of madrassas,[10] which imparted religious education to young men. During the Zia period the number of madrassas increased phenomenally from 868 in 1975 to 3,289 by 1988. Thereafter their number increased to 6,000 by 2000.[11] In due course, Jamaat preachers imparted religious education to army units. Some of the madrassas even provided military training to the civilians.[12] At a later stage the army personnel and militarily trained elements got together in promoting religious extremism and violence in the neighbouring countries.

Externally, Zia was recognized as the saviour of the Islamic faith. His regime received all help and assistance from conservative forces in fighting against the Soviet forces in Afghanistan. Saudi Arabia extended economic aid to Pakistan through the Jamaat-e-Islami to look after Afghan refugees. Subsequently, Zia gave a call for jihad proclaiming that Islam was in danger in Kabul and converted Afghan refugees into the Mujahideen to fight a holy war. Following the Saur revolution in Afghanistan, the Zia regime encouraged Afghan Islamist groups based in Pakistan – Jamaat-e-Islami of Burhanuddin Rabbani and Hezb-i-Islami of Gulbuddin Hekmatyar – in launching a movement against the Afghan government led by the People's Democratic Party, a leftist political party.

During the Afghan crisis, more than 80,000 jihadis were trained and about $ 6.8 billion worth of weapons flowed into the hands of jihadis.[13] Kabul became a free-for-all with the regional and global powers involving heavily. The Afghan state itself came under the hold of a group, which was radical in its policies and extremist in its religious beliefs and views.

Following the Soviet withdrawal from Afghanistan, the Islamic militants of Mujahideen captured power. In the power struggle that followed, various Mujahideen groups tried to wrest power from each other. Finally, the Taliban, created and trained in madrassas in Pakistan, could overthrow other groups and occupied most of Afghanistan and slowly consolidated on Afghan soil with Taliban religious extremism and jihad became state ideology in order to create a pure Islamic Society. In due course, the Taliban spread its ideology to various other regions – Central Asia, Russia, West Asia, Africa, South Asia and Europe. As a result, there came into existence a number of organizations and groups championing the ideology of jihad and other forms of extremist religious forms in different parts of the world. Most of these groups adopted violence and terrorism as a means to spread their activities. A Rand Corporation Study revealed that till 1980 there were no religious groups that could be classified as terrorist organizations. In the year 1980, only two out of sixty-four terrorist organizations were of religious character. By 1992 their number increased six-fold. They increased their number further to 26 by 1995. It further increased to 64 out of 96 active terrorist groups, being identified as religiously motivated.[14] The list heavily tilted towards Islamic groups.

II

In the post-Cold War period, a new dimension has been added to the genre of terrorism with the rise of the Islamic Jihad. It has become a serious destabilizing factor in plural states. Unlike other terrorist groups whose goals are definable in distinct political terms, the goals of jihadi elements are no less than to establish a pure Islamic society in the regions once ruled by Muslim rulers. It is these jihadis who are at the forefront of militancy and violent movements for establishing independent Islamic states in a number of countries. Kashmir, Kosovo and Chechanya are a case in part. Such movements are also encouraged and actively assisted by militant Islamic fundamentalists from Islamic countries. These fanatic elements claim that they are the protectors and promoters of 'pure Islam'. However, their sympathy for separatism and support to terrorist activities in a number of countries, appeared to damage the reputation of their faith, which they try to glorify.

The fundamentalist groups not only launched a movement to liberate their brethren from the Kafirs but also aspire to establish pure Islamic regimes in Muslim countries. With the success of the Taliban in Afghanistan, fundamentalists tried to convince others that their objective is not far off. They have been successful, to some extent, in indoctrinating, motivating and organizing a few individuals who are prepared to sacrifice for the cause of faith anywhere in the world. They look up to Mullah Mohammed Omar and Osama bin Laden in Afghanistan.

South Asia is one of the regions directly involved and affected by religious terrorism. For almost two decades the region has become the epicentre of all kinds of violence and terrorist activities. This has been recognized and taken into account by the American foreign policy establishment in their fight against terrorism after 11 September. Thereafter the region has also assumed a key role in the American foreign policy in combating terrorism.

Terrorism in South Asia

South Asia has witnessed various types of terrorism. There are many religious, ethnic and sectarian groups that are adopting violent and terrorist means and seeking to destabilize civil societies. In the recent past jihadi and extremist Islamic forces have become active in India, Pakistan, Bangladesh and Nepal. They have also established closer links with the insurgent movements in the north-eastern parts of India. Other forms of terrorist activities were precipitated by Muslim and Hindu zealots in India. There are also revolutionary movements like Maoists and ethnic insurgencies led by the LTTE in Nepal and Sri Lanka respectively.

The unique feature of terrorism in South Asia is the strong state support it receives. Almost all the South Asian states seems to officially sponsor and encourage terrorism as an instrument of state policy to pressurize others. Pakistan-sponsored terrorism in Kashmir is a known fact for the last two decades. Bangladesh has encouraged and sheltered many groups from north-east India against the Indian government. Often, Bangladesh played a conduit to ISI-supported activities against India. Similarly, India encouraged and supported Tamil militants in Sri Lanka by providing money and ammunition to LTTE cadres before the India–Sri Lanka accord was signed. Even smaller states like Bhutan and Nepal are no exception. Nepal increasingly faces Maoist insurgency. Bhutan faces a nexus between militant groups and Nepali refugees. Tensions between Bhutan and Nepal have been increasing on account of suspected Nepal's suspected support to the Nepalese in Bhutan.

Another feature of terrorism in South Asia is religion-fuelled terrorism practised by a number of groups and organizations in the name of jihad actively supported by the states in the region. Most of the jihadi groups made Pakistan as the centre for their activities and use hit-and-run tactics. Their activities are supported by both political and military leadership of Pakistan. In due course, the Jihadi elements spread their tentacles into neighbouring countries in raising similar organizations.

Role of Pakistan in Abetting Terrorism in South Asia

Pakistan has been the driving force of terrorism in South Asia. It supports, encourages and aids all types of miscreants' elements in the name of the right to self-determination in Kashmir, Islam and Jihad. From the 1980s onwards, Pakistan has become a base and a transit point for outside operations for many Islamic groups.

Pakistan has never been able to accept Kashmir as a part of India. Having failed to resolve the issue through negotiations and war, Islamabad found a new way in the form of low-intensity conflict by training and encouraging militancy in Kashmir. It has been spreading the cult of militancy and terrorism to create ethnic and sectarian divide and communal backlash.

During the Zia regime, Pakistan launched 'Operation Topac' a code name for proxy war against India. The operation aimed at exploiting the religious sentiments of the Kashmiri people, whipping up passion on communal lines and raising the flames of religious fundamentalism and finally creating conditions for waging a jihad. The features of 'Operation Topac' were: (a) initiate low-level insurgency; (b) exert pressure along the line of control by infiltrating mercenaries and special forces to attack vital targets; (c) using religion as a motivating and binding factor and giving a nudge to the jihad.[15] The programme also envisaged support to militant and insurgent groups in north-east India and spreading it to other parts of India in a gradual manner.

The militancy that took innumerable lives in Punjab in the 1980s was the handiwork of the Pakistani establishment. On the role of Pakistan during the Punjab crisis, Sanjoy Hazarika observed that "over the years, the ISI (Inter Service Intelligence) had stirred the Punjab insurrection arming and training Sikh extremists".[16] It is Islamabad that recruited, trained, equipped and coordinated financial transactions to support Sikh extremist activities in India.

After unsuccessful attempts in Punjab, Pakistan turned its attention to other parts of India. It has been encouraging and supporting insurgency movements in north-eastern states of India. The ISI personnel tried to bring together the ULFA leaders and Afghan Mujahideen groups for the supply of arms to the ULFA cadres. Hazarika, notes that in 1988 Munim Nobis made ULFA's first effort to internationalize its campaign by travelling to Pakistan along with a Bangladesh businessman who had connections with the top leadership of military and politics in Bangladesh. In 1990 the top leadership of ULFA was flown to Pakistan when the Indian government tried to crackdown the ULFA. Thereafter Pakistan has taken the ULFA men to the North-West Frontier Province (NWEP) where the world's biggest open and illegal arms are sold. [17]

Pakistan upgraded its policy towards Kashmir and changed tactics there in the 1990s having failed to realize the establishment of an independent Khalistan. Islamabad recognized the effectiveness of cross-border terrorism in achieving its goal in Kashmir after the Cold War. The ISI began assuming a role behind the scene. It recruited hundreds of refugees from the war-torn Afghanistan and used them to ferment terrorism in India. It took over direct control of the so-called liberation movement of Kashmir and made available weapons to the youth fighting against India in Kashmir. The ISI turned Karachi into a centre for Islamic international terrorism involving people of different nationalities such as Palestinian, Bangladeshi, Afghan, Burmese, Thais, Sri Lakan and Philippines.[18] It also used the slogan that Islam is in danger in India to recruit mercenaries from Pakistan- occupied Kashmir, Saudi Arabia, Iraq, Egypt, Libya, Algeria whose percentage among the militants gradually increased year after year and reached to 40 per cent in 1998.[19] These mercenaries are used as manpower for the development of terrorist operations in India. In addition to encouraging terrorism, the ISI has also taken up the activities of : (a.) propagating religious fundamentalism to promote separatism and communal outlook; (b) training the Kashmiri people to raise militant cadres and (c) training the youth in the use of automatic weapons, sabotage and attacks on security forces.

In addition to training the mercenaries, Pakistan infiltrated the trained mercenaries through the porous line of control with the support of the army. The Pakistan army provided a safe passage to terrorists, either hiring the Kashmiri shepherds living in the border areas or providing a cover of fire by drawing away of attention of the Indian troops on the LoC. Following infiltration, a flexible command was set up to coordinate operations of mercenaries in various areas with Kashmiri militants. S.M. Zafar, former law minister under Benazir Bhutto and former Chairman of Pakistan's Human Rights Commission, while speaking at a conference of pro-Pakistani groups in London in September 1996 said that "everything is being done by Pakistan in Kashmir. The Kashmiri movement is the official jargon for armed violence and terrorism in the state (Kashmir)." [20]

Schools of Jihad and Terrorist Organizations

Violence and terrorism in Kashmir are the by-products of jihad taught in Pakistani religious schools popularly known as madrassas. Madrassas are located all over Pakistan and provide not only free education but also free boarding and lodging. Many madrassas are financed by the government. In course of time, more and more madrassas have come to be financed by wealthy Pakistanis at home and abroad. Most madrassas offer only religious instruction. Some of the madrassas preach extremism and jihad. They equate jihad with guerrilla warfare. These religious schools encourage their graduates to fulfil their spiritual obligation by fighting others. Former interior minister of Pakistan, Moinuddin Haider, observed that "The brand of Islam they (madrassas) are teaching is not good for Pakistan." He added "Some, in the garb of religious training, are busy fanning sectarian violence, poisoning people's minds."[21]

According to an estimate, there are about 40,000 to 50,000 madrassas in Pakistan. Only 10 per cent of them are registered with the government and most of the remaining are controlled and run by the Jamiat-e-Ulema-e-Islam under whose supervision the Taliban evolved and received education. It is also roughly estimated that about a million students are receiving education and training in these madrassas.[22] In Karachi alone, there are about 29 madrassas with 2,000 studying in each of them. Most of these schools inculcate the spirit of jihad in their students. It was even reported that every madrassa has been supplied books on jihad and war front reports from Kashmir, Chechnya, etc. Some of the students were even sent to the warfront.[23]

The leadership of madrassas is opposed to any reform plans describing them as "against Islam". Any takeover of them by the state is also opposed on the ground that the madrassas are the supply line for jihad.[24]

Many madrassas are used as the recruiting centres to fight for the cause of Islam. They not only preach jihad but the concept of jihad is identified with warfare and terrorism against other societies. They justify terrorism in the name of fighting for the rights of Muslims anywhere in the world. President Musharraf in a speech made on 5 February 2000 justified jihad in Kashmir by supporting the terrorist organizations' fighting in Kashmir. Many of the militant leaders and organizations often proclaim their plans to bring jihad to India and plant the Islamic flag. Osama bin Laden said on 27 August 2000 that "Fighting jihad against India is a the duty of such and such world." The Kashmir issue cannot be resolved by any other means other than jihad, said Osama. Masood Azhar, who was released on account of Indian Airlines plane's hijack to Kandahar, had said that "our mission is not Srinagar; we have to capture New Delhi". One of the Harkat activists had also said: "We won't stop-even if India gave us Kashmir— we will bring jihad here (Pakistan)— to see a Taliban style regime—"[25] The Chief of another organization, Markaz-ud-Dawawal-Irshad in November 1998 had stated that the goal of jihad is to turn the world into Darul-ul-Islam beginning with India.[26]

The mushrooming of madrassas and the rise of jihad culture in Pakistan have their impact on the South Asian region. Pakistani political and military establishment forged an alliance with madrassas and jihadi elements in nurturing them and exporting terrorism in the name of Islam to the neighbouring states. The goals of Pakistani government and jihadi groups have become more or less similar. It is doubtful whether the militant jihadi organizations could have achieved whatever they have been doing in South Asia in general, and India in particular, without the active support extended by ISI and the Pakistan government. In course of time, a new breed of religious fanatics trained in madrassas with the zeal of jihad arose who are ready to give up their lives for the cause of Islam. Pakistan motivated and sent them to Kashmir for committing sabotage, subversion, assassination and later on all kinds of terrorist activities. The militants also developed a global network of information and communication to spread the rationale of their cause, mobilize support and coordinate their operations. There also developed a number of terrorist outfits to carry out various activities in Kashmir and other parts of India with the clandestine support from the ISI of Pakistan. They are:

Harkat Ul-Ansar : Harkat Ul Ansar is a militant organization created in October 1993 with headquarters in Muzaffarabad in Pak-occupied Kashmir. It conducts terrorist operations targeting Kashmir and enjoys the backing of Pakistan. It also has linkages with many foreign terrorist outfits at the global level, most notably with Al-Faran. In 1995 the organization claimed that it had trained more than 4,000 militants. Another 8,000 members were associated with the Kashmir struggle. The Harkat was declared a terrorist organization by the US when it kidnapped five Western tourists in Kashmir in 1995.[27]

Harkat ul Muzahideen: Harkat ul Muzahideen is a terrorist organization of a Wahabi group under the influence of Jamiat-ul-Ulema-Islam leader Maulana Samiul Haq. Rivalry between the leaders of Harkat ul Ansar resulted in a group parting and starting a new organization called Harkat ul Muzahideen.

After the Afghan war the group turned its attention towards Kashmir. It is reported to have many Kashmiris, Pakistanis, Afghans and Arabs on its rolls. It is also said that the ISI has played a major role in strengthening the organization. The Pakistani establishment is said to support Harkat ul Muzahideen because of its proven record of militancy in Kashmir. A number of training camps in Hazara, Pak-occupied Kashmir are run by the members of the Harkat along with other outfits.

Harkat ul Muzahideen group was responsible for the hijacking of the Indian Airlines flight from Kathmandu. It was also involved in the seizure and the burning of the Charar-e-Sharif mosque in 1995 and the Wandhama massacre in 2000.

Harkat is believed to have links with Osama bin Laden's International Islamic organization for propagating jihad. It had said that jihad would be ended only on the day that the Indian army withdraws from Jammu & Kashmir.[28]

Laskar-e-Toiba: Laskar-e-Toiba is the most prominent and active terrorist group involved in terrorist activities across the entire Indian subcontinent It is the military wing of the Markaz Dawa wal Irshad under the leadership of Hafiz Muhammad Saeed. The Toiba is considered to be the largest jihadi organization of Pakistan with highly trained militants who are willing to go to war wherever and whenever the commander (Amir) orders.

Laskar's parent organization, Markaz Dawa wal Irshad

had a humble obscure beginning but had grown into a formidable force. In 1997, the group was running 30 schools with 5000 students geared towards producing Muzahideen to wage jihad. The head of the organization had said that "jihad is carried out to establish the system of Allah in the world."[29]

The main objective of the Laskar is to establish a political system based on the Shariat law. Its tentacles are spread to various parts of India in addition to Kashmir to achieve its pan-Islamic agenda. It created fidayeen or suicide squads to carry out its operations. Between April 2000 and November 2001, there were thirteen fidayeen attacks in Kashmir in which five were led by Laskar-e-Toiba.[30] It is also believed to have links with Osama bin Laden's International Islamic organization. One of its spokesmen, Abdullah Muntazir, claimed setting up a few hundred training camps in Pakistan and POK to provide military training to those who were willing to fight across the LoC between India and Pakistan.[31]

Laskar's popularity has grown since its role in the Kargil conflict and sending suicide missions into Kashmir. Its annual gatherings draw thousands of new followers who would be willing to go to Kashmir to fight. Periodically its leadership whipped up emotions at annual congregations in the name of Islam and Jihad. At one of the congregations, the Commander of the Laskar announced that its "next target is New Delhi." Similarly, in an interview to a journalist, the commander of the Laskar said that "not only has the need for Jihad always existed, the present conditions demand it more than ever". He further proclaimed, "jehad is confined strictly to non-Muslims, and particularly Hindus and Jews, the two main enemies of Muslims. Those two powers are creating problems for Muslims and for Pakistan. To my mind, Hindus are what the Koran terms as mushriks (polytheists). This Hinduism is the worst form of shirk (polytheism) in which 30 million gods are worshipped. And from here shirk has been smuggled to other parts of the world". [32]

Jaish-e-Mohammad: Jaish-e-Mohammad is the new form of Harkat ul-Ansar. It came into prominence when its members hijacked the Indian Airlines flight to Kandahar for the release of Moulana Azhar Masood. This group also claimed responsibility for the attack on the Kashmir Assembly. Now it is headed by Masood. He claims responsibility for killing 1500 people in Kashmir since his release. After 11 September the organization changed its name to Tehrik-ul-Furqah. [33]

Jamaat-i-Islami: Jamaat-i-Islami is a conservative, religious and semi-political group encouraged by Zia ul-Haq in the early years of his regime. During the Afghan crisis, Jamaat received economic aid from the US and Saudi Arabia to look after the refugees. In the subsequent period it gave the call for Jihad and raised the bogey that Islam is in danger and had taken militant Islam to a high pitch.

From the 1990s onward, Jamaat-e-Islami has collaborated with the Pakistani political and military establishment especially with ISI in raising a Taliban type force with the purpose of fighting Indian forces in Kashmir. It also forged a tactical alliance with the secessionist forces and engaged in terrorist acts like assassinations, bomb explosions and subversion in Jammu & Kashmir.

JKLF: The Jammu-Kashmir Liberation Front (JKLF) was

established by Maqbol Butt, a Kashmiri escaped to Pakistan and Major Amanullah Khan of POK with the object of securing the right of self-determination for the Kashmiris. From the beginning the JKLF engaged in violent acts like looting, kidnapping and hijacking. In the late 1980s it forged an alliance with the Jamaat-e-Islami of Pakistan and intensified the pro-Islamic religious movement and infiltrated Pak-trained Kashmiri youth into the Indian territory. With the kidnapping of Rubiya Sayeed, the daughter of Mufti Mohammad Sayeed in December 1989, terrorism took a new turn. Thereafter the JKLF killed a number of Hindus and Sikhs in Jammu & Kashmir resulting in the mass exodus of people from the valley.

In addition to these major groups there are many other informal terrorist outfits operating in Kashmir with the encouragement and support from Pakistan in cross-border violent and terrorist activities. Most of these groups are created for a specific purpose and are dismantled as and when required, depending on the situation. They are Al Foran, Mahaz-e-Azadi, Al Jihad Forces, Tehrik-e-Jehad, Laskar-e-Jabbar, Hizbul Mujahideen, Hizbe Wahadt, Sipahe Sahaba and Sipahe Mohammad. Recently women also floated their terrorist organizations. One such organization is Dukhteran-e-Millat headed by Asiya Andrabi. Members of the organization support Jihad and act as couriers and messengers and enforce a dress code for women. They treat the Kashmir issue as primarily a religious one and its accession to Pakistan is possible only through Jihad. It receives money from ISI to carry out its operations.[34] Some of these groups recruit their members from different nationalities. The only binding factors are Islamic brotherhood and Jihad.

The goals of Jihadi groups are compatible with those of the Pakistani government. Both hope that they can force a settlement in Kashmir on their terms in the name of Islam and Jihad. It is roughly estimated that ISI spends about Rs. 60 to Rs. 80 crores every year for persecuting a low-intensity proxy war against India. Almost all the terrorist groups working in Kashmir have connections and share resources with international terrorist networks such as Al Qaeda[35] and ISI. The networks such as Al Qaeda and ISI in turn spread their influence and activities to other South Asian countries especially Bangladesh. The existing political environment and the role of madrassas in Bangladesh society in recent times helped the international and regional terrorist organizations to begin and carry out their activities from there.

Bangladesh and Terrorist Network

A silent revolution has been taking place in Bangladesh that may disturb peace in the region and may create trouble for the region as well as beyond. The rise of Islamic fundamentalism, religious intolerance, militant Muslim groups' linkages with international terrorist groups, a powerful military ties with militants and the mushrooming of madrassas churning out militant and radical students are transforming the Bangladeshi society and nation.

The transformation of the politics of Bangladesh has started when General Zia ur Rahman deleted secularism from the Constitution in 1977 and lifted the ban on religious parties to broaden his political base. He carried the process forward by making Islam the State religion. This resulted in an alliance between the elements of radical Islam and transnational Islamic forces.

The politics of Bangladesh took a U-turn with the arrival of the exiled assassins of Sheik Mujibur Rahman to Dhaka in the early 1980s. They formed a militant Freedom Party and promoted militant Islam and developed closer relations with other militant groups.

The second half of the 1980s witnessed a phenomenal rise of madrassas and hundreds of Bangladeshi youth joined the Mujahideen. According to an estimate, there are roughly 64,000 madrassas in Bangladesh, most of which mushroomed only during the last decade. [36] Most of these are funded by proselytizing Arab charity organizations as in Pakistan. Most of the Muslim youth joined the Mujahideen to fight against the Soviet Union in Afghanistan later on turned as 'holy worriers' or 'Jihadis' to fight against Serbs in Bosnia and Herzegovina, and Indians in Kashmir.

In recent times the rise of Islamic fundamentalist parties to power raised alarm bells in the South Asian region. In the recently held elections two Islamic parties with a history of links to Jihadi terrorist groups not only gained a few seats but also became electoral partners and coalition partners of the government headed by Prime Minister, Begum Khaleda Zia's Bangladesh Nationalist Party (BNP). These two parties' –Jamaat-e-Islami and Islamic Okiya Jote-sympathy and support to Islamic fundamentalism and the Taliban and Al-Qaeda are well known. Islamic Okiya Jote, more or less reflects the ideology and membership of the Harkat-Ul-Jehad-al-Islami (HUJI – the largest terrorist group allied with Al-Qaeda in Bangladesh), a group formed by the Bangladeshi Mujahideen to transform the moderate Islamic state into a nation of true believers. Similarly, during elections, the Jamaat leaders spoke of breathing the "Islamic Spirit of Jihad". Further they extended support to HUJI's slogan "we will all be Taliban and Bangladesh will be Afghanistan". [37]

Today, Bangladesh has become a safe haven for hundreds of Jihadis. They find natural allies in Muslim extremists and ULFA activists from India. The border between India and Bangladesh has become a hot spot for all kinds of terrorists, Islamic militants and gunrunners. Over the years, Muslim Rohingyas, who fled the ethnic suppression of the Burmese military rule, also established military camps. These camps have become training centres for guerrillas fighting in Kashmir, Chechanya and Central Asia. Rohingyas are accused of having links with Islamic Jihadis. [38]

Jamaat-e-Islami and Islamic Oikaye Jote are the main forces in spreading Islamic Jihad in Bangladesh. They are behind the growth of a number of unlicensed madrassas known as quami madrassas run by the Mujahideen. Jamaat and Jote also maintain not only closer contacts but also coordinate their activities with Pakistan's ISI. They also support rebels such as ULFA and National Socialist Council of Nagaland (NSCN) rebels fighting Indian rule across the border. [39] After the recent elections, a greater number of radical Islamic groups shifted their operations from jungles to like-minded madrassas. At a meeting held on 9 and 10 May 2002, the representatives of nine Islamic groups met and formed the Bangladesh Islamic Manch under HUJI leadership to unite and carry forward their Islamic agenda of creating "a larger Islamic land than the territorial limits of Bangladesh to include Muslim areas of Assam, North Bengal and Burma's Arakan Province".[40] The Jamaat also nurtures an ambition of carving out a "Greater Bengal" – a demand raised in intellectual circles. The idea is articulated even among government circles. Now and then their politicians say that Bangladesh is a small country and it has to expand its living space. A cabinet member of Begum Zia's first government, General Mir Shaukat Ali, stated: "The problem is Bangladesh is a small country, so we need to expand eastwards to gain more living space for our people". [41] Ali was obviously referring to India's north-east. If any such designs and dreams are allowed to be nurtured, it could be a nightmare for the countries of the region.

Jamaat and HUJI and their alliance partners not only entertain extra-territorial ambitions but also organizing violent secessionists. The best example is that the Jamaat was successful in organizing the Rohingya Muslims in the Arakan Province of Burma. It has been trying to expand its influence among the Muslims of north-east India by supplying arms to wage Jihad. There are press reports that HUJI maintains six training camps near Chittagong where piracy, smuggling, arms dealings and gun running take place. [42] It is suspected that both the Jamaat and HUJI are involved in a series of blasts. Indian officials strongly believe that it is Harkat gunmen who were involved in the attack of the American Cultural Centre in Kolkata. They also believe that Harkat has links with Laskar-e-Toiba and Jaish-e-Mohammad of Pakistan. It is also believed that Jamaat is aiming at establishing bases in Assam, Tripura and West Bengal for its operations in India. They also encourage the ULFA and NSCN activists to travel to Pakistan for training and operational guidance from the ISI.[43] Further, it was brought to light that a large group of Al-Qaeda arrived in Bangladesh by a boat in December 2001. The reports were confirmed by a senior member of the Harkat-ul-Jihad-al-

Islami.[44] Such a development raises pressing concerns for India, as Bangladesh may become a centre of international terrorist network posing serious problems to the security of India.

Thus, Bangladesh has become a hot spot and home for the Jihadi extremists and terrorists in the recent past. The Jihadi elements' activities are not only challenging the integrity and security of India and others but are undermining the very base of Bangladesh civil society. Religious and right wing parties are not only raising the issue of Islam and Jihad but are also trying to forge transnational linkages with like-minded groups at the global level to wage Jihad and carry out terrorist attacks. After the American war against terrorism and the overthrow of the Taliban in Afghanistan, Bangladesh is becoming a safe haven for terrorist groups of different kinds. It is also slowly emerging as a transit point for arms and weapons.

Conclusion

Terrorism is an inter-state problem in South Asia. Its threat to the region is multi-dimensional. It is a complex intermix of religious–separatist–communal overtones. Though no state is free from terrorist activities, regional cooperation is not forthcoming to deal with it. This is because almost all the states seem to have consciously adopted the policy of supporting extremist outfits against the neighbours. In spite of the issue being raised at the very first summit of the SAARC in 1985 and again in 1987 and adopting a Convention on Suppression of Terrorism, there has been a lack of political will to implement the convention on the part of the signatories. The South Asian states have not come forward to meet the challenge collectively as they used support to terrorism to pressurize neighbours. In the post-Cold War period terrorism assumed the form of Frankenstein as the global community is emphasizing respect for human rights, right to self-determination leading to strengthening insurgency and autonomy movements of various types in South Asia.

In South Asia, India has been the major victim of militancy and terrorism. Many groups both within and outside the country employ terrorist tactics championing their cause. Some of the left wing and secessionist groups acquired considerable firepower and forged links with other militant outfits outside India. From the mid-980s onwards the extremist activities took a new turn with the rise of fundamentalist groups in Pakistan, Bangladesh and elsewhere. Islamization of those societies further provided an impetus to cross-border terrorist activities of fundamentalist and religious elements. The end of the Cold War, rise of Mujahideen and subsequent capture of power by the Taliban resulted in the rise of madrassas and jihad forces in Pakistan as well as Bangladesh. The result was, India becoming a major victim of Islamic militancy and terrorism. Slowly other countries are also becoming victims of terrorist operations on their own soil. Jihadi extremism and terrorism are becoming an obstacle for regional cooperation. Islamic forces can be controlled only if the madrassas are regulated and training camps are closed down. Though such a measure is not an easy task, it is not impossible when the political will is strong. It is also high time Pakistan and Bangladesh recognized that terrorism is harming their national interests in the form of sectarian violence destroying their own social fabric. They have to realize that Islamic extremism and terrorism are threats not only to others but also to the cause of Islam in the long run.

Jihad and cross-border terrorism as ideology, challenge and undermine democracy as a value. The use of force and counter-violence by the security forces is also likely to create a gap between the theory and practice of democracy. This may raise the question on the feasibility of democracy when neighbours follow dictatorship and encourage cross border terrorism. It may create a dilemma in the minds of policy makers while choosing options between national integrity / security and social peace and counter-terrorism tactics. The question is which should precede which?

Notes

1. Cited in P.M.Kamath, "Terrorism in India: Impact on National Security", *Strategic Analysis*, vol. 25, no. 9, December 2001, p. 1081.
2. Paul Wilkinson, *Terrorism and the Liberal State* (New York: John Wiley & Sons, 1977), p. 49.
3. Brian Jenkins, *International Terrorism: A New Mode of Conflict* (Los Angeles: Crescent Publications, 1975), p.1.
4. Raymond Aron, *Peace and War* (London: Weidenfeld and Nicolson, 1966), p. 170.
5. US Department of State, *Patterns of Global Terrorism: 1998* (Washington, DC: Department of State, April 1999), pp. vi – vii, cited in Michele L. Malvesti, "Explaining the United States' Decision to Strike Back Terrorists", *Terrorism and Political Violence*, vol. 13, no. 2, Summer 2001, p. 103.
6. S. Andreski, 'Terror', in *A Dictionary of the Social Sciences* (Glencose: UNESCO Fress Press, 1964), cited in Wilkinson, n. 2, pp. 52-53.

7. "Terrorism: A Global Survey", *Jane's Information Group,* 1999, cited in Tara Kartha, "Countering Transnational Terrorism", *Strategic Analysis,* vol. 23, no. 11, February 2000, p. 1833.

8. Sudhir Kumar Singh, *Terrorism: A Global Phenomenon* (New Delhi: Authors Press, 2000), p. 179.

9. O.N. Mehrotra, "Madrassas in Pakistan: The Chief Promoter of Islamic Militancy and Terrorism', *Strategic Analysis,* vol. 23, no. 11, February 2000, p. 1882.

10. Kumar Singh, n.8, p. 247.

11. Shaukat Qadir, "Threats of Religious Extremism in Pakistan and India", *South Asia Politics,* vol. 1, no.2, June 2002, p. 14.

12. According to Shaukat Qadir, about 8 to 9 per cent of madrassas provided military training to 48,000 to 54,000 students studying in them annually, see *ibid.*

13. Kumar Singh, n.8, p. 13.

14. *Ibid.*, pp. 13-14.

15. "Proxy War by Pakistan in Kashmir", *Sainik Samachar,* 1-15 August, pp. 15-18, cited in Gurmeet Kanwal, "Proxy War in Kashmir: Jehad or State-sponsored Terorism?", *Strategic Analysis,* vol. 23, no. 1, April 1999, pp. 57-58.

16. Sanjoy Hazarika, *Strangers of the Mist: Tales of War and Peace from India's Northeast* (New Delhi: Penguin Books, 1994), p. 170.

17. *Ibid.*, pp. 170-172.

18. Clifford E. Simonsen and Jeremy R. Spindlove,

Terrorism Today: The Past, The Players, The Future (New Jersey: Prentice Hall, 2000), p. 217.

19. The *Times of India*, 14 January 1999.

20. Cited in P.M. Kamath, "Terrorism in India: Impact on National Security", *Strategic Analysis*, vol. 25, no. 9, December 2001, p. 1083.

21. Jessica Stern, "Pakistan's Jehad Culture", *Foreign Affairs*, vol. 79, no. 6, November-December 2000, p. 119.

22. The estimate on the number of madrassas functioning in Pakistan and the number of students receiving education varies from source to source. Most of the reports are based on the new paper reports see Stern, *ibid*; Rahimullah Yusufzai, "Here come the Taliban", *Newsline*, February 1995, p. 28 and *The Tribune*, 26 June 2000. Cited in Ajay Darshan Behera, "The Supporting Structures for Pakistan's Proxy War in Jammu and Kashmir", *Strategic Analysis*, vol. 25, no. 3, June 2001, p. 400 and Shaukat Qadir, "Threats of Religious Extremism in Pakistan and India", *South Asia Politics*, vol.1, no. 2, June 2002, pp. 14-15.

23. Owais Tohid, "The Jehad at Home", *The Herald*, December 1997, pp. 63-64 and Owais Tohid, "The New Recruits", *The Herald*, December 1997, p. 68, cited in O.N. Mehrotra, "Madrassas in Pakistan: The Chief Promoter of Islamic Militancy and Terrorism", *Strategic Analysis*, vol. 23, no. 11, February 2000, pp. 1883-1884, and *The Hindu*, 16 August 1999.

24. Stern, n.21, p. 120.

25. *Ibid.*, pp. 121 and 124 and Arun Jaitely, "Let Us Not

Abdicate Our Responsibility", *Seminar,* Issue no.512, April 2002, p. 59.

26. Behera, n.22, p. 401.

27. See P. B. Sinha, "Pakistan: The Chief Patron-Promoter of Islamic Militancy and Terrorism", *Strategic Analysis,* vol. 21, no. 7, October 1997, pp. 1020 & 1025 and Sumita Kumar, "Pakistan's Jehadi Apparatus: Goals and Methods", *Strategic Analysis,* vol.24, no.12, March 2001, p. 2187.

28. See Mehrotra, n.23, p. 1887; Kumar, *ibid.,* 2188 and Kshitij Prabha, "Terror Enterprise: Organization, Infrastructure and Resources", *Strategic Analysis,* vol. 29, no. 9, December 2001, p. 1051.

29. See Zaigham Khan, "Allah's Army", *The Herald Annual,* January 1998, pp. 124-125, cited in Mehrotra, n.23, pp.1885-1886.

30. Prabha, n.28, p. 1053.

31. Mehrotra, n.23, p. 1888.

32. Khan, n.29, cited in Kumar, n.27, p. 2180.

33. See *The Hindu,* 31 December 2002, Prabha, n.28, p. 1054, and Kamath, n.20, p. 1083.

34. *The Statesman,* 17 July 2002.

35. See Rohan Gunaratna, "Next Stop for Al-Qaida", *The Times of India,* 16 September 2002

36. Bertil Lintner, "A Cocoon of Terror", *Far Eastern Economic Review,* 4 April 2002, p. 15 and Bibhuti Bhushan Nandy, *The Statesman,* 25 June 2002.

37. See *Time,* 21 October 2002, p.25.

38. Lintner, n.36, p.17.

39. *The Hindu,* 14 October 2002.

40. *Time,* 21 October 2002,p.25.

41. Cited in Nandy, n.36.

42. Lintner, n.36, p.17.

43. *Ibid.,* p.16 and Nandy, n.36.

44. See *Time*, 21 October 2002, p.22.

Financing Terror: Dealing with the Transnational Networks

M.J. Vinod

The increase in the volume of terrorist activity has been matched by its geographic spread. Terrorism is likely to persist as a mode of political expression for various groups and also as a means of warfare among states. Terrorists want many people to be 'watching'. It is the continuation of war by other means for the purpose of compelling an adversary to submit to specific demands. Terrorists have introduced into contemporary life a new brand of psychological warfare and propaganda in terms of combined threat and victimization. The damage done to the individual human being and the fabric of public order is tremendous.

The export of terrorist skills and weapons across borders has added an entirely different dimension. Moreover if the political and ideological intention is the strengthening of one state vis-à-vis another, then transnational terrorism has important strategic consequences too. The underground network that funds terrorist activities in different parts of the world is complicated and secretive. Exporting terrorist skills and weapons across national borders represent an entirely new dimension. 'Transnational terrorism' has important strategic consequences too. Terrorism is the continuation of war by other means for the purpose of compelling an adversary to submit to specific demands. The terrorist networks are amorphous and transnational in their outlook and functioning. Unravelling this network constitutes one of the main challenges in the ongoing campaign against terrorism and hence deserves a deeper study.

Terrorism has cast a shadow across the globe. The global resolve to tackle it and defeat it has never been greater. The events of 11 September 2001 were epoch-making, changing the landscape of geopolitics as visibly as they have changed the skyline of Manhattan. The terrorists struck at the symbols of America's political, economic and military might. The attacks were essentially on democracy and America's 'way of life'. Incidentally, 11 September 1922 was the day when the British mandate came into force in Palestine. Perhaps the attack will transform forever the way the US looks at itself and the world.

Terrorists are not born. They are what they are owing to a variety of factors. It could be the product of a 'sick mind' often nurtured by a sense of 'injustice', which could be 'real' or 'imaginary'. Among others, an adverse social environment, along with biological and emotional state of mind are also contributory factors. Terrorist incidents have increased more than 300 per cent in the past three decades, escalating from 8,100 incidents in the 1970s to over 27,000 in 1999-2000. The 11 September 2001 incident brings into sharp focus the "new breed" of terrorists, viz. the religious and political extremists in the US hand-in-glove with their counterparts in other countries.

Terrorism today largely runs on the wheels of:

- religious and sectarian fundamentalism
- narcotics trade
- arms trafficking

- ideological extremism and
- money laundering.

The terrorists operate "cheek by jowl" with transnational criminal groups. As a result, terrorism today has an independent power base, thanks to these transnational linkages. Connections between the terrorist groups occur for a variety of reasons:

- shared ideology
- shared enemy
- shared financing techniques
- shared training facilities.

In the case of the Taliban, this network is reflected in the cosy relationship between the Islamic militants, Pakistani madrassas and Afghan training camps on the one hand, and the gun runners, narcotics traffickers and smugglers on the other. These linkages need to be probed a little deeper.

Drug Trafficking and Terrorism

The war against terrorism and the war against drugs are clearly linked. Organized crime, drug trafficking and terrorist acts are no longer insular distinct activities that can be eradicated through traditional enforcement measures alone. We see the merging of 'terrorism, militancy and war'. They finance each other. Perhaps the Taliban would not have existed, but for the opium trade. Recent studies show that in the year 2000, Afghanistan produced 70 per cent of the world's opium supply and 80 per cent of the opiate products bound for Europe. Today 95 per cent of Europe's heroin comes from Afghanistan. Drug trafficking has become the prime sponsor of the conflict, since the trade is largely confined to criminal elements. The International Narcotics Control Board based in Vienna has in its various reports brought out the link between illegal drug production, trafficking in illegal arms trade and international terrorism. Drug trafficking has affected the socio- economic and political fabric of Afghanistan and Pakistan. The UN task force estimates that the narcotics trade generates 5 per cent of Pakistan's GDP. These 'realities' and 'linkages' deserves a deeper analysis.

The background to these developments will be in order. It may be recalled that following the ban on the Khomeini regime in Tehran, the drug barons from Iran had shifted their base to the Helmand Valley in Afghanistan. The entry of Soviet troops into Afghanistan in 1979 had greatly altered the drug trafficking scenario in Pakistan and Afghanistan. The Afghan refugees were converted into freedom fighters or the Mujahideen. The Mujahideen were provided money and weapons to fight the Soviet Red army. They were also provided an ideological framework by declaring the fight against the Soviets as a 'Jihad' or holy war. The Soviet invasion in the late 1970s altered the narcotics trade scenario in two ways:

One, the US and Pakistan began to support the Afghan Mujahideen. It is reported that the US Central Intelligence Agency (CIA) and Pakistan's Inter-Services Intelligence (ISI) had clandestinely assisted the Mujahideen drug trade to help them procure more arms. The CIA eager to humble the Soviets, invested billions of dollars in weaponry and training to turn these young warriors of Islam into a cadre of freedom fighters to drive out the Soviets. Those who survived the war turned Afghanistan into a boot camp for terrorists. Since then carrying a kalashnikov in Afghanistan has been as common as wearing a wrist watch in the US.[1] The Pushto-speaking tribal belt bordering Afghanistan were patronized in order to ensure that the Mujahideen supply line was secure. Secondly, the Soviet presence resulted in the closure of the traditional routes to Europe, and resulted in the opening out of many new routes.

These developments led to an increase in poppy cultivation, and poppy-refining factories came up all along the Pakistan-Afghanistan border. As a result during that phase, opium production in Afghanistan increased from 200 metric tons in 1980 to about 400-475 metric tons in 1983. Much of it was largely grown in the eastern part of the country. Laboratories in Afghanistan had been converting opium into morphine base, white heroin or one of the three grades of heroin, depending on the order. The primary market for the Afghan morphine base is traffickers based in Turkey. Afghanistan is also a major producer of cannabis, much of which is processed into hashish. INTERPOL contends that Pakistan and Afghanistan together produced about 1000 metric tons of cannabis every year. Hashish that had originated in Afghanistan was trafficked throughout the region and international markets. Studies suggest that approximately two thirds of the world's heroin (made from opium) came from Afghanistan.[2]

The most powerful professional drug traffickers in Pakistan are the Afridis, who are sub-divided into eight sub-clans. They are involved right from cultivation to processing, to transporting and marketing. In the North West Frontier Province, the prominent centres dealing with drugs are Landikotal, Jamrud, Bara Bazar and Dara Adam Khel. The Dara community is perhaps the most prominent and influential outlet in Pakistan for heroin. In Baluchistan, the Notezai and Bugti tribes were largely involved in drug trafficking.

Afghanistan produces the world's second largest amount of opium, ranging from 650 – 800 metric tons. In this context Pakistan is a major producer and a transit point. Much of the cultivated drugs are processed in factories located in the North West Frontier Province and Baluchistan. Ironically most of these factories are mobile, based on a few trucks. In 2001 Afghanistan produced approximately 74 metric tons of opium, a substantial reduction from the 3,656 metric tons produced in 2000.[3]

The war against terrorism and the war against drugs are still being couched in military terms only. 'Symptoms' are attacked rather than the 'causes'. What are targeted are the 'supply' and not the 'demand'. An estimated 14.8 million Americans over the age of 12 used illicit drugs in 1999. This amounts to 6.7 per cent of the US population. Besides, 1.5 million Americans were arrested for drug-law violations in the same year (Report of the National Control Strategy released by the National Drug Control Policy in January 2001).

The Phenomenon of Narco Politics

Nacro-politics refers to the linkages between the 'world of politics' and the 'world of narcotics'. The nexus between the politicians, the drug barons and the terrorist outfits began in the 1970s. This trend got consolidated later. The nexus between the army and narcotics was yet another disconcerting development. Both these resulted in:

- personal ties between politicians and drug barons, irrespective of political affiliations.
- The drug barons also began funding political parties and leaders.
- As time elapsed, many drug barons themselves turned into politicians.

We see the close linkage between 'belligerent states' and the 'terror networks'. Terrorism has to be fought on several fronts. The time has come to address the realities that underpin terrorism. These include:

- the trafficking of narcotics
- the trafficking in arms, and
- the large reserve of 'religious mercenaries'

Regional instability has contributed to enhanced drug cultivation and trafficking. The fact is that support to terrorist groups has been done covertly. In the process, states have resorted to covert means to raise financial resources. Hence states sponsoring terrorism have sponsored insurgencies, terrorist groups and armed resistance in the neighbouring states. Much of the required funds for this purpose have been generated through drug trafficking. The money generated in this form has been used to procure arms.

Politicians now seem to have limited control over this Frankenstein monster that was released by them. Needless to say that the disturbed conditions provided an "ideal cover" for increased smuggling of narcotics. It has also helped the drug and arms barons to "legitimize" some of the money acquired through this trade. All this has happened as the State was busy fighting the terrorists. Though all drug dealers are not necessarily terrorists, yet the war on drugs is a war the state can ill afford to use. Drug trafficking threatens both the rule of law and human rights. The time has come for taking the following measures:

- Initiate supply-reduction measures
- cracking down on international criminal organizations
- strengthening of democratic institutions, and
- the need for the international community to honour various drug-control commitments.

What is required is an inclusive strategy that emphasizes both 'supply disruption' and 'demand reduction'.

Money Laundering and Terrorism

The capital that terrorists require comes from several sources. There exists 'strategic partnerships' between terrorist groups and organized criminal groups, especially narcotics traffickers. The IMF has estimated the amount of money laundered annually at between $600 billion and $1.5 trillion, or 2-5 per cent of the world's annual gross domestic product. Approximately a third of that amount it is believed passes through US financial institutions at least once on its clandestine journey. In the words of Ambassador Stuart E. Eisenstat, "Stopping money laundering and the syndicates it finances, is critical to the fight against narcotics trafficking, organized crime, foreign corruption and software counterfeiting and other intellectual property crimes, as well as preserving the health of the international financial system."[4]

The Pakistan-Afghanistan belt has become the 'money launderer,s dream', popularly called 'hawala transactions'. The hawala or hundi bankers have been providing funds to militant outfits in the region for a number of years. Money laundering is a system that operates:

- Underground
- Through informal networks
- Through traditional transactions
- Through the globalized financial network
- The transactions are largely unregulated

Money laundering largely emanates from illicit narcotics trade. It is estimated that a kilo of heroin, 40 per cent pure, sells for up to $290,000 on the streets of the US, enough to buy a Rolls-Royce car. On American streets after changing hands a number of times, the retail price for a kilo of cocaine works out to $110,000. In Europe it costs substantially higher. The official estimate of retail drug sales in the US is $60 billion, making America the most valuable market.

In the Pakistan-Afghanistan belt, money laundering can be divided into three categories:

- White money, which is generated through legal economic activity
- Black money, which arises out of tax and duties evasion. The money is held and operated in secrecy to circumvent economic laws.
- Dirty money which arises from illegal activities like

drug trafficking, arms trafficking and the nefarious criminal activities of the underworld.

Money laundering can be examined from the following perspectives:

1. The proceed of narcotics money "inside a country". In this case the proceeds are in the local currency, and laundering goes on through the channels of the local economy.
2. Proceeds of narcotics sales 'outside the country/region", whereby commission is paid for transporting the narcotics outside the country/region, i.e. to further destinations. Payment in this case is normally paid in US dollars.
3. Where there is a barter system. In this case narcotics trafficking is done by armed insurgent groups, and the mode of payment for the "services' rendered is in the form of 'small arms' and 'explosives'.

For the past decade, Al Qaeda's money had moved freely through banks in money laundering havens like Dubai, Sudan and Bahrain. Often Al Qaeda's money completely bypassed the banking system, passing from one hand to another via suitcases full of $100 bills or informal networks of remittances that usually left no paper records.[5] In the case of Afghanistan, narcotics and its illegal trade had become "part and parcel of statecraft". The implications of this on the State, the region and the world community are as follows:

- It is becoming increasingly difficult to distinguish between white/black and dirty money.

- Dirty money is being used to sustain the terrorist network.
- Dirty money is being used to achieve the 'strategic objectives' of the terrorists.
- Money laundering threatens the integrity and stability of financial and government institutions worldwide.
- The growth of money laundering reflects the dark side of globalization.

Observations

Terrorist groups cannot sustain themselves without substantial patronage; financial support of states; logistical support of states and moral support of states. The greatest danger is when organized crime is the 'state apparatus' itself, and when it operates in tandem with a variety of 'non-state' actors. The terrorists have operated 'cheek by jowl' with transnational criminal groups. Terrorism today largely runs on the wheel of the narcotics trade, religious and sectarian fundamentalism, arms trafficking, ideological extremism and money laundering. It has to be fought on several fronts with different tools, postures and strategies. The partnership between organized crime, drug trade and the terror network is well established. Drug profits can be used in a variety of ways once they have been laundered. Like-minded countries have to get together, through multilateral arrangements to collectively fight this menace. The time has come to explore options to get to the 'source' of the problem. In the words of Meghan L.O'Sullivan, "in the new campaign against terrorism, the United States will have to consider the whole range of foreign policy instruments – from military force to diplomacy –and find the proper mix to achieve its goals. In strengthening the potential of non-military tools and widening opportunities for their use, changes in the international environment since 11 September ensure that policy-makers have a range of robust options to deal with state sponsors of terrorism."[6]

All these developments have clear-cut extra-regional inputs and global dimensions. The events of 11 September 2001 are epoch-making which have changed the landscape of geopolitics. The attacks were essentially on 'America's way of life'. The larger question is how the US without compromising on an open society, can defend itself against such elusive threats. We see a dangerous mixture of 'political paranoia', 'messianic fervour' and an obsession with 'apocalyptic prophecy'. The terrorist now has the capacity to disrupt society on an unimaginable scale. In the days to come one can imagine that counter-terrorism will come to occupy centre-stage in America's reordering of its defence priorities. There is need for balance, breadth and long-term consistency in the US approach to counter terrorism. The most effective measures are those that are developed in the context of a multifaceted policy, with political, social, legal, diplomatic, economic and military elements. Overemphasis on the military element could undermine the others. The need of the hour is a broad-based, effective and sustained response.[7]

The time has come for like-minded countries to negotiate agreements committing themselves to sharing intelligence information; permit 'hot pursuit' of terrorists across international borders and establish clear-cut and workable extradition agreements.

Terrorism is obviously perceived differently by

perpetrators, victims and observers. In combating and coping with terrorism, there is need for considerable "domestic" and "international" consensus. It requires national, regional and international strategies. Terrorism has to be fought on several fronts, with different tools, postures and strategies. Counter- terrorism strategies need to get at the root of these terror networks especially the criminal groups involved in drug peddling and money laundering. There is the need for perpetual vigilance against the threats being posed by these networks. The greatest advantage that terrorists have is a virtually unlimited range of targets. Terrorists can attack anything, anywhere, anytime limited only by operational considerations. International terrorism is fanning out as a form of 'global guerilla warfare'. The aim of the terrorists and the ultimate objective of those who sponsor, train and supply them is to shatter self-confidence, undermine values and blunt the response. There is no choice but to meet this threat.

Notes

1. Harvey W. Kushner, *Terrorism in America: A Structured Approach to Understanding the Terrorist Threat* (Springfield: Charles Thomas Publishers, 1998), p. 28.
2. "A Survey of Illegal Drugs", *The Economist*, vol. 79, no. 6, 28 July 2001, p. 6.
3. Statement made by ASA Hutchison, Administrator Drug Enforcement Administration: US Department of Justice, *FDCH Congressional Testimony Before the House Government Reform Committee*, 3 October 2001.
4. Statement made by Ambassador Stuart E. Eisenstat, *FDCH Congressional Testimony before the Senate Banking,*

Housing and Urban Affairs Committee, on 26 September 2001.

5. Peter Carbonara and Borzou Daraghani, "Financing Terror", *Money*, November 2001, p. 122.

6. Meghan L. O'Sullivan, "Dealing with State Sponsors of Terrorism", *Brookings Project on Terrorism and US Foreign Policy*, Analysis Paper-6, 25 October 2001.

7. *The Diplomacy of Counter Terrorism: Lessons Learned, Ignored and Disputed*, Special Report-80 (Washington: The United States of Peace, 14 January 2002).

Suicide Terrorism: An Enquiry

Suba Chandran

Suicide terrorism has assumed greater significance after the attack on the US in September 2001. In South Asia, Sri Lanka and India (Kashmir) have been witnessing this phenomenon. In Sri Lanka, the Liberation of Tigers of Tamil Eelam (LTTE) began their suicide offensive in the late 1980s, whereas Kashmir has been witnessing suicide bombing and fidayeen attacks after the Kargil war in 1998. Other than these two in South Asia, none of the other countries, which are facing terrorism-related problems are not facing any suicide bombings.

What makes an individual to make this supreme sacrifice? It should be emphasized that these suicide terrorists are neither fanatics nor uneducated. Most of the suicide bombers seem to have come from a higher economic and educational background.

Defining the Features of Suicide Terrorism – An Analysis of Events during the 1980s and 90s

Suicide terrorism, to a great extent, is a post-1980 phenomenon. In the past, there were a number of isolated incidents, in which the individuals had given up their lives in committing a terror act. But the major difference between them and the modern day suicide bombers is that the latter covers himself with explosives and attacks the target, thus acting as a human bomb, whereas the former were using bombs and other related weapons.

It can be said that the attack in October 1983 in Beirut killing more than 250 American and French peace keepers as the first suicide terrorist attack. Since then, there have been nearly 300 suicide terrorist attacks especially in the Middle East, Europe and Sri Lanka.

How to define suicide terrorism? Since the phenomenon is new and not many works have been done on this subject, there are no ready-made definitions for suicide terrorism. Any attempt to define suicide terrorism and bombings should be based on the various features. What are the features of suicide terrorism and bombings? An analysis of the suicide attacks over the last decade would reveal the following four major features of suicide terrorism.

Suicide terrorism was closely related to the Khomeni revolution in Iran. *Hizballah* (Army of Allah), the first to carry out a suicide attack was a *Shite* terrorist group, and had very close links with Iran. In fact the Hizballah became the leasing group in the 1980s along with the *Amal*, another *Shite* terrorist organization to carry out maximum number of suicide bombings in the Middle East.

The second major feature of suicide terrorism is that among the various groups that had carried out suicide bombings till now, most of them belong to the Muslim community, belonging to both Shia and Sunni sects. Besides the LTTE, the rest – Hizballah, Amal, Hamas, Kurdistan Worker's Party (PKK), Palestinian Islamic Jihad (PIJ), Egyptian Islamic Jihad, Gama'a al-Islamiya and Al-Qaeda – adhere to the Islamic faith. Does this mean that Islam as a religion promotes or supports suicide terrorism? This has been one of the major discussions in the post-1 September suicide attacks on the US. Those who view that suicide terrorism as a part of jihadi instruments consider the phenomenon very much to be of Islamic. Those who oppose base their views on the fact that Islam does not support suicide, hence suicide terrorism is un-Islamic. The community is divided on the whole issue of whether suicide terrorism is Islamic or not.

The next major feature of suicide terrorism is that the final objectives are political and not religious. Religion is used only as a means to achieve political objectives, in terms of gaining support. Hizballah, which carried out the first attack was to threaten the UN Peace Keepers, mainly the Americans and the French, and prevent any future deployment of UN troops in Lebanon. Additionally, chasing the Israeli troops away from Lebanon was also an objective of these attacks, one in which the Hizballah did succeed; the UN Peace Keeping Forces were withdrawn and Israel, finding it difficult to cope with a series of such attacks, retreated. The attacks by the two Egyptian groups, Egyptian Islamic Jihad and Gama'a al-Islamiya, were primarily acts of revenge or of disapproval. For example, the suicidal attack on the Egyptian Embassy in Pakistan in November 1995 was aimed against any possible cooperation between Pakistan and Egypt in extraditing the terrorist leaders to Egypt. The attacks of the Hamas and the PIJ were purely political and were mainly aimed at disrupting the peace process between Israel and the PLO (Palestine Liberation Organization). The Al-Qaeda, a recent addition, which is funded by Osama bin Laden and accused for the terrorist attacks against the US, is in fact anti-West and, in particular, anti-US though it proclaims of waging a jihad against the infidels. All these groups use Islam merely to gain religious legitimacy for their acts and in the PKK, its women cadres had undertaken more number of suicidal attacks than their male counterparts.

Suicide Terrorism: A Sociological Enquiry

Emile Durkheim, the first sociological thinker to propound a systematic and structured theory on suicide, lists three basic types of suicide. When an individual fails to integrate himself with his family and society he commits, what Durkheim calls as egoistic suicide. In this type of suicide, the belief and value systems of the individual are not approved by the value and belief systems of the society (which includes one's own family). Also in this type of suicide the individual does not approve of society, resulting in his alienation from society.

Anomic suicide forms the second form, in which the individual commits suicide because of anarchy in society. Any breakdown of life due to unforeseen factors such as a crisis related to industrial, financial and social aspects play a significant role in influencing the decision of the individual to commit suicide.

The final category of suicide, according to Emile Durkheim is altruistic. An individual commits suicide due to over integration of himself with the society. Suicide terrorism falls in this category, in which the individual feels that he is a part of a whole. He also believes that the "self" has no relevance, if the "whole" is under threat. The individual gives his "self" so that his "whole" would survive.

The following factors mould the "self" to give way for the "whole." The primary agency in this is that of the family. In terms of any actions taken by the government and its security forces in a conflict situation, the primary implications on the adverse side have always been that on the family. Either in terms of economic or in terms of social factors, the families bear the primary brunt. Events such as arrest, killing, torture and rape affect the social side of the family, while loss of employment and other related events affect the economic side of the family. Either social or economic, the result is always the same in terms of developing a negative perception towards the state. This negative perception of the state by the family especially affects the psyche of the younger generation. The younger generation either believes on its own or is made to believe that the protection of the family values against the state is one of its primary duties.

The second factor that aids the self to sacrifice for the whole is that of the education system in the conflict areas. In most of the conflict areas, the educational structure is outside the sphere of the state due to economic and political factors. Where the education system of the locality in a conflict region is not under the control of the State, then the non-state actors such as the local social and religious groups, militant organizations and others take over running the educational system. Whether run by the religious groups, or Marxist groups or militant groups, educational systems under these non-state actors result in these groups exploiting education to impose their version of history. For example, in the Kashmir valley, a number of madrassas have proliferated in the last two decades that inculcate a value and belief systems; the Naxalite groups in select areas in Andhra Pradesh, Bihar and Jharkand in India; and the LTTE in the northern region of Sri Lanka, all these groups impart their own versions of social, economic and political history to their students. In other words, in conflict areas, where the educational system is not under the control of the state and is controlled by non-state factors, the younger generation has no other alternatives to know about his environment. Hence the decision to decide what is right and what is wrong, to a great extent is based on what those non-state actors consider as right or wrong.

The role of secessionist leaders and their success also play a vital role in suicide terrorism. In some cases, the leaders define the history, objectives and future of the society. Especially when there are no second layers of leaders, then the society looks to a great extent to its only leader as a saviour and as a messiah. Prabhkaran, leader of the LTTE, decides what constitutes the "Tamil Eelam" and how to achieve it. He is worshipped in Tamil society and there are many LTTE cadres, who are ready to become Black Tigers, since this would ensure an exclusive meeting and dinner with him. There is a direct linkage between the leadership and suicide bombings, as could be seen in the case of the PKK. After the arrest of its leader, Abdullah Oclan in March 1999, there have been no suicide attacks by the PKK. There were around 20 suicide attacks carried out by the PKK between 1966 and 1999 killing 19 persons and wounding more than 100 persons, but there are no suicide attacks since then.

Suicide bombers, thus, are the result of the individual's assimilation into society, especially in a conflict environment. Education and leadership also play an increasing role in mulding the psyche of the suicide bombers.

Suicide Terrorism in South Asia

Suicide terrorism in South Asia has manifested in two countries – Sri Lanka and India (Kashmir). The LTTE in Sri Lanka and the so-called Fidayeens in Kashmir are significant while talking about suicide terrorism in South Asia.

The Black Tigers of the LTTE

The LTTE is one of the few groups in the world to have an elite suicide squad known as Karumpuligal (Black Tigers). The other groups to have these distinctions are the Hizballah, the Hamas and the PKK of Turkey. However, the LTTE occupies a unique position in terms of suicide bombings which could be seen from the simple fact that, out of an approximate 300 suicide attacks by various groups all over the world since the first attack in 1983, the Black Tigers alone had carried out 150. Secondly, the Black Tigers are the only group in the world to assassinate two former Prime Ministers – Rajiv Gandhi (India) and Ranasinghe Premadasa (Sri Lanka).

There is an overt glorification of the Black Tigers is Sri Lankan Tamil society and within the LTTE for the following factors.

It could be argued that in a sense the entire LTTE as a suicide squad. Every cadre of the LTTE carries a cyanide capsule when he goes for any operation or ambush. Worse, he never hesitates to use it when captured or faced with an adverse situation. However, the Black Tigers assume significance and respect among the LTTE, as the mission of a Black Tiger is to give up his or her life. This difference in the objectives of the mission provides the Black Tigers an elite status inside the LTTE. By giving them an elite status, the LTTE leadership, as shall be seen subsequently prepares its other cadres indirectly to aspire for that status.

July 5 is celebrated every year by the LTTE as the day

of the Black Tigers. It was on July 5, 1987, that the first suicide attack was perpetrated by the LTTE, when its 'Captain' Millar drove a truck full of explosives into a Sri Lankan Army camp, killing nearly forty soldiers. On this particular day, an eternal lamp is lighted in front of the tombstone of every Black Tiger, who had lost his or her life. The LTTE flag is hoisted and the parents of the Black Tigers, who had sacrificed their lives, are honoured. Which is why, when the Sri Lankan Army took over Jaffna from the LTTE, the first thing it did was to bulldoze this cemetery which eulogized the Black Tigers.

The success rate of the Black Tigers also makes them very popular. In most of the cases, except on a couple of rare occasions, the Black Tigers have succeeded in achieving their mission. Chandrika Kumaratunga was one of the few targets, who escaped the Black Tigers. The ability to penetrate the tough security not only in Colombo, but also in other places and carry out its mission, make the Black Tigers invincible in their mission.

The presence of women cadres in the Black Tigers is a significant factor. Other than the LTTE, only the PKK has women cadres in its suicide wing but nearly one-third of the Black Tigers is composed of women. The presence of women in the suicide squad asserts the gender equality, which the LTTE preaches.

The Black Tigers thus form the backbone of the LTTE, which in turn eulogize the former and this overt glorification ensures the continuous inflow Black Tigers have.

The *Fidayeens* of Kashmir

Suicide terrorism in terrorism needs to be carefully analyzed, as there are many misperceptions regarding the recent dare-devil acts that have been perpetrated by the various militant groups. A clear distinction needs to be made between the attacks of two individuals at different periods and the so-called "*fidayeen*" attacks by militant groups.

The former attacks are in fact suicide attacks, in the sense that both the individuals made themselves as the bombs. The first suicide bomb attack in Kashmir occurred when a student rammed his car in front of the Badamibagh cantonment in April 2000. The second attack also took place in the same place in the same manner in December 2000. Whereas the so-called fidayeen attacks are in fact hit and run attacks in which the militants were killed in the encounters. The militant groups, especially the Lashkar, which conducted most of the fidayeen attacks, preferred to call it "fidayeen", for various psychological and media benefits.

These fidayeen attacks have been perpetrated for many reasons. First and foremost have been the intense internal dynamics and objectives of the militant groups that have been fighting against the Indian security forces in Jammu and Kashmir. Besides the major militant groups such as the Hizbul Mujahideen, Lashkar-e-Toiba, Jaish-e-Mohammad and Harkat-ul-Mujahideen, there are more than a hundred minor militant groups. There are a number of differences among these militant groups in terms of objectives and support. These two factors force the various militant groups to involve in certain attacks that would increase the prestige of the group inside Kashmir and also among those who have been sponsoring them, both politically and economically.

These fidayeen attacks also earn huge publicity for the

militant group, which is essential for any militant organizations. The publicity also results in securing more funds, especially from abroad, from a number of religious and fundamentalist organizations and boosting its recruitment drive inside Kashmir.

Reviving the support for militancy at the grass root level is another objective behind these fidayeen attacks. The participation of Kashmiris has been on decline in the last half of the 1990s because of many factors. It is essential for those who support militancy in Kashmir to revive it at any cost. The human bomb that drove the vehicle into the Srinagar Legislative Assembly complex was a citizen of Pakistan, and Jaish and the Lashkar have been regularly carrying out the so-called fidayeen attacks, with Pakistanis.

Combating Suicide Terrorism?

How to con suicide terrorism be combated in Kashmir? Suicide terrorism is not a new phenomenon. Ever since the first suicide attack in Lebanon by the Hizballah in 1983, Israel, Sri Lanka and India are the countries that were affected the most by the suicide terrorists. How did / do these countries cope with suicide terrorism? What options does India have in combating this new menace?

Given the short history of suicide terrorism, so far no state has been able to effectively deal with suicide terrorism. Israel, Sri Lanka and India are the three main states that have been affected with this menace. Suggestions that have been made so far have proved to be ineffective in combating. The real question is how to stop a person, who is willing to give his or her life.

Section-V: Legal Regime and Terrorism

Elimination of International Terrorism: International Legal Regime and Perspectives

V. Nageswara Rao

Terrorism – National and International

Terrorism as a phenomenon has a national or domestic dimension and international dimension and the distinction has to be kept in mind both for the purposes of definition and of evolving the measures and mechanism for combating it. Though both may have overlapping elements, it is desirable to keep the two separate and distinct as they may fall within two different jurisdictions—domestic terrorism may be of purely local concern and hence a matter of maintenance of internal law and order whereas international terrorism may require active cooperation and action at international level. The paper is mainly concerned with international terrorism and the legal regime that is being sought to be evolved to define it and to suppress and eliminate it.

Traditional International Law

Terrorism, in the sense it is understood now, was not known in the earlier times and traditional international law simply treated any forcible interference by one State in the affairs of another State as impermissible unless it is justifiable as an act of self-defence. In fact every State is under a duty not to interfere in the affairs of another State as a necessary sequel to the principle of sovereign equality of States.

Article-2, clause 1 of the United Nations Charter of 1945 says that the "Organization is based on the principle of the sovereign equality of all its members". Article- 2, clause 4 of the Charter enjoins "all its members shall refrain in their international relations from the threat or use of force against the territorial integrity or political independence of any state or in any other manner inconsistent with the purposes of the United Nations." Any use of force is consistent with the Charter only when it is used by a State in the exercise of its right of self-defence under Article- 51 or in pursuance of the coercive measures undertaken by the Security Council under Chapter 7 of the Charter against any State for committing threat to the peace, breach of peace or act of aggression.

In the ***Corfu Channel Case*** (UK v Albania), the International Court of Justice observed that a State was under an obligation "not to allow knowingly its territory to be used contrary to the rights of other States." Oppenheim, the noted jurist, would characterize such interference as intervention, which was an international delinquency for which a State might to have to pay reparation. In fact he defined intervention as a dictatorial interference by a State in the affairs of another State. J.G. Starke states that a State is under a duty: a.) not to perform acts of sovereignty on the territory of another State; b.) to abstain and prevent its agents and subjects from committing acts which violate the sovereignty of another State and c.) not to intervene in the affairs of another State. He also classified Intervention under four categories: 1. internal, i.e. intervention in the internal affairs of another State; 2. external, i.e. intervention in the external affairs of another State; 3. subversive, i.e. intervention aimed at causing subversion in the other State and 4. punitive, i.e. intervention by way of punitive measures against another

State for causing an injury to a State.

Article- 4 of the Draft Declaration on the Rights and Duties of States prepared by the International Law Commission in 1949 also mentioned the duty on the part of a State not to interfere in the affairs of another State, which was also reiterated in the Declaration on Friendly Relations and Cooperation among States adopted by the General Assembly in 1971.

Definition of International Terrorism

Definition of terrorism under international law is beset with many problems. Some even question the very motives of the countries in seeking to define it in a manner to suit their national and strategic interests and others charge some countries with downright hypocrisy in trying to adopt a holier-then-thou attitude. Noam Chomsky, for instance, relates a story: St. Augustine tells the story of a pirate captured by Alexander, the Great, who asked him "how he dares molest the sea". "How dare you molest the whole world?" The pirate replied, "because I do it with a little ship only, I am called a thief, doing it with a great navy, you are called an emperor." Chomsky proceeds to observe: "It captures with some accuracy the current relations between the United States and various minor actors on the state of international terrorism."[1] After the 1972 Munich Olympics killings, Ambassador Charles W. Yost said: "The fact is, of course, that there is a vast amount of hypocrisy about the subject of political terrorism. We all righteously condemn it—except when we ourselves or friends of ours are engaged in it. Then we ignore it or gloss it over or attach to it tags like 'liberation' or 'defence of the world' or 'national honur' to make it seem other than what it is."[2] However, hypocrisy is an equal opportunity employer and almost all States, big or small, indulge in it.

Definitional Problems

Some of the definitions that have been attempted by conventions and commentators may appear to be adequate for the limited purpose for which they have been made but, on analysis, they would not serve the purpose of a comprehensive and acceptable definition. Yonah Alexander defines terrorism as "the use of violence against random civilian targets in order to intimidate or to create generalized pervasive fear for the purpose of achieving political goals." The term 'random', 'civilian' and 'political' have a very limiting connotation. Walter Laquerur defines the term as "an attempt to destabilize democratic societies and to show that their governments are impotent."[3] The obvious implication of this definition is that terrorism can be committed against democratic societies only. Article-1 of the 1937 Convention on Terrorism states that terrorism consists of "criminal acts directed against a State and intended or calculated to create a state of terror in the minds of a particular person, a group of persons or the general public." This convention obviously confines terrorism to situations where the State per se is the target. We shall now refer to possible elements that may be taken into account for formulating a workable definition of the term terrorism.

Private Acts or State Acts ?

One of the many issues that dogged the definition of terrorism is whether it should be confined to terrorism indulged in by private individuals and organizations or if it should also include terrorism sponsored by one State against another State. The term came into use first at the time of 'reign of terror' in France during the Revolution to describe the intimidating practices of the government in power from 1789-1794. But as stated by a study prepared by the UN Secretariat the above meaning of terrorism has undergone a major change so that it "now seems mainly applied to actions by individuals or a group of individuals."[4] In their preliminary comments submitted to the UN Ad Hoc Committee on Terrorism, most States confined their comments to terrorism of individuals or groups. However, some Arab States like Syria and some non-aligned States wanted that international terrorism be discussed from the stand point of State terrorism also. But Venezuela and several States clubbed both. The Venezuelan proposal defined the term as "any threat or act of violence which endangers or takes innocent human lives or jeopardizes fundamental freedoms, committed by an individual or group of individuals" as well as "inhuman repressive measures carried out by colonial or racist regimes."[5] The United States representative, however, opposed the inclusion of State terrorism as an attempt to blur the nature of the problem "as to ensure that no meaningful action would be taken with regard to either."[6] The US argument was that State terrorism was being discussed by other fora of the UN.

Other Factors

Various factors were considered relevant for a comprehensive definition of international terrorism. They are:

a) General or specific definition

b) Difference between intimidation and terrorism

c) Whether to include acts committed in struggle for self-determination

d) Whether to include all criminal activities and political violence

e) Range of acts

f) What constitutes international element

g) Identity of perpetrators

h) Identity of victims

Any definition that is too general might secure wider acceptance but may not serve any practical purpose in the actual implementation. Too specific a definition might get bogged down in national susceptibilities and may ultimately fail to get the required support. In fact India even suggested that instead of focusing on definition, concrete measures of cooperation should be devised to prevent and deter terrorism.

Range of Acts

The Convention on Terrorism adopted under the auspices of the League of Nations in 1937 was too comprehensive and included a whole gamut of acts but the Convention could never come into force as only one State ratified it. But Leo Gross considers that the Convention was not ratified for a variety of reasons and thinks that the wide cover was 'thorough' and 'coherent.'[7] But the fact remains that even this wide cover could not include the bewildering variety of tools of modern acts of terrorism that range from very handy small weapons to nuclear, radio-active, biological, and chemical weapons and a deceptive technique of funding.

Motive of the Acts

The issue of the motive of the acts of terrorism has deeply divided the international community with regard to an acceptable definition of the term. Here we may have to make a distinction between the legal concept of 'intention' and the behavioural concept of motivation. As Leslie Green observes, "little is to be gained by analyzing the political or ideological nature of the motivation of the actor. Any activity of this character can be associated with some type of idealistic purpose...." [8] In its draft articles on the Protection of Diplomats etc, the International Law Commission (ILC) states that the phrase "regardless of motive" in Article 2 "restates to the universally accepted principle that it is the intent to commit the act and not the reasons that led to its commission that is the governing factor." The OAS Convention on Terrorism also uses the phrase "regardless of motive" in Article-2.

The Ad Hoc Committee on Terrorism of UN thought that motive is necessary. France observed that acts, which spread terror in population, might be done for ordinary motives like extortion. For defining terrorism 'political motive' was important. But Sweden thought that it was difficult to define 'political' as some states might consider all acts directed against their governments as political.

But questions regarding motive may be relevant not only in defining terrorism but also in quantifying the punishment. Hijacking by a person as a mode of escape from a repressive regime at home should get lesser punishment than other hijackers.

International Component

Various factors may be relevant for determining when terrorism should be treated as 'international'. They are: (a) acts taking place in more than one State; (b) acts affecting citizens in more than one State; (c) acts taking place in areas that are treated as common property (high seas, etc.); (d) acts affecting internationally protected persons like diplomats and (e) acts affecting internationally protected objects like international civil aviation, mail and other means of communication.

Brian Jenkins proposes that to be characterized as international the acts must have "clear international consequences". This test obviously excludes acts directed against one's own State or citizens without any foreign connection.

The 1937 Convention on Terrorism covered only acts directed against a foreign State. OAS Convention and the ILC Draft Articles were confined to acts directed against internationally protected persons like diplomats. This offence is however a crime under domestic as well as international laws. The anti-hijacking conventions of Tokyo, Hague and Montreal applied the 5th test referred to above (e). The 1972 Draft Articles submitted by USA to the UN Ad Hoc Committee on Terrorism proposed the following tests:

a) Act must be committed or take effect outside the State of which the offender is a national, or

b) Act must be committed or take effect against a foreign national even within the State where the act is committed and of which the offender is a national, or

c) Act must not be committed by or against a member of the armed forces in the course of military operations, since these acts are covered by other rules of international law relating to war

d) Act must have been committed to damage the interests of or for obtaining concessions from another State or international organization.

Targets of Terrorism

In the context of defining terrorism with an international dimension, it would be necessary to identify the targets of terrorism. Jordan Paust classifies the targets under the following categories: (a) Instrumental targets—human and non-human; (b) Primary targets (victims); (c) Secondary targets and (d) Spill over victims.

But attack against one category may affect another category, whether intended or not. Attack on a military headquarters may also cause intense anxiety to military top brass also, both of which may be intended. Similarly attack on power stations may also affect civilians dependent on the power supply.

However there is a general agreement among States that terrorism should not affect "innocent" lives. But its implied opposite "guilty" may bring in hazy components like political, moral, and ideological factors. It can be argued that the civilians of a State by not 'resisting' the 'repressive regime' are condoning the acts of the government and, hence, are not 'innocent'. Is a foreigner 'guilty' if he trades with a State, which is the target of terrorism?

Terrorists are often very selective in choosing their

target whether it is a leader or a governmental establishment. Or they can be purposefully indiscriminate and kill at random civilians also. This is called "pure terrorism". Sometimes it is said that terrorism should not extend to countries and their civilians who are not involved in the conflict. But this formula would ignore the humanitarian need to protect the 'innocent' civilians of even the State, which is the target of terrorism. So Israel proposed that the definition should also comprehend "acts directed against a State.... its nationals, interests or property, including its means of transport." But South Africa would like to make a distinction between terrorism and other unlawful use of force and confine the former to acts "aimed directly or indirectly at a State or an international organization."

The 1937 Convention for the Prevention and Punishment of Terrorism applied to the following acts directed against: (a) Heads of State, etc; (b) Wives and husbands of (a) and (c) Persons charged with public functions when the acts are directed against them in that capacity.

Incidental Terrorism (Collateral Damage)

The question of collateral damage was sought to be skirted in some international instruments by specifically identifying the targets. The ILC Convention on Prevention and Punishment of Crimes against Diplomatic Agents and Other Internationally Protected Persons tried to avoid the problem of targets by focusing exclusively on a single category, i.e. diplomatic agents. The same was also done by the OAS Convention. But the international community must come to grips with the problem of incidental terrorism in a more pragmatic manner as this variety is bound to affect the 'innocent' lives. The so-called collateral damage can be much more callous and inhuman than the damage to real targets.

Manifestations of International Terrorism

Even a cursory review of the terrorist acts will reveal a variety of ways in which terrorism has manifested itself. Some of them are: Class struggle; Caste struggle; Liberation struggle; Separatist movements; Undeclared wars; Power struggles; Sectarian struggle; Religious Fundamentalism; Tribal Warfare; Revenge and Organized Crime like drugs, smuggling, etc.

The so-called definitions, observes V.S. Mani, "have endeavoured to stigmatize terrorism without directing attention to the need for curing the deep-seated societal maladies, the permanent breeding grounds of terrorism."[9] Brian Jenkins, on the other hand, thinks that the main cause of terrorism is the reaction to the general trend towards increasing centralization of authority in modern States. The UN Secretariat Study already referred to above "concluded that origins and underlying causes of terrorism were complex and various but that many of them lay in international political and social situations which the United Nations was founded to improve. The efforts to eliminate those causes should be inter se and continuous." Whatever may be the real or perceived injustices suffered by individuals or groups that seem to fuel the flames of criminal behaviours in domestic societies or of terrorism in the international arena, human societies will have to evolve a multi-pronged approach to tackle the menace of crime and terrorism so as to deal with it, in the short run, as a deviant behaviour and, in the long run, as a manifestation that is symptomatic of deeper social maladies that call for urgent curative measures. It will be a folly to treat it in a uni-dimensional manner.

Conclusion

It is evident from the above that it will be very unwise to expect the international community to agree on a universally acceptable and comprehensive definition of international terrorism. The reasons for it are not far to seek. The causative factors for the emergence of terrorism are not only the perceived injustices shared by individuals and States but also the fact that certain States, overtly or covertly, sponsor terrorism as a means of achieving goals that they think would not be possible to attain by fairer means. In the US, Frank Camper openly runs a school for training terrorists. Control Risks Limited and Ackerman and Palumbo Inc., two risk consultancy firms, rake in more than $4,000,000 per year for advising clients on how to avoid terrorism.[10] Every State has skeletons in its cupboards, which it wants to hide and any definition of international terrorism will have to cater to these nefarious needs to be acceptable to them. In the interim, the only solution is what India proposed at the Ad Hoc Committee on Terrorism, that is, to shift the focus from definition to the adoption of measures to tackle the menace at the national and global level.

One such measure that readily strikes the mind is to enter into binding bi-lateral, regional and global conventions that oblige the signatories to adhere to the time-honoured principle of international law—***aut punier, aut dedaere,*** i.e. either you punish or surrender the offender. The SAARC Regional Convention on Suppression of Terrorism of 1987 attempts to arrive at this solution by obliging the member-States to extradite the offenders and to make provision in their respective extradition treaties and national legislation to that effect. That all is not well even in this relatively small regional group is evident from the fact that Article-VII of this Convention leaves many backdoors open by providing:

> "Contracting States shall not be obliged to extradite, if it appears to the requested State that by reason of the trivial nature of the case or by reason of the request for surrender or return of a fugitive offender not being made in good faith or in the interests of justice or for any other reason it is unjust or inexpedient to surrender or return the fugitive offender."

This, in short, epitomizes the dilemma faced by the international community in arriving at an agreed definition of international terrorism with an adequate enforcement mechanism. Terrorism will prove to be a greater scourge to mankind than a regular war if the States persist in their attempts at watering down any meaningful definition by grafting exceptions that will eat away the very substance of definition.

Notes

1. Noam Chomsky, *Pirates and Emperors—International Terrorism in the Real World* (Montreal, New York: Black Rose Books, 1991), p. 1.
2. See V.S. Mani, "International Terrorism—Is a Definition Possible?", in Verinder Grover (ed), *Encyclopaedia of International Terrorism—History and Development*, vol. 1, (New Delhi: Deep & Deep Publications, 2002), p. 66.

3. Walter Laqueur, "Reflections on Terrorism", *Foreign Affairs*, vol. 65, no.1, Fall 1986, p. 87
4. UN General Assembly, *Secretariat Study for the sixth Committee, UN General Assembly*, A/C. 6/418, 2 November 1972, p. 6
5. "Report of Ad Hoc Committee on International Terrorism", *General Assembly Official Records*, 28th Session, Supplement No.28 (A/9028), New York, 1973, p.23.
6. *General Assembly Official Records*, A/C. 6/SR 1581, 4 December 1975, p. 82.
7. Leo Gross, "International Terrorism and International Criminal Jurisdiction", *American Journal of International Law*, vol. 67, 1973, p.503.
8. Leslie Green, "International Terrorism and its Legal Control", *Chitty's Law Journal*, vol.21, 1973, p. 294.
9. Mani, n.2, p.66.
10. See Kent Layne Oots, *A Political Organizational Approach to Transnational Terrorism* (New York: Greenwood Press, 1986), p, 109.

Indian Legal Regime Relating to Prevention of Terrorism: An Analysis

G.B. Reddy

Introduction

Disregard and contempt for human rights have resulted in barbarous acts which have outraged the conscience of mankind, and the advent of the world in which human beings shall enjoy freedom of speech and belief and freedom from fear and want has been proclaimed as the highest aspirations of the common people.[1] Many international covenants on human rights and national constitutions guarantee the right to life, liberty and security of the person.[2] The movement for securing human rights to all gained strength after the conclusion of the Second World War. On the other hand, the states are under an obligation to maintain the sovereignty, unity and integrity of those countries from internal disturbances as well as external aggression. The ultimate goal of the human rights and also of sovereign powers is to ensure that the human beings wherever they are living are guaranteed the right to live in a peaceful and harmonious society by enjoying the right to life, personal liberty, safety and security.

The great scourge on humanity in recent times is the menace of terrorism. Even though it is not a new phenomenon, it attracted increased attention after the terrorist attack on the World Trade Centre in New York on 11 September 2001. India has awakened to the threat of terrorism a long time ago, but the attack on the Indian Parliament on 13 December 2001 has prompted the Indian policy makers to take fresh notice of this desperate behaviour of certain sections of the society. It is with this backdrop that an attempt has been made in the paper to locate the various laws in India that aim at tackling extraordinary situations like terrorism and extremism.

Terrorist act is the use of violence when its most important result is not merely the physical and mental damage of the victim but the prolonged psychological effect it produces or has the potential of producing on the society as a whole. The extent and reach of the intended terrorist activity travels beyond the effect of ordinary crime capable of being punished under the ordinary penal law of the land. Its main objective is to overawe the government or disturb the harmony of the society or terrorize people and the society with a view to disturb the even tempo, peace and tranquillity of the society and create a sense of fear and insecurity. The various terrorist techniques and methods include bombing operations, hijacking and kidnapping, hostage taking, assassinations, use of rockets and mortars, chemical weapons and nuclear terrorism. Ordinary criminal law may not be adequate to tackle the above situations and therefore it may be necessary to pass certain extraordinary legislation to deal with such extraordinary situations. Insofar as India is concerned, after the commencement of the Constitution many special legislations came to be passed to deal with certain extraordinary crimes like terrorism and extremism.

Intention of the Framers of the Constitution

At the time of framing of the Constitution, there was a lot of discussion on the present Article 22 of the Constitution dealing with the safeguards available to the arrested persons and the detenues detained under the preventive detention laws. While supporting the necessity to pass preventive detention laws, G. Durgabai Deshmukh observed :

> "...the question before us is this, whether the exigencies of the freedom of individuals or the exigencies of the state is more important. When it comes to a question of shaking the very foundations of the State, which state stands not for the freedom of one individual but of several individuals, I yield the first place to the state.... The new Article 15-A[3] ...is a very happy compromise.[4]"

Another learned member P.K.Sen, a member from Bihar also supported such a measure and observed :

> "...there may be certain things in the provisions of the articles which appear to be rather against the fundamental rights, but an awareness of the troubled times which not only this country but also all other countries in the world are passing through, some special measures for the security of the state are necessary..."[5]

However, certain other members like Mahavir Tyagi had opposed the law of preventive detention on the ground that " life, liberty and pursuit of happiness are the three fundamental rights. The State comes into being not because it has any inherent right of its own, but because the individual, who has inherent rights of life and liberty, foregoes a part of his own rights and deposits it with the state....the state is thus organized and constituted not by depriving the people of their inherent rights....the introduction here of a (detention) clause changes the chapter of fundamental rights into a penal code worse than the Defence Rules of India of old government.....it is not the business of the Constituent Assembly to vest in the hands of future governments power to detain people..."[6] B.R.Ambedkar supported the preventive detention law totally by overruling the objections of members like Mahavir Tyagi. Thus, the Constituent Assembly took cognizance of the extreme situations like terrorism and provided certain measures to curb the same.

The Legal Regime Relating to Terrorism

The legal regime to control terrorist activities may be classified into (i) International legal regime and (ii) National legal regime. As regards the international law, the laws of war are considered as a potential legal regime for the control of terrorist activities. The issues that arise at the international level include the principle of double criminality, the doctrine of political offences, the extradition, the right of asylum and the war crimes, for which there appears to be no uniform and universally acceptable approach.[7] Since the scope of the present paper is confined to the domestic legal regime related to terrorism in India, it is proposed to take a cursory look at the similar regimes in some of the South Asian countries.

Position in South Asian Countries

In Bangladesh, the Parliament enacted the Special Powers Act, 1974 (SPA) with the objective of crushing black marketeers and smugglers said to be responsible for the food shortages throughout the country. The Preamble to the SPA states that its purpose is to provide special measures for the prevention of certain prejudicial activities, speedy trials and effective punishment for certain grave offences and matters connected therewith. This law is based on the assumption that the existing Penal Code and Criminal Procedure Code are insufficient to address terrorism and criminal conspiracies. The definition of 'prejudicial act' u/s 2(f) of the Act is very broad and includes any act that is intended or likely to prejudice the sovereignty or defence of Bangladesh, to prejudice the maintenance of friendly relations of Bangladesh with foreign states, to prejudice the security of Bangladesh or to endanger public safety or the maintenance of public order and to cause fear or alarm to the public or to any section of the public, among other acts. This act gives vast powers to the State. There has been criticism that the law is draconian and violates the provisions of the International Covenant on Civil and Political rights, the Universal Declaration of Human Rights and the Convention Against Torture and other Cruel, Inhuman or Degrading Treatment or Punishment.[8]

In Pakistan, the Legislature has passed the Anti Terrorism Act, 1997 intending to 'provide for the prevention of terrorism, sectarian violence and for speedy trial of heinous offences and for matters connected therewith and incidental thereto.' The law has been made more draconian by the amendments made in 1999 and 2002. The 2002 Amendment includes even 'military officers' in the panel of judges to try 'terrorist' offences. It is said that the existing legal and judicial system is already equipped to deal with offences referred to in the Act. The problem then, seems to be a lack of implementation and not a lack of laws. However, in an attempt to conceal this inefficiency, Pakistan adopted the anti-terrorist acts which provide speedy trial without necessary guarantees for the accused, unfair trials and license to kill, etc.[9]

In Nepal, on 26 November 2001, the King promulgated the 'Terrorist and Disruptive Activities (Prevention and Control) Ordinance 2001, because "it had become necessary to make necessary legal provisions to control terrorist and disruptive activities so as to provide security to the general public and ensure peace and order in the Kingdom of Nepal". The Ordinance grants wide powers to arrest people involved in terrorist activities". It may be mentioned in this context that the TADO appears to be similar to the TADA of India.

In Sri Lanka, there are a number of anti-terrorist legislations, viz. the Public Security Ordinance, the Prevention of Terrorism Act, and the Emergency Regulations (Collectively, the 'Emergency Laws'). These laws enable political and security officials at all levels to participate in counter campaigns of terror. The Prevention of Terrorism Act (PTA), 1979 addresses the threat to public security by the insurgence of the LTTE by outlining the ways in which the government may issue emergency regulations of oppression without sufficient justification. It has been criticized that under the emergency regulations, public security has not improved. Rather, the island, particularly the war-torn areas of the north and north-east, has witnessed a virtual collapse of the law enforcement system.[10]

On a clear analysis of the above laws, it becomes clear that the socio-political backgrounds in the above countries are not uniform and vary from each other. The fact is that the terrorist-related laws are stringent and there are numerous allegations of their misuse and abuse by the State machinery. However, good legislation is no substitute for political will and statesmanship in the struggle against terrorism, legislative protections are no substitute for the efficient and accountable enforcement of the laws. Similarly there is no guarantee that even ordinary criminal laws are exempted from being abused and misused, in any civil society, in spite of a number of human rights and freedoms.

The Preventive Detention Laws in India

Article-22 of the Indian Constitution provides protection to the persons arrested and detained in police custody. This implicitly shows the powers of Parliament and the State Legislatures to pass laws relating to preventive detention including the so-called terrorism. A number of legislations came to be passed after 1950 under this category and the relevant Entry in the Union List contained in the Seventh Schedule of the Constitution is Entry 9 which reads "Preventive Detention for reasons connected with defence, foreign affairs or the security of India; persons subjected to such detention." The relevant entries in the State List are Public Order and Police.[11] In the Concurrent List, the relevant entries are Criminal Law, Criminal Procedure and Preventive Detention.[12] By exercising the power vested as above the competent legislatures have passed many legislations. They include the Armed Forces (Special Powers) Act, 1958; the National Security Act, 1980; the Special Courts Act, 1978; the Unlawful Activities (Prevention) Act, 1967 and the Disturbed Areas(Special Courts)Act, 1976.The two legislations which are directly relevant to the prevention of terrorism are: (1) The Terrorist and Disruptive Activities (Prevention) Act, 1987[13] (TADA) and (2) The Prevention of Terrorism Act, 2002.[14]

A. The Terrorist and Disruptive Activities (Prevention) Act, 1987

This Act was passed to make special provisions for the prevention of and for coping with terrorist and disruptive activities in the background of terrorist activities in many parts of the country at that time. As it was expected that it would be possible to control the menace within a period of two years, the life of the Act was restricted initially to only two years. Some of the existing provisions were amplified in 1993 taking note of the fact that the terrorism, which was initially confined to the states of Punjab, Jammu and Kashmir and the north-east, has spread its tentacles to the states of Uttar Pradesh, Madhya Pradesh, Himachal Pradesh, Maharashtra, and West Bengal. Apart from this, the sophisticated weapons, remote control devices, rocket launchers, professional training and international involvement have added a new and disturbing dimension to the problem. Further the agreement entered into by India with the UK for mutual assistance in the investigation and prosecution of the terrorist crimes was also instrumental in this amendment.

This legislation defined terrorism in its Section 3 in an exhaustive manner. An analysis of Section 3 clause (1) shows that whoever with intent

(i) to overawe the government as by law established; or

(ii) to strike terror in the people or any section of the people; or

(iii) to alienate any section of the people; or

(iv) to adversely affect the harmony amongst the different sections of the people, does any act or things by using

    (a) bombs or dynamites; or

    (b) other explosive substances; or

    (c) inflammable substances; or

    (d) fire arms; or

(e) other lethal weapons; or

(f) poisons or noxious gases or other chemicals; or

(g) any other substances (whether biological or otherwise) of a hazardous nature in such a manner as to cause or is likely to cause (i) death; or (ii) injuries to any person; or (iii) loss of or damage to or destruction of property; or (iv) disruption of any supplies or services essential to the life of the community; or (v) detains any person and threatens to kill or injure such person in order to compel the government or any other person to do or abstain from doing any act, commits a terrorist act punishable under Section 3 of TADA.

This is a very comprehensive definition of a terrorist act and it is self-explanatory in nature, as it covers all the forms and consequences of terrorism.

It has been made clear that an activity, which is sought to be punished under the above provision, has to be such which cannot be classified as a mere law and order problem or disturbance of public order.[15] The Supreme Court declared that the TADA is an extreme measure to be resorted to when the police cannot tackle the situation under the ordinary penal law. The intendment is to provide special machinery to combat the growing menace of terrorism in the different parts of the country.[16] The Act prescribed special procedures aiming at speedy disposal of cases, departing from the procedure prescribed under the ordinary procedural law. For obvious reasons, the prevalent ordinary procedural laws were found to be inadequate and not sufficiently effective to deal with the offenders indulging in terrorist and disruptive activities, secondly the incensed offences or arising out of the activities of the terrorist and disruptionists which disrupt even the sovereignty and territorial integrity of India or which may support any claim for the cession of any part of India or a secession of any part of India from the Union.

The TADA was criticized by many on the ground that it was a draconian law capable of violating human rights and of even being misused. The constitutionality of legislation was challenged in many cases and the courts have upheld its validity except the validity of a few provisions.[17] This Act defined the disruptive activity as any action taken whether by an act or by speech or through any other media or in any other manner, which questions, disrupts or intended to disrupt the sovereignty and territorial integrity of India or which causes or supports any claim for the cession of any part of India or the secession of any part of India from the Union.[18] Further the Act provided for the punishment of persons found with unauthorized arms in notified area. The experience of working of the Act appears to be not so satisfactory even though the provisions of the Act are quite capable of handling the challenges arising out of terrorism and disruptions. Ultimately the Act was repealed some time in 1995, ironically after the Supreme Court upheld its validity on the whole in the Kartar Singh Case.[19]

B. The Prevention of Terrorism Act 2002

The Criminal Law Amendment Act, 1995 to replace the TADA had been lying pending in the Rajya Sabha since 1985. As the existing criminal justice system was not designed to deal with terrorism, the Prevention of Terrorism Ordinance, 2001 was promulgated on 24 October 2001 and it became an Act (POTA) after the Parliament had passed the same in a joint sitting on 26 March 2002. Thus, POTO has become POTA after considerable political controversy.

It is relevant to note in this context that the UN Security Council Resolution 1373 adopted on 28 September 2001 has called upon the state to assume that any person who participates in the financing, planning, preparation or perpetration of terrorist act or in supporting terrorist acts is brought to justice and ensures that in addition to any other measures against them, such terrorist acts are established as serious criminal offences in domestic laws and that the punishment duly reflect the seriousness of such terrorist acts. There appears to be global consensus on the need for enacting special laws to deal with terrorism. The President promulgated the Prevention of Terrorism Ordinance 2001 on 24 October 2001. This POTO has come under severe criticism. It has been criticized on the ground that (i) the definition of terrorism is too wide and could be used against strong protests outside Government Buildings; (ii) Bail will not be granted unless he is not guilty of committing the offence;[20] (iii) The investigation period can be stretched to 120 days;[21] (iv) the 'citizen spy' provisions requiring even journalists (but not lawyers) to reveal information of material assistance carries a punishment of three years and unlimited fine[22] compared to the normal punishment of three months and Rs.200/- fine with bail and (v) it permits confessions to the Police.[23] The general criticism from some quarters was that POTA is wider and worse than TADA and that the safeguards are insufficient.[24] Another criticism has been that the POTO (present POTA) "obliterates the distinction between innocent and guilty. Social visionaries and anti-socials, civil libertarians and crooks, poets and conmen, secessionists and scoundrels, peasant revolutionaries and thieves – all coalesce into one category: Terrorists."[25] The main ground on which POTO is opposed appears to be that it is a new garb of TADA that was allegedly notoriously misused and abused. The critics point out that ordinary laws like the Indian Penal Code, 1860; the Arms Act, 1959; the Explosives Act, 1884; the Explosive Substances Act, 1908; the Unlawful Activities Act, 1967, the Anti-Hijacking Act, 1972 and the Code of Criminal Procedure, 1973 can take care of the various terrorist activities and that there is no need for the laws like the POTA. Justice Krishna Iyer, the eminent Judge and commentator also opposed POTA in spite of admitting that "terrorism is dangerous and its ubiquity makes the menace a cause for consternation." He warned that in the guise of anti-terrorist enactment, everything precious in our constitutionally sanctified criminal justice couldn't be subverted. He approvingly quoted the UN High Commissioner for Human Rights Mary Robinson who warned governments that 'measures to eradicate terrorism must not lead to excessive curbs on human rights and fundamental freedoms.'[26]

On the other hand, the supporters of POTO argue that extraordinary situations like the acts of terrorism require extraordinary and stringent laws exclusively made to tackle the menace. Arun Shourie argued that "under the Unlawful Activities Act, 1967, only those individuals or organizations that aim at disrupting the sovereignty and territorial integrity of the country can be proceeded against. The terrorist don sitting in Dubai exercising murderous control over the film world is not threatening the sovereignty of the country...?"

He further asks that "can it be anyone's case that while it is all right to require a person on whom some computer hard disks are found to prove his innocence, it is wrong and diabolic to require him to do so if RDX and AK-47 are found?"[27] The BJP led Central Government maintains that the general people appreciate the efforts of the government to totally eliminate the activities of terrorists and also understand the need for a comprehensive legal Act of Parliament to deal with the situation.

In this background some of the so-called controversial provisions of the POTA can be referred to. They are: (i) 'an act of terrorism' has been broadened to include membership, support, assistance or furthering the activities of any terrorist organization including the raising of funds for the purpose of terrorism; (ii) Provisions incorporating "Proactive duty" clauses making it mandatory for citizens to furnish information about terrorist activities that the police suspect them of possessing; (iii) Provision requiring the charge sheeted to lose passport for a period;[28] (iv) forfeiture of proceeds of terrorism[29] and (v) forfeiture of property of certain persons. [30]

Because of the controversy generated, the Prevention of Terrorism Bill 2001 to replace the POTO could not be introduced in the House of People; it was repromulgated on 30 December 2001 with some minor changes. Some of the changes are:

1. deletion of punitive action for failure to disclose information of material assistance in preventing the commission of terrorist activities
2. limiting the duration of the ordinance to *three* instead of *five* years

3. doing away with the concurrent jurisdiction of the designated authority and the Special Courts; and

4. vesting the power of forfeiture of proceeds of terrorism in the Special Court instead of the designated authority etc.

While the amended POTO (present POTA) deletes one of the controversial sub sections, i.e. Section- 3(8), that makes it mandatory for citizens to disclose information connected with a terrorist group or act to the police it leaves the more sweeping section 14 requiring any individual, officer or bank etc. to furnish information in their possession in relation to such offence of terrorism, intact.

It is in the fitness of the things that the Bill on the Prevention of Terrorism Ordinance which has been passed by Lok Sabha on 18 March 2002 was introduced in Rajya Sabha, on 21 March 2002 but due to the opposition from the parties like Congress I and CPM the same could not be passed in to Act. Consequently, a joint sitting of the Parliament had to be summoned and on 26 March 2002, it has become an Act.

A clear analysis of the POTA shows that, the law is a stringent legislation, which puts the onus on the citizens to prevent terrorism. It arms the investigating officers to intercept communication in certain cases, authorises the Central Government to declare an organization as a terrorist organization, provides forfeiture of property of a person accused of a terrorist act, and of proceeds of terrorism, and also provides for impounding of passport and arms licence of person charge sheeted under law.

One unique and extraordinary provision in the POTA

is making the confession made to police officers not below the rank of a Superintendent of Police admissible in the trial of such person for an offence under the ordinance.[31] This is an exceptional measure but enough safeguards are provided to the accused making such confessions.[32]

Conclusion

The Opposition to the POTA comes from certain political parties and organizations on the following among other grounds that:

a. the law is draconian;

b. the human rights of citizens are violated thereby;

c. it is likely to be misused;[33] and

d. it is likely to be misused against the minorites etc.

However the same argument can be advanced against any legislation including Indian Penal Code or Criminal Procedure Code. Since the law is supposed to be dynamic, it has to change in accordance with the changing times. Our lawmakers never envisaged extraordinary situations like terrorism in the past and there appears to be nothing unreasonable in passing such extraordinary laws like POTA to tackle with this new menace.

India is not alone in passing such legislations. Many countries in the West and North America have already passed such legislations. Similar legislations were passed in United Kingdom, Canada and US. The Uniting and Strengthening America by Providing Appropriate Tools Required to Intercept and Obstruct Terrorism Act of 2001 (US Patriot Act) expresses the sense of US Congress among other things that (i) the civil rights and liberties of all Americans, including Arab Americans, must be protected and that every effort must be taken to preserve their safety, (ii) any acts of violence or discrimination against any American be condemned and (iii) the nation is called upon to recognise the patriotism of fellow citizens from all ethnic, racial and religious backgrounds. Political considerations should not be allowed to overtake other important considerations like national security and human rights of the majority people. Terrorism is a menace of monstrous proportions and is a crime against humanity on the whole. Since it is transnational in nature, it has to be tackled at the national as well as the international level. As no state can foster international cooperation single-handedly due to many constraints, the best way of tackling the terrorism is to have a strong legislation like POTA, to suppress this inhuman practice. It may not be out of place in this context that certain States in India like Andhra Pradesh have passed special legislation, viz. the Andhra Pradesh Control of Organized Crime Act of 2001 which *inter alia,* aims at preventing organized crimes including promotion of insurgency. However, enough safeguards can be insisted upon against the abuse and misuse of such legislation.

The concept of Secularism and humanitarian jurisprudence should not come in the way of national unity, integrity and sovereignty and also the greatest happiness of the greatest number of people. After all Bill Of Rights cannot be converted into a suicidal pact under the guise of human rights and secularism. The critics of the stringent laws enacted to deal with terrorism appear to forget that the victims of terrorism also are entitled to the human rights like the right to life, personal liberty, safety and security.

Whether the law alone can tackle the menace of terrorism all by itself is a moot question, but any country that fails to enact necessary laws to prevent one of the greatest national security threats on any ground whatsoever, would be abdicating its sovereign duty. It is gratifying to note that Indian Lawmakers have discharged their constitutional obligation. Their next most serious challenge would be to ensure that the law is used effectively for the objects for which it is enacted and not to permit its abuse.

Notes

1. *Preamble to the Universal Declaration of Human Rights,* 1948.
2. Like Art.3 of Universal Declaration of Human Rights, 5th and 14th Amendments to US Constitution and Article 21 of the Indian Constitution.
3. The present Article 22 of the Indian Constitution, dealing with safeguards to arrested persons and detainees and exceptions thereto.
4. *Constituent Assembly Debates,* vol. 9, p. 1543, 16 September 1949.
5. *Ibid.*
6. *Ibid.*
7. Paul A. Tharp, Jr., "The Laws of War as a Potential Legal Regime for the Control of Terrorist Activities", *Journal of International Affairs,* vol.32, no.1, Spring/ Summer 1978, pp.91-100.
8. See Cathy Mcwilliam, "Exercising the Bigstock", *Seminar,* Issue no. 512, April 2002, pp. 41-47.

9. See Jekkue Irtegam "Anti-Terrorist Laws in Pakistan", *Seminar*, Issue no. 512, April 2002, p. 48 ff. See also "Legalizing the impermissible: The new Anti terrorism Law", *Amnesty International*, 1 October 1997, ASA 33/03401997.

10. See Abizer Zanzi, "Sri Lanka's Emergency Laws", *Seminar*, Issue no. 512, April 2002, p. 33 ff.

11. Entries 1 and 2 respectively.

12. Entries 1, 2 and 3 respectively.

13. Which has been repealed in 1995.

14. Which has become an Act after the Parliament in its joint session passed the POTA Bill in place of the second Ordinance on Prevention of Terrorism.

15. Hithendra Vishnu Thakur v. State of Maharashtra, (1994) 4 SCC 602.

16. Usman Bhai Dawood Bhai Memon v. State of Gujarat, (1988), 2 SCC 271.

17. Usman Bhai Dawood Bhai Memon v. State of Gujarat, (1988) 2 SCC 271; Kartar Singh v. State of Punjab, (1994), 3 SCC 564; Hithendra Vishnu Thakur v. State of Maharashtra, (1994), 4 SCC 602, etc.

18. Section 4 of the Act.

19. (1994) 3 SCC 564.

20. Section 48(7).

21. Section 48(2).

22. Section 3(8) and 14.

23. Section 32.

24. See Rajeev Dhavan, "POTO: An Assault on Democracy", *The Hindu*, 16 November 2001, p. 12.

25. See Gautam Navlakha, "POTO: Taking the Lawless Road", *Economic and Political Weekly*, vol. 36, no. 49, 8 December 2001, p. 4522.

26. See Justice V.R.Krishna Iyer, *Legally Speaking* (Delhi: Universal Law Publishing Co.Ltd, 2002), p. 242.

27. See his interview "TADA was Never a POTO Prototype-Clearing Some More Misapprehensions about the New Terrorism Ordinance", *The Hindustan Times*, 12 November 2001.

28. Under Section 58.

29. Under Section 8.

30. Under Section 16.

31. Under Section 32.

32. Under the provision of the Indian Evidence Act, 1872, such confessions are generally not admissible under Section 27.

33. However under Section 58 of the POTO, any police officer who exercises powers corrupting or maliciously knowing that there are no reasonable grounds for proceeding under the Act, shall be punishable with imprisonment upto two years or also fine or both. Further the victim can also be compensated.

Akshardham and Beyond: Redefining Police and Public Order Maintenance in the Face of Terrorist Hyper-Violence

Satya Narayan Pradhan

"... we can afford – we must afford – to preserve our liberties and our unity at the same time as we deal with threats to our society. For a great democratic nation what is needed is a strategy, not unbridled anger" Phillip B. Heyman[1]

Introduction

On 24 September 2002 India was to relive the shock and agony of a nation under attack by forces of destabilization that employ unmitigated terror as the modus operandi and are willing to die in the process. They create bloodbath and mayhem. What is worse the whole idea seems to be aimed at perpetuating a sense of countrywide insecurity and disorder. After the attacks on the American Consulate in Kolkata and the daring attack on the Indian Parliament, the events at Akshardham have suddenly but surely made the average Indian citizen wonder if the foreseeable future will be witness to several such attacks on symbolic targets around the country? Already the media is speculating on the possible soft target that may be picked up in the future for isolated acts of terrorist violence.[2] The question that follows rather predictably is not whether the police in the States across the country are prepared to face such eventualities (the answers are declaredly on the negative) but whether we can afford to continue being unprepared and flat-footed in our responses to a new terrorist strategy of attacking soft targets at unexpected places and getting away with it? Whatever the answer, the moot point is that it is undeniably an item highest on the police agenda-the sworn agenda of any policeman being to provide a sense of security and safety to the average citizen. We are not about to call in the Armed forces to cordon off the temples across the country where thousands, sometimes lakhs throng! Public order maintenance is the core duty of the police. From crowd control to handling terrorist situation they have been at the forefront of their duties either by design or by default. But the problem at hand has special ramifications for public order maintenance. Before we seek to understand how it is a unique challenge we may first appreciate the role of the police as the prime instrument of governance in maintaining public order and tranquillity.

State and Public Order Maintenance

All states are faced with the imperative of maintaining public peace and order. This concept seems to be accepted universally by us without much thought. It is usually not well-appreciated that the police and the security forces are burdened with the onerous responsibility of ensuring public order in the face of myriad challenges to internal security. They are the prime state apparatus to maintain and uphold a sense of safety and security. From day-to-day crowd control to maintenance of public peace and order in the face of terrorist hyper violence, involving large-scale destruction of life and property, the police continues to be at the forefront of the state machinery that tackles such challenges.

The efficacy with which the police rise to such challenges is often the prime criteria for judging the internal security scenario in the state. The multiplicity of tasks that the police has to perform, including crime prevention and control often detracts from the readiness of the police to face these situations of sustained violence in society. Besides, there is the all-important question of resource, training and attitudinal preparedness. Often the police have been found wanting on all the parameters and the sense of security has thereby diminished in the context of situations of protracted violence. But, there is one elementary criterion that is given the go by even in enlightened circles: the active involvement and participation of civil society in creating a desirable security climate for itself. It has been noted, not without significance, that the society in which the citizenry is generally aware and alert about its security concerns and responsibilities in the context of the overall security of the nation, is able to adapt quicker and more effectively to terrorist violence or any other kind of public disorders including disasters. In short, we are talking about a desirable degree of national security consciousness in the average citizen or if that is too tall an order, at least in the educated citizen. To repeat the old saying—eternal vigilance is the price of liberty. In such a scenario the state and its machinery including the police is able to produce visibly better results. In any case, the state sustains its legitimacy of actions only on the basis of the weal of the civil society.

The Supreme Court of India has defined public order as the even tempo of the life of the community. This is to distinguish public order from the ordinary connotation law and order. According to the honourable Supreme Court any contravention of law affects order and therefore can be referred to as a law and order matter. But it becomes a public order issue the moment it affects the even tempo of the life of the community at large. To cite an example, the murder of a man during the quarrel between two neighbours over a piece of land is a serious and illegal act. The law has been broken and a crime is said to have been committed. But it may not necessarily affect the even tempo of life of a big town. On the other hand, the murder of a social worker in the busy central bazaar area of the town might spark off a chain reaction involving bandobusts, large-scale demonstrations, citizen protests and so on. This would affect the even tempo of life in the entire town and thereby would become an issue of public order. Sometimes a relatively insignificant incident in a big city when replicated in a small hamlet may turn into a public order problem in that hamlet. Therefore, we should bear in mind that it is not the problem per se but the consequential effect of the problem on a community that determines the nature of the contravention of law, i.e. whether this contravention is a routine law and order matter or does it amount to public disorder.

The police are the missing link between the law and the implementation of the law to obtain order. A more meaningful way of understanding this is to see police work as work aimed at ensuring peaceful and orderly life in a community through faithful observance of the good laws with a view to upholding the quality of life for the citizens of that community. The above definition of policing or police work sums up the nature of duties that the police are authorized to perform.

The issue at hand is whether this civil force has the attitude and the resources to face situations of extreme disorder triggered by terrorist strikes or man-made disasters like widespread explosions. Interestingly, even disasters like train accidents as well as natural disasters like earthquakes enjoin a great amount of responsibility on the police as first responders. The import of the analysis above, points in the direction of the inadequacy of police preparedness in our country to tackle extreme situations of disorder. An event like the one in the Akshardham temple in Ahmedabad recently has opened up the debate as to the probable need to have commando strike units in every state police with an expertise level on par with NSG commandos. Are we adequately equipped in strategy and capability to handle simultaneous countrywide attacks of such a nature on selected soft targets? Will it be the police or the army who will come in to do it? If it has to be the police to fight at the forefront of this war by other means we desperately need a rethink.

Terrorist Violence and India's Security Scenario: Defining the Role of Police

Indian security concerns are inextricably linked with its strategic location in the heart of the Asian Continent. Its emergence as an economic and technological power and the socio-political military scenario obtaining around its borders in the subcontinent. The ethnic insurgencies in the north-east, the proxy war in Kashmir, and the emerging underground structures and narcotics, arms and organized crime add up with the above to make a very disturbing national security scenario externally as well as internally. To the most optimistically minded it represents a highly challenging agenda for India to come up with a consistent policy on all fronts perhaps. What is more necessary is an integrated and proactive approach across the board on all national security issues.

India has borders with six countries of which China and Pakistan have traditionally been adversarial. Sri Lanka and Myanmar are affected by serious internal disturbances. While Sri Lanka is seized with the problem of tackling insurgency with the LTTE campaign strongly, Myanmar is affected throughout its length and breadth by violence from several insurgent groups. Nepal and Bhutan have only referral strategic identities because they are not only economically dependent on neighbouring big brothers like India and China but are also sought by the neighbourhood as a strategic buffer. Indeed Pakistan has also found cause to use the porous borders of Nepal as well as its open economy to its own operational advantage against India. Finally there is Bangladesh weighed down by ever increasing population and backward economy as a result of which trans-border migration from Bangladesh into India has, in itself became a security issue to reckon with. This subcontinental picture contains enough disturbing evidence all around for Indian security concerns. Yet this is not the big picture. The big picture starts to emerge in clear relief when we consider the following:

Geopolitically speaking, India occupies not only the strategic centre of the Asian Continent, but also of the Indian Ocean. The geo-strategic and economic significance of the Indian Ocean region cannot be over-emphasized. The sweep from the Persian Gulf in the West to the South-East Asian Region is an area containing not only the substantial portion of oil and natural gas resources of the Gulf and also significantly the booming economies of the Asian Tigers. On the other side this is also the source of area for terrorism worldwide and of course it is host to the narcotic mega zones – the golden crescent on the one side, and the golden triangle on the other.

Against the above backdrop, India has to reckon with the following:

1. Ethnic insurgencies in the North-Eastern states with active support from neighbouring countries like China and Pakistan.
2. Left extremism in the heartland right from Andhra Pradesh in the South up to the Indo-Nepal borders in Bihar running through Madhya Pradesh, Maharashtra and Orissa.
3. Small and medium-seized arms and narcotics coming in through land borders and the sea route as supplies to terrorists and insurgent groups and criminal gangs.
4. Pumping of counterfeit currency into India by the ISI to undermine its economy.
5. Illegal migration across the borders.
6. Rampant smuggling along the borders.

The above challenges to internal security in India can be placed in perspective once we realize that the line between terrorism and insurgency of the so-called wars of liberation are quite blurred in the subcontinent. Often therefore the problem arises where a certain act can be that an acceptable definition of terrorism is yet to be formulated. But terrorism like all crimes has its tell-tale signatures or fingerprints, the most obvious of which is to inspire pure terror and unmitigated fear through violence and bloodshed. The difficulty here is terrorism is not a problem for the terrorist, it is in fact a solution to his angst. It is for the police that it is problem number one. Steven Segallar calls the terrorists Invisible Armies.[3] He points out very pertinently that terrorism is from a purely legal point of view just another crime and often the governments of the day do dismiss it as such. It offers governments and leaders a unique problem in modern politics. But more than that it is the biggest problem in public order maintenance for the police. "There is a crime, with victims (usually innocent), public outrage, accusations and demands. The state is attacked for some policy other, or the absence of a policy, but it is not the state, which suffers directly – indeed states are only composed of their people and their public and private property. The government must react somehow to reassure its citizens and to present an image of calm. What usually occurs is rather more, however: the Prime Minister or President promises that terrorism will not influence policy; that terrorists will be subject to justice (sometimes meaning retaliation upon other unrelated victims); that terrorism will never pay. The problem is that these claims are almost always false. Terrorism does produce results – it gets issues into the public consciousness..."[4]

In a political context, terrorism has started questioning legitimacy of the state itself. Many scholars and political thinkers feel that there is nothing surprising in this. Indeed it may be one of the pointers to the fact that the concept of sovereignty of the nation state has itself taken a beating in recent times. As mentioned earlier, there has been a conspicuous lack of overarching strategy to fight terrorism and its newfound technology and tactics. Especially the police and the security forces have not been primed to take on this new challenge in their own stride confidently. Yet this very issue has come to symbolize the cutting edge of public order maintenance today.

In all the areas of concern above, it is warranted that the Indian police in its various manifestations at the State and the Central level formations fight the challenges as an integrated machinery of prevention and control. This has brought to fore the issues of inter-state coordination in fighting terrorism and insurgency, organized crime and the menace of arms and drug running and of course communalism and caste-related violence. That law and order continues to be a state subject has only complicated matters. This is only one of the many structural and functional problems that face the Indian police today. In short, the work agenda for the Indian police in the context of a global network of terrorism and subversive activities across the border has not yet materialized. One gets the impression that when we should be prepared and raring to face the prospect of several sustained attempts at destabilization from within and without, the very moribund and militarized nature of policing is affecting police efficiency. Continued lack of public goodwill and indeed a negative image has detracted from whatever good work it might have done. Moreover, events like the turmoil in Gujarat where the role of police is put under the microscope prove to be reference points in the already negative balance of opinions against the police as an organization dedicated to the maintenance of internal security, among other things.

Indian Police: The Road Ahead

The increasing use of the army in maintenance of national security has been an area of concern. The magnitude of the problem can be realized from the fact that the army is increasingly called for IS duties which are not strictly its brief. A majority of the para-military forces are in the North-East and J&K trying to fight terrorism and insurgency alongside the army. Of course, Gujarat today is the most recent example of the lack of faith in the police, both on part of the public as well as the State. Apart from the huge budgetary burden on the common man every time the army is deployed for IS duties, the matter for concern is that these internal security issues are showing no signs of going out of the agenda in the near future. The sensitive scenario of communal violence including anti-Christian and anti-tribal violence has compounded this. A pronounced lack of community support has become symptomatic of the lack of civil society's involvement in day-to-day policing. Not to speak of public order policing in disturbed areas. The gulf separating police from the public seems to have widened with each passing year of independent India. This has belied the ideal of an autonomous and intrinsically democratic police system. Patrick Colquohoun, a founding father of modern police in Britain has underlined the need for democratic policing in a free society. "Next to the blessings which a nation derives from an excellent Constitution and a system of general laws are those advantages which result from a well-regulated and energetic plan of police conducted and enforced with purity, activity, vigilance and discretion. The police have a fair claim, while they act properly, to be esteemed as the civil defenders of the lives and properties of the people. Everything that can heighten in any degree the respectability of the office of constable adds to the security of the State and to the safety of the life and property of every individual."[5] So, amidst all these signs of a deteriorating security scenario and the diminishing faith of the common man, whither the Indian Police?

Terrorism expert Richard Clutterbuck has stressed the importance of the following measures to empower the police forces to tackle terrorist tactics in the new millennium:

1. Forming of specialized anti-terrorist squads and

hostage rescue squads. He has given the example of the German GSG 9, British SAS, etc. In India we have the special intervention groups raised for various situations in NSG. But today there is a need to multiply this in all states.

2. Reorganizing the anti-terrorism intelligence units, if necessary by coordinating operations across various intelligence agencies. In view of the proxy war being launched across the border there have been attempts in India to form a joint intelligence committee to tackle terrorist activities across the country. This needs to be systematized and integrated into an overall policy to fight terrorism.

3. Standardization of weapons in the fight against terrorism.

4. Standard practices for security of premises and vital installations.

5. Improving training and technology in interrogation techniques

6. An upgraded approach to airlines security as one of the most vulnerable but potentially most devastating theatre of terrorist attack.[6]

In view of the above the right thinking police officer's agenda for the future would perhaps read something like this:

1. Training: The police force acquires its image not from the 10 percent officer cadre but from the 90percent cadre of constabulary who directly interface with the public. The imperative is to train them thoroughly and continuously throughout their careers. A good training in attitudes, skills and behaviour is a force multiplier. If this sort of exercise seems too burdensome and costly, perhaps the State and the civil society should compare this to the cost it has to pay when an ill-trained police force fails to control a public order situation and there is an enormous impact on life and liberty and the sense of security! So, train the men well and train repeatedly. Isn't it worth the effort, especially when the entire efficacy of policing is contingent upon how the average constable exercises his enormous discretion that he is legally endowed with?

2. **Providing Adequate Technological and Resource Backup**: The principle of giving the necessary resources and then demanding performance rightfully cannot be overemphasized. Today, along with an absence of standardization of resources that a police force must have, there is also a disturbing lack of concern among policy makers as to the basic needs of policemen on the streets. When it comes to elementary issues like non-lethal riot control and mob control equipment there is very little thinking, not to speak of R& D efforts that have gone into it. Yet it is well-known that non-lethal weapons have a great significance for day-to-day policing in democratic societies with the attendant concerns for human rights and dignity of human life.

3. **Involving and Educating the Citizen in His Own Security Concerns**: This should be the perpetual agenda of any police organization. After 11/9 in the US or 13/12 in India, the average citizen has woken up to the fact that these

are times of impending violence in our lives. Hence the common man will live with a perpetual sense of insecurity. At no point of time has the need for a proactive partnership of police and citizenry been more important than now. Police is the civil force in the society. Events like Gujarat may have affected the sense of viability of a police-public partnership. But, in the same breath it has to be said that ultimately it is the police in such situations, which has to restore the faith. If it cannot, the entire gamut of civil life is affected.

4. **Transnational Policing:** Policing can no more be effectively carried out within the confines of national boundaries. Today when crimes and criminals have no boundaries, policing has to reach out beyond national limits to forge partnerships in fighting subversive and criminal elements that affect public order in the country. Increasingly the nature of policing will be transnational, especially in the backdrop of a need to fight jointly the war against terrorism, organized crimes and narcotics. Aren't we talking of a global war on terrorism?

5. **Privatization in Policing:** Privatization in policing is the dominant trend worldwide. So is increasing civilianization, i.e. increasing use of non-police agencies in what has been traditionally police work to be carried out by police personnel ?

6. **Specialized Forces:** Specially trained outfits to tackle special security needs may be the order of the day in the none-too-distant future. Forces may be raised separately to handle operations like hostage rescue, disaster rescue and relief, VIP security, security of vital installations, anti hijacking, etc. After Akshardham, there seems to be a case for raising specialized anti-terrorist squads in all the states

specifically trained in commando operations involving high risk assault and rescue tasks.

7. **Special Laws:** The enacting of special laws for special situations has not always been a welcome step. However, there are bound to be more of such enactments as our security concerns and needs evolve. The POTO being dismissed as a draconian law is the easy option response. The hard part is to answer the poser about tackling terrorists within the present inadequacies of our legal system. The inadequacies are not necessarily with respect to the slow delivery of justice or the loopholes in our present laws. The issue is one of relative deterrence. The terrorist who finds reasons to kill innocents for a cause should be faced with a greater amount of immediate deterrence than the criminal who indulges in robbery or even armed dacoity. The ordinary criminal generally kills for gain. The terrorist goes well beyond his pecuniary exigencies. He kills for the publicity gains of the act itself and seeks to make a political statement through the blood of the innocents. Indeed, in cases like the attack on Akshardham the sole motive is to destabilize the civic society. Such acts warrant special laws as adequate deterrence and punishment mechanisms. No wonder then that the champions of democracy and representative governments—France and Great Britain—have the most stringent anti-terrorism laws. The citizenry of these countries is aware of the needs as well as the limitations of these laws and are willing to be a part of the evolution of any such law towards a universally acceptable form within the confines of democracy and a society facing considerable security risks. In India, the degree of awareness in the common man on the street, as opposed to the intellectuals and ideologues, about the emergent security concerns and needs of this

country, will be the true reflection of the felt needs of a society faced with the real and happening threat of terrorist hyper violence.

Conclusion

The march towards a community-oriented policing has been at best a series of isolated and hesitant steps in a country like India. On the other hand, challenges to our integrity and public order at the dawn of the new millennium has magnified the internal security problems that police have to confront. While nobody can rightly predict to the last detail what India's security concern would be in 2010 or 2020, it is time to cultivate a vision and a strategy to counter effectively all the problems that are threatening the very basis of India's national integrity and sovereignty. From a purely internal security perspective, one would be justified in believing that a crucial and central factor in this vision and strategy will be the Indian Police and Security Forces. As outlined above, the changes that are sweeping through the democratic world in the nature of policing are bound to affect India and later on the South Asian subcontinent. In trying to come to terms with isolated issues like fighting terrorism in a region and handling the security concerns arising from there we are often guilty of glossing over the fundamental issues facing the security forces and the police themselves. As is often said but perhaps, the import of which is not fully understood—policing is too important to be left to the police. In the context of a scenario of terrorist violence or from the perspective of routine policing, effective police functioning is primarily contingent upon the physical involvement and the moral backup of civil society. Policing as an isolated function is a misnomer. When police and public chalk out a joint strategy for fighting crime and maintaining law and order, it becomes the hallmark of an evolved citizenry. It is time the citizenry and the opinion leaders therein realized that the terrorists seek to destroy democracy by using the very instruments of democracy. The people of Jammu and Kashmir realized this and turned up to vote in large numbers realizing that the hands-off attitude of the local population would be ultimately to its own great detriment. In such a case there is a palpable consciousness of the security concerns of the community in the average citizen. Such an alertness and sustained vigilance keep the police on its toes and is perhaps the most potent weapon against security threats to order in a civil society. In a developing country like India, that should be the direction towards which we must strive unerringly.

The shape of terrorism that is emerging now and that is bound to induce public disorder in India will be an isolated terrorist act committed by a single individual or small group of individual terrorists with more and more miniaturized but highly lethal and destructive weapons. The trend that is emerging now is very disturbing because at the cutting edge of the terrorist incident it is the state apparatus and the police may be able to apprehend or kill only one or two terrorists. But once the conspiracy is revealed it will be found that behind the lone perpetrator will be a terrorist group with its links to a bigger terrorist outfit, which may be transnational. A further investigation into the conspiracy may link the so-called international terrorist group with an agency of an enemy state (most probably an intelligence agency trying to engineer disruptive activities in the enemy state). Next, it is bound to be revealed that such a state agency has the full backup and approval of its government for all its actions and operations. Finally, it may be alarming to see that the government and state in question may itself be a part of a bigger political and strategic linkage to undermine the sovereignty and integrity of the target state. The incident at Akshardham in Ahmedabad is much more than the act of two terrorists entering a religious shrine in some corner of India. It is a proverbial tip of the iceberg at the base of which lies the dynamics of international real politic and jostling for power in the subcontinent between India and Pakistan. Thus we see that today an isolated incident of terrorism that disrupts public order and brings the local police face to face with a novel challenge of violence and disorder. The alarming thing is that such acts are in fact linked with an umbilical cord to the drawing board where deliberately subversive operations are planned out by an enemy state hell-bent on creating disorder. Messianic terrorism and fundamentalism, irrespective of community and religion, will release more and more "mad dogs" to trigger off incidents of terrorism. These will, in the main, be seen as police problems and accordingly an appropriate response will be expected. To quote William Maley, "if a mad dog invades one's house, it is rarely an adequate response to write out a cheque for rabies research. For that reason, it is vital that those confronted by messianic terrorism have an adequate range of response mechanisms available to them: police, military back up, intelligence gathering, forensic assets, mechanisms to manage the consequences of a terrorist strike, security for appropriate targets, appropriate penalties, and judicial procedures which – while consonant with the rule of law and the rights of the state – do not prevent relevant evidence from being different before courts that suspected terrorists are being hold to account."[7]

The moral of the story therefore is that the police being the foremost line of defence for a liberal democracy must rise to the occasion and prepare to take on terrorism in its new and sinister form. The obvious bottom line here is if policing does not face up to this disorder, civil society may come under the grave threat of experiencing the anxieties of war without the real war! It is only the practising of public order maintenance through policing, which provides citizens with one of their most immediate and tangible experiences of the protective presence of competent State machinery that gives the unequivocal signal of having things under control and one that underscores order in the societal life.

Notes

1. *Terrorism and America: A Common Sense Strategy for a Democratic Society* (Manchester: The MIT Press Cambridge, 1998), p.x.
2. *India Today*, 7 October 2002, p.34 and *The Weekly*, 6 October 2002, p.32.
3. Steven Segaller, *Invisible Armies: Terrorism into the 1990s* (London: Stephen Segaller Films Ltd, 1986)
4. *Ibid.*, p.6.
5. Cited in C.C.H. Moriarty, *Police Procedure and Administration* (London: Butterworth, 1944), pp.14-15.
6. Richard Clutterbuck, *Terrorism in an Unstable World* (London: Routledge, 1994), pp.180-193.
7. William Maley, "Messianism and Political Action: Some Contextual Characteristics", in K.P.S. Gill and Ajai Sahni (ed.), *The Global Threat to Terror* (New Delhi: Bulwarks Books for Institute of Conflict Management, 2002), p.15.

Section-VI : Terrorism in Kashmir

Kashmiri Ethnic Identity and Terrorism

P. Sanjay

Political movements based on ethnic identities have gained momentum after the end of the Cold War. Bosnia, former Yugoslavia and Kashmir are a few examples. The disintegration of Soviet Union and the end of the Cold War provided the stimulus and space for ethnic separatism in various nation-states. Apart from the international context in which these ethnic movements take place, a closer examination of domestic politics helps us in having a better understanding of these ethnic movements. Such an approach will not only highlight the various factors that prompt violent ethnic uprisings but will also reveal that 'identities', on the basis of which militant movements derive legitimacy, are themselves subject to change. It is in this context this paper examines the rise of terrorism due to the de-institutionalization of democratic institutions and the impact of terrorism in transforming the Kashmiri ethnic assertion into an Islamic Jihad.

De-institutionalization and Rise of Terrorism

In trying to understand the decay of democratic institutions it is imperative to look into the context in which these institutions took root. In September 1947 Sheik Abdullah was released from prison and the Maharaja invited Sheik Abdullah to form an interim government. On 27 October 1947 the Indian Government accepted the Maharaja's desire to accede to India, with a promise that the accession would be settled by referring it to the people of Kashmir. On 1 January 1948, with Pakistani troops inside Kashmir, India took the Kashmir issue to the UN Security Council. The promise of plebiscite and reference to Security Council continued the uncertainty over the status of Jammu & Kashmir (J & K). It was during this period of uncertainty that Abdullah took the reigns of administration. The Maharaja's administration collapsed during 1947's turbulent days and Abdullah supplanted it by his party National Conference. The distinction between a political party and government got erased and they became synonymous. Abdullah extended the same framework to Jammu and Ladakh, where the National Conference had a weak organizational network. With the absence of clearly defined constitutional powers, National Conference workers functioned without any checks and balances. Abdullah conducted the administration in an authoritarian fashion and he allowed little dissent. With a party-state organizational framework, Abdullah implemented his party manifesto Naya Kashmir,[1] which promised land to the tiller without giving any compensation to the landlord. The attempts to impose a monolithic political system, which had evolved under special circumstances in the valley on the Jammu and Ladakh regions provoked stiff resistance and became an additional cause of regional tension in J & K.[2]

In 1951, with the plebiscite appearing as a distant reality Abdullah organized elections to the Constituent Assembly of J & K. The National Conference under his leadership won all 75 seats unopposed, and in Jammu where the National Conference had weak organizational structure, the Hindu nationalist group Praja Parishad was not allowed to contest the 1951 elections.[3] The denial of free and fair elections and nominal representation in Abdullah's cabinet created discontent among the people of Jammu. The possibility of rejecting India by a Muslim majority state in the event of plebiscite further exacerbated fears among minority Hindus of J & K prompting the Praja Parishad of Jammu to make demands for division of state on religious lines and then holding zonal plebiscite. The Praja Parishad demanded abrogation of Article-370, a demand that was supported by the Bharatiya Jan Sangh and Hindu the Mahasabha. The agitation provoked the angry reaction in the valley. In average Kashmiri minds the agitation created the impression of annexation of Muslim Kashmir by Hindu India and for the National Conference leadership, who had fought Jinnah and repudiated his Two-Nation theory based on religion, was confronted with the same type of forces, this time Hindu instead of Muslim in a country with which they had thrown their lot.[4]

Even as the regional tensions were brewing within J & K, Abdullah's authoritarian leadership resulted in discontent among certain sections of the National Conference. The discontent assumed the form of pro-Pakistan sentiments in the absence of a secular opposition party and lack of support from political parties outside Kashmir. National leaders felt that the presence of an opposition party in Kashmir would be detrimental to national interests as long as it remained a subject of international dispute. Even Nehru maintained that nothing should be done to weaken Abdullah as India's Kashmir polity revolved around him.[5] Contrary to their beliefs too much centralization of power in the hands of Abdullah and denial of regional autonomy created intra-regional conflict in J & K. This intra-regional conflict sowed the seeds of communal and secessionist politics in the state.

In early 1953, the Praja Parishad launched a nationwide agitation for complete integration of the state of J & K with India. In order to stem the growth of Karra and sufficiently provoked by the Praja Parishad, Abdullah started emphasizing the distinct Kashmiri identity and argued that accession of Kashmir to India was not final.[6] Abdullah was arrested in 1953 and Bakshi Ghulam Mohammed was installed as the new Prime Minister.[7] This marked the beginning of active intervention of the centre in the affairs of the state. The Government of India in 1954 passed a constitutional amendment act, which empowered the central government to legislate all matters, mentioned in the Union list.[8] The charade of unopposed elections continued even after the 1951 election in which the National Conference won all the 75 seats unopposed; in 1957 contest took place only for 32 seats; in 1962 contest took place only for 41 seats, mostly in Jammu; in the 1967 elections the unopposed return of Congress candidates in 22 out of 42 constituencies in the valley was ensured by the rejection of 118 nomination papers.[9] Further, Articles-356, 357 and 249 were made applicable to J&K in 1964-65.[10] Thus in reality the autonomous nature of Article-370 was never enforced. Application of Articles-356, 357 and 249 to J & K in 1964 led to discontent among Kashmiris. The emergence of a viable functioning opposition seemed possible in 1972 when the Plebiscite Front, which came into existence immediately after Abdullah's arrest in 1953, decided to contest elections. The fear that an opposition party, would not be in the interest of the nation led to banning of the Plebiscite Font. Moreover in the ensuing election Congress colluded with a communal party called Jamaat-e-Islami. It was the first occasion when Jamaat received constitutional recognition and political legitimacy in Kashmir as Congress won 57 seats and 5 by Jamaat.[11] For almost two decades after independence many opportunities for emergence of a functioning opposition party were squandered.

By the mid-1960s and early 1970s there was growing discontent in Kashmir due to the excessive interference of the Union Government in the matters of the State of J & K. In order to alleviate Kashmiri discontent, the central government started being generous in the perusal of licenses, quotas, loans, contracts, etc and the central assistance to the Kashmir Five Year Plan expenditure rose to 97 per cent during the Third Plan period.[12] The subsidized economy failed to generate productive forces that could create substantial employment opportunities for the educated unemployed, which aggravated discontent among the educated unemployed. The neo-rich class skilfully, Riyaz Punzabi states, passed the blame for all Kashmiri ills on 'India' and held the 'centre' responsible for everything that was going wrong in Kashmiri society and in common Kashmiri perception of the distinction between the government at centre and 'Union of India' got excessively blurred.[13] Discontent arising out of exploitation or presumption of exploitation by an indigenous or an alien group may give rise to assertion of ethnic identity in a secessionist form. But the discontent of the 1970s in Kashmir did not take the form of a secessionist movement because of the rise of democracy in 1977, which successfully mediated Kashmiri ethnic identity within the national framework.

After the 1971 war, India emerged as a dominant power in South Asia. Pakistan got bifurcated and conceded the Kashmir issue as a bilateral issue. Realizing the impossibility of plebiscite in a changed scenario, Abdullah gave up his demand for self-determination. Abdullah was released and was reinstated as chief minister of J & K and his deputy

Mira Afzal Beg signed the Delhi Agreement.[14] The Delhi Agreement paved the way for the 1977 election, which is generally considered as the most free and fair elections ever held in Kashmir. The National Conference led by Abdullah won impressively and the Janata Party got routed. Communal and secessionist voices got subdued because of these elections and normal politics functioned for almost a decade.

With the death of Abdullah in 1982, Farooq Abdullah became the leader of the National Conference and the Congress Party occupied the position of a main opposition party in Kashmir. In the 1983 elections contest revolved around the National Conference and Congress and the former secured two-thirds majority. Before the elections of 1983, Farooq hosted an opposition conclave in Srinagar, and Indira Gandhi perceived Farooq's victory as a serious setback to her party. Across the country, as Congress failed to accommodate newly emergent sections of society, it started decaying rapidly. Indira Gandhi increasingly depended upon the executive arm of the state for her political gains. She implemented the tactics of depending upon the executive organ of the state to deliver political goods in Kashmir. In 1984, within a year of elections in Kashmir, Congress engineered defections from the National Conference. Under the leadership of G.M.Shah, 12 National Conference MLAs parted company with Farooq and formed a government with Congress support. Governor Jagmohan dismissed Farooq without even an opportunity to prove his majority resulting in statewide protests. With deterioration of law and order in the state, G.M.Shah was dismissed. Increasing misuse of Article-356 and dismissal of duly elected government led to disillusionment and contempt towards democratic institutions and towards the centre respectively. Farooq mobilized public opinion around Kashmiriyat and in the parliamentary elections that followed all Farooq candidates were returned with huge majorities. However in 1986, Farooq entered into an accord with Prime Minister Rajiv Gandhi, which proved to be a political blunder. According to the accord the then Chief Minister G.M. Shah was dismissed and Farooq was reinstated as Chief Minister in return for contesting elections in alliance with Congress.

As the National Conference and Congress, the two major parties came together; the dejected and disappointed populace looked for an alternative to express their discontent. Fundamentalist and secessionist parties like the Muslim United Front (MUF) provided the outlet for this discontent, which was an alliance of diverse parties. But in 1987 election MUF could manage only four seats, while the rest were taken by National Conference. Congress alliance. There were reports of malpractices and malfeasance. The administration worked blatantly in favour of the National Conference-Congress alliance and the police refused to listen to any complaint.[15] The rigging of elections, biased attitude of the administrative apparatus and absence of an opposition party that professed loyalty to the Indian Union led to complete alienation of Kashmiris from the Indian State.

From the above discussion it becomes clear that a viable function political opposition did not take root till 1977. The National Conference did emerge as a viable political party in 1977, however, it decayed rapidly within a decade. Sumantara Bose brings out the importance of a functioning political opposition quite succinctly in this context. Bose points out that providing the institutional space for opposition is essential for ensuring that discontent and dissatisfaction can be directed at a particular government rather than at the regime itself. Unless there are such institutional outlets for dissent within the regime's institutions, Bose adds, those discontented (for whatever reason) with the status quo may not distinguish a particular government from the political system as a whole in expressing their anger and frustration.[16] In Kashmir by the late 1980s, with all the avenues for expressing loyal opposition closed, the discontent metamorphosed into total alienation and legitimacy of Indian State to rule was questioned.

According to James Manor, in India, the unparalleled heterogeneity and tendency of most people to shift their preoccupatios from one identity to another results in tensions not becoming concentrated along single fault line.[17] The presence of democratic politics with strong institutions such as functioning political parties facilitates in shifting in loyalties from one identity to another. In the case of Kashmir a single fault line did emerge due to the absence of democratic politics and institutions required to carry out such politics. While grappling with community conflicts Amrita Basu and Atul Kohli observe that the growth of community conflicts, has coincided with a de-institutionalization of the Indian State as the normative and organizational pillars of the post-independence Indian State-secularism, socialism and democracy of Nehruvian type, as well as the Congress Party and civil and political bureaucracies have weakened.[18] This is more so in the case of Kashmir. After the initial spurt of socialism, which was seen in implementation of land reforms, socialism did not make much progress in Kashmir. As a result, disparities between rich and poor increased. Democracy faltered due to lack of functioning opposition. Communal politics replaced secular politics. The organizational structure of the National Conference was not democratic. Principles of federalism were by and large ignored. The growing nexus between politicians, bureaucrats and businessmen resulted in the decay of both civil and political bureaucracies. With immediate political gains becoming paramount, with the federal structure coming under increasing stress due to decaying of existing parties, and increasing misuse of Article-356 culminated in de-institutionalization in the context of increasing political mobilization. Consequently perception about ethnic discrimination replaced the cross-cutting cleavages with a single fault line in 1989. The result – the transformation of Kashmiri ethnic identity into Kashmiri ethnic nationalism expressing itself in a most virulent form.

Kashmiri Identity, Islamic Fundamentalism and Terrorism

When insurgency came to the fore in 1989, it was not based on Islamic religious identity but on Kashmiriyat or secular Kashmiri ethnic identity shared by the region's Buddhists, Muslims, Hindus and others. Organizations that reflected this composite identity Jammu Kashmir Liberation Front (JKLF) were at the forefront of the movement that aimed at the establishment of the independent state of Kashmir. However, in the 1990s the argument that Kashmiri identity is nothing but an Islamic religious identity gained credence. It does not mean that the religious dimension manifested itself suddenly and gained credibility. The identity of Kashmiriyat faded from the political scene in the 1990s. The death of Sheik Abdullah and decline of NC provided the space for Islamic parties such as MUF, with their religious interpretation of Kashmiri identity, to make their presence felt.[19] Organizations like JKLF were a dominant force with substantial support among the Kashmiri Muslims when Kashmir ethnic nationalism expressed itself in a virulent form in 1989. The JKLF propounded the establishment of a free democratic, secular nation-state based on Kashmiri ethnic identity. However, the growth of Islamic fundamentalism in Pakistan, the principal benefactor of the militancy of Kashmir, altered the nature of militancy in Kashmir and blunted the secular dimension of Kashmiri identity.

The rise of Islamic fundamentalism in Pakistan in 1990s can be traced back to the events that resulted from the invasion of Soviet troops of Afghanistan in1979. Soviet intervention in Afghanistan also resulted in the exodus of millions of Afghan refugees, which erased the boundary between Afghanistan and Pakistan. In the early 1980's various religious parties in Pakistan such as the Jamait-ul-Ulema-e-Islam, a Pakistani Deobandi political party used the war to set up hundreds of madrassas in Pakistan's Pushtun belt, offering Afghan refugees and young Pakistani's free education, food, shelter and military training.[20] These Deobandi madrassas, however were run by barely literate mullahs untutored in the original reformist Deobandi agenda. Moreover, Saudi funds and scholarships brought them closer to ultra conservative Wahhabism.[21] The Pakistani state under Zia ul-Haq promoted these madrassas in order to garner support for his rule and to recruit troops forthe anti-Soviet war in Afghanistan.[22] However, in spite of its claims of Islamic universalism, the Islamization General Zia project was based on narrow Sunni interpretations of Islamic law. With huge funds coming from wealthy Pakistani industrialists at home and abroad, Persian Gulf states and

Saudi Arabia, Pakistan witnessed the proliferation of Sunni madrassas with students from various countries. For instance, Khudamudeen madrassa trained students from Afghanistan, Myanmar, Nepal, Yemen, Bangladesh, Mongolia and Kuwait, while nearly half of the students at Darul Uloom Haqqauma madrassas were also from Afghanistan, Uzebekistan, Tajikistan, Russia and Turkey.[23] The spread of these madrassas in the context of the Afghan war resulted in the militarization of various religious organizations in Pakistan. Approximately 10 to 15 per cent of madrassas in Pakistan encourage their students to fulfil their 'spiritual obligations' by fighting the Hindus in Kashmir or carrying out Jihad in Afghanistan.[24] By showing the cause of Jihad, many Islamic organizations in Pakistan thrive on donations given by wealthy Pakistanis and the Arabs all over the world.[25] Therefore continuation of hostilities in Kashmir provides many Islamic organizations the means of sustenance and a source of employment. Apart from the direct support of the Pakistani government to militancy in Kashmir, various Islamic organizations and political parties in Pakistan such as the Jamaat-e-Islami, and Jammat-e-ulama-Islam sponsored militancy in Kashmir in cooperation with Pakistan's intelligence agencies.[26]

With various religious parties and organizations in Pakistan working closely with Pakistan's armed forces in fostering militant groups in Kashmir, JKLF fell out of the Pakistan's patronage list as its goals of establishment of secular democratic nation-state were at complete variance with the goals of Pakistan's Islamic parties and organizations. As a result, sponsorship to militancy in Kashmir was extended to various Islamic militant groups such as Hiz-bul Mujahidin (HM), which is a militant wing of Jamaat-e-Islami J & K (JIJK). Organizations such as HM and JIJK do not see the struggle in J & K as a struggle for Kashmiri independence but rather portray it as war between the Muslims and Hindu community as a whole. The withdrawal of Soviet Union from Afghanistan and the formation of independent Central Asian republics was consistently displayed by Islamic militant groups leading to the perception that the formation of Islamic Caliphate would not be a formidable challenge, thereby strengthening the Islamic fundamentalist organization in Kashmir.[27] Further the use of violent means to silence the moderate voices in Kashmir and the active support from the Pakistani government and various organizations resulted in the establishment of the HM version of Kashmiri struggle as a dominant discourse by the mid-1990s. The growth of Islamic fundamentalism in Pakistan and the close relationship between Islamic militant groups and religious parties in Pakistan provided the Islamic militant groups in Kashmir with a constant flow of personnel from various countries to carry out their agenda. According to Indian government estimates, 40 per cent of the militants in J & K are from Pakistan and Afghanistan and many Afghan war veterans are fighting in Kashmir.[28] On the other hand, organizations such as JKLF not only lost patronage across the border and had a limited area of recruitment, i.e. Kashmir. Consequently organizations such as JKLF along with its arguments for establishing a secular independent Kashmir were pushed into the margins of the struggle so much so they were compelled to adopt non-violent means for survival.

The marginalization of organization such as the JKLF and the rise of Islamic militant groups gave impetus to the attempts aimed at giving an Islamic orientation of Kashmiri identity.[29] One of the striking manifestations and a tragic outcome of the Islamic orientation of Kashmiri identity was the attacks on Kashmiri Pandits and flight of thousands Kashmiri Pandits from Kashmir in the early 1990s to escape the attacks of the Islamic militant groups. Islam, not Kashmiriyat and accession to Pakistan not independence were the rallying points of the Islamic parties such as JIJK.[30] Pakistani Islamic militants in Kashmir organizations such as HM, Al-Badr and Lashkar-e-Taiba aggressively contest the concept of the Kashmiri nation and argue that Kashmiri independence of Kashmir is merely a stepping-stone for the establishment of Islamic Caliphate. The concept of Islamic Caliphate, popularized by the Jammaat-e-Islami Pakistan (JIP), an Islamic party in Pakistan was adopted by Islamic militant groups operating in Kashmir reflecting complete congruence of goals between them.[31] For instance, HM in a press release in 1992 stated:

> "Our aim is the establishment of an Islamic Caliphate the world over. We do not believe in ideological or geographical boundaries.... The demand of the right to self-determination was distorting the image of the ongoing struggle for the establishment of Caliphate. Any other solution, except the merger of Kashmir with Pakistan would be deemed as a sell out."[32]

And in 1993 JM stated:

> "The slogan that the future of Kashmir wou d be decided by Kashmiris has given rise to an evil which was distorting the Islamic identity of the present movement and reducing it to a mere democratic movement."[33]

The above statements amply demonstrate that Kashmiri right to self-determination (with an option choosing an independent Kashmir) on the basis of which militant movement started in Kashmir, was denounced by the Islamic militant organizations such as HM. In consonance with the Islamic orientation to Kashmiri identity, the militant organizations started implementing various measures such as banning all forms of public entertainment, Islamic code of conduct for women, compulsory attendance in morning prayers and establishment of Darul Sharia-the Central authority for adjudication of disputes according to Sharia laws.[34] By the late 1990s, the establishment of Islamic Caliphate became the primary goal of various militant organizations. Militancy started to spread to from the Kashmir valley to Muslim majority regions of Jammu such as Poonch, Rajuari, and Doda.[35] And with characterization of the ongoing struggle in Kashmir as one between believers of Islam and non-believers, Islamic militants increasingly targeted the civilian Hindu population in the Jammu region. As Jonah Blank notes, approximately 90 attacks were carried out on the civilian population in Doda region in 1998.[36] Due to the complete support of Pakistan armed forces, Islamic militants in Kashmir increased the firepower and started carrying out large-scale operations culminating in the Kargil war in 1999. In 1999, Islamic militants along with the Pakistan Army occupied strategic positions in the Kargil region. Owing to the successful Indian military operations and pressure from the international community, Pakistan withdrew its forces. However the Islamic militant organizations were reluctant to obey the withdrawal proposals as they saw it as betrayal of their Jihad and started a new means of violent attacks in Kashmir such as the suicide attacks.[37] The Kargil war was symptomatic of the transformation of Kashmiri identity and the nature of militancy in Kashmir. Condemning the withdrawal of militants and Pakistani forces from Kargil, most of the militant leaders in Kashmir stated that liberation of Kashmir alone was not their objective, rather it was establishment of the Islamic Caliphate through pursuance of Jihad was their final goal. Thus the growth of Islamic militant organizations attempts at altering cultural attributes and imposition of Sharia, growing salience of 'Jihad' and relegation of demand for right to self-determination on to the margins of the militant movement amply demonstrated the transformation of Kashmiri identity based on cultural sensibilities of Hindu, Muslim and other religious groups into an identity that is solely based on religion.

Conclusion

The above study has attempted to explain the mutation of Kashmiri ethnic identity. However, an important concern that emerges from this study is that the Islamic orientation of the Kashmiri identity portends trouble to the peace and stability of South Asia. The terrorism based on Kashmiriyat can be addressed by giving more constitutional concessions. However, the terrorist movement based on Islamic fundamentalism can be dealt with only through coercive means by the Indian State, as such demands cannot be accommodated through constitutional measures.

Notes

1. Naya Kashmir was a blue print of the National Conference to build a new society, economy and polity. See Riyaz Punjabi, "Kashmiri: The Bruised Identity", in Raju G.C.Thomas (ed), *Perspectives on Kashmir: The Roots of Conflict in South Asia* (Colorado: West View

Press, 1992), p. 139.

2. Balraj Puri, *Kashmir Towards Insurgency* (Delhi: Orient Longman, 1995), p. 44.

3. Sumantara Bose, *The Challenge in Kashmir* (Delhi: Sage Publications, 1997), p. 31.

4. Punjabi, n.1, p. 140.

5. Puri, n. 2, pp. 45-46.

6. Sisir Gupta, *Kashmir Dispute: A Study in Indo-Pak Relations* (New Delhi: Asia Publishing House, 1996), p. 384

7. *Ibid*.

8. Punjabi, n. 1, p. 141.

9. See Balraj Puri, "Kashmiri Muslims, Islam and Kashmiri Traditions", *Economic and Political* Weekly, vol. 25, no.6, pp. 44 -50, and Bose, n. 3, pp. 44 -45.

10. Article 356 says that the President of India shall be entitled to assume to himself all or any of the executive powers of the state upon the failure of the constitutional machinery of the state. According to Article 357, Parliament of India may confer legislative powers of the State on the President and authorize him to delegate these powers to any other person and Article 247 postulates that the Parliament of India will become a competent authority to legislate on state matters if the Rajya Sabha passes a resolution to that effect with two-thirds majority. See Durga Das Basu, *Introduction to the Constitution of India* (Delhi: Prentice Hall India, 1990), pp. 245-254.

11. Puri, n. 9, p. 50.

12. Punjabi, n. 1, p. 142

13. *Ibid.*, p. 143.

14. Bose, n. 3, p. 40.

15. Cited in *ibid.*, p. 46

16. *Ibid.*, p. 49.

17. James Manor, "Ethnicity and Politics in India," *International Affairs*, vol. 72, no. 3, July 1996, pp. 459-475.

18. Amrita Basu and Atul Kholi, "Community Conflicts and State in India," *The Journal of Asian Studies*, vol. 56, no. 2, May 1997, pp. 320-324.

19. Riyaz Punjabi, "The Concept of Islamic Caliphate: The Religious and Ethnic Pulls of the Kashmiri Militant Movement," *Journal of Peace Studies*, vol.1, no.1, November-December 1993, p. 42.

20. Ahmed Rashid, "The Taliban: Exporting Extremism," *Foreign Affairs*, vol. 78, no. 6, November-December 1999, p. 26.

21. *Ibid.*

22. Jessica Stern, "Pakistan's Jihad Culture," *Foreign Affairs*, vol. 79, no. 6, December 2000, pp. 118-119.

23. Sumita Kumar, "Pakistan's Jihadi Apparatus Goals Methods", *Strategic Analysis*, vol. 24, no. 12, March 2001, pp. 2179-2198.

24. Stern, n. 22, p. 119.

25. *Ibid.*, p. 120

26. Yoginder Sikand, "Changing Course of Kashmiri Struggle, From Liberation to Islamic Jihad?" *Economic*

and Political Weekly, vol. 36, no.3, 20 January 2001, p. 222

27. Punjabi, n. 19, p. 43.
28. Stern, n. 22, p. 118.
29. Sikand, n. 26, p. 218.
30. *Ibid.*, p. 220.
31. Riyaz Punjabi, "Kashmir Realizing the Dream of an Islamic Caliphate," *World Affairs*, vol. 4, no. 2, April-June 2000, p. 67
32. Punjabi, n. 19, pp. 44-45.
33. *Ibid.*, p. 45.
34. *Ibid.*, pp. 43-45.
35. Jonah Blank, "Kashmir: Fundamentalism Takes Roots," *Foreign Affairs*, vol. 78, no. 6, November-December 1999, p. 45.
36. *Ibid.*,
37. Sikand, n. 26, p. 224

European Union's Response to Terrorism in Kashmir

B. Krishnamurthy

Introduction

Initially, the European states tried to take measures to control the terrorist problem at the national level. Aware of the growing concern caused by the increase in acts of terrorism and wishing to take effective measures to ensure that the perpetrators of such acts do not escape prosecution and punishment, the Council of Europe (of 21 states at that juncture) set up a Committee of Experts in June 1975, to study international terrorism and to find ways and means to combat it. This resulted in the drafting of the European Convention on the Suppression of Terrorism, which was opened for signature on 27 January 1977 and entered into force on 4 August 1978.[1]

The Europeans who were convinced that extradition is a particularly effective measure for achieving this result, tightened their extradition laws and procedures. The European Convention adopted the pragmatic approach of identifying specific offences of a "predominately criminal character" most likely to be committed by terrorist offenders as extraditable, notwithstanding its so-called political motivation or political character (thus, moving away from attempting a definition of the term 'terrorism' with all its political complexities), thereby setting an important precedent for other international initiatives to follow.

The most noticeable impact of the convention on

development of legal principles relating to extradition or prosecution lies in the fact that it substantially restricted the scope of the traditional "political offences exception" in respect of well-defined serious crimes involving the use of indiscriminate violence against innocent civilians. Moreover, it augmented and supplemented the provisions of existing international conventions on specific aspect of terrorism. It also provided for an "extradite or prosecute" regime (*aut dedere aut punire*), when due to domestic, constitutional or other legal constraints, a contracting state finds itself unable to extradite a fugitive offender. In such instances the contracting state is obliged "without exception" to submit the case to its competent authorities for purposes of prosecution.[2]

The group of offences categorized as "non-political" in the European Convention included the offences covered by the international conventions on specific aspects of terrorism such as hijacking of aircrafts. In this sense it cured a major deficiency in the earlier conventions. Thus, the impact of the European Convention in the draft of international legal norms had been of a far-reaching nature. Its major contribution was in respect of precluding the application of the traditional "political offences exception" in respect of "terrorist crimes".[3] However, there were several negative elements in the Convention, which impair its effectiveness as a legal instrument for the extradition of terrorist offenders.

I

European Countries Views on Terrorism

Besides their activities at the national and bilateral

levels against the terrorist outfits, the member states of the EU have cooperated and coordinated among themselves as well as with other international organizations to formulate and codify international norms and measures to contain and eradicate the terrorist menace. The Ministerial Conference of the Group-7 countries on Terrorism was held in Paris, on 30 July 1996, which agreed on 25 important measures to curb terrorism. Thorough review of new trends in terrorism throughout the world was undertaken and it was concluded that there could be no excuse for terrorism. The Conference also resolved to condemn terrorism in whatever shape or form and regardless of its motives, to make no concessions to terrorists, to implement means consistent with fundamental freedoms and the rule of law, and to effectively fight terrorism with all means at its disposal. It was also decided to establish among the G-7 countries a directory of counter-terrorism competences, skills and expertise to facilitate practical cooperation and to adopt internal measures to prevent terrorism and to improve counter terrorism cooperation and capabilities. It also discussed prosecution and punishment of terrorists, efforts to prevent terrorist fund raising, to prevent the free movement of terrorists-individuals and groups and to deny them asylum and refugee status. It was also resolved to intensify exchange of operation information.[4]

The International Convention on the Suppression of the Financing of Terrorism of 9 December 1999, which drafted a convention making it a criminal offence in signatory countries to provide financial assistance to terrorist organizations, was the next crucial step.[5] It was a French initiative and the convention was opened for signature on 10 January 2000. This Convention tried to curb the flow of the much-needed funds for the terrorist outfits from its sympathizers and compatriots.

The European Community has already complied with the obligations contained in UNSC Resolutions 1267 (1999) and 1333(2000) requiring certain restrictive measures to be taken – including the freezing of assets-against the Taliban and against Osama bin Laden and Al-Qaeda organization, with the adoption of Regulation-467(2000) and subsequent amendments further to the decisions adopted by the Sanctions Committee set up by Resolution 1267.

As a reaction to the 11 September terrorist attack on the US, the European Council at its extraordinary meeting, on 21 September 2001, declared that terrorism is a real challenge to the world and to Europe and that the fight against terrorism would be a priority objective of the EU. As a part of their anti-terrorist drive, the EU member states resolved to bring in anti-money laundering measures in their effort to curb the fund flows to the terrorist organizations. On 8 October 2001, the Council reaffirmed the determination of the EU and its member states to play their full part, in a coordinated manner, in the global coalition against terrorism and to attack the sources, which fund terrorism, in close cooperation with the United States. Agencies on both the sides of the Atlantic are committed to giving the "widest possible assistance" to investigations and legal proceedings against those named on the list of 27 groups and individuals linked to Osama bin Laden and his Al-Qaeda network. It was also decided that the list of terrorist groups would be subject to review every six months. The EU member states have undertaken the process of streamlining procedural methods for better coordination among pan-European security agencies and police. A pan-European arrest warrant was expected to become effective by the end of 2001.[6]

On 19 October 2001, the European Council declared that it was determined to combat terrorism in every form throughout the world and that it would continue its efforts to strengthen the coalition of the international community to combat terrorism in every shape and form, for example by the increased cooperation between the operational services responsible for combating terrorism: Europol, Eurojust, the intelligence services, police forces and judicial authorities.

On 27 December 2001, the European Council adopted the common position on combating terrorism and on the application of specific measures to combat terrorism. It called for measures to criminalize the wilful provision or collection of funds meant for terrorist groups; to freeze their funds; to suppress the recruitment of new members and to eliminate the supply of weapons to terrorists. It also provided for exchange of information on terrorist groups among member states and between member states and third countries. The common position also advocated denial of safe haven to those who finance, plan, support or commit terrorist acts or provide safe havens to those offenders.[7]

The Organization for Security and Cooperation in Europe, a body of 55 member countries and the continent's top-security establishment, too intends to join front against terrorism. It stressed close attention to the links between organized crime and terrorism, particularly the financing side and to deal with them appropriately.

As a follow-up to these conventions, individual

member states of the EU have taken measures to tackle terrorist outfits active on their own soil and the German police have arrested individuals belonging to these terrorist groups, who were indulging in trafficking in arms and explosives and in recruiting trainees for terrorist camps in Afghanistan. The German government is planning to change the law that gives special protection to clubs and groups with a religious character and to tighten laws to crack down on suspected terrorist organizations. Britain's new Anti-Terrorism, Crime and Security Act allow foreign suspects to be detained without trial.

Endeavour to arrest members of terrorist outfits as well as those individuals who finance terrorist activities residing in the European countries continued unabated and the Spanish police have arrested a suspected Al-Queda "Chief financier" Ahmed Brahim, who has allegedly been distributing cash worldwide, in April 2002. On 3 May 2002, the EU has added to the already existing list of some 27 terrorist groups and individuals, 11 more terrorist groups and seven individuals, including three groups operating in India such as the Lasker-e-Taiba, and blocked their assets. Again. Spain has finalized a new law that allows the Supreme Court to ban any political party considered to give "active or tacit support to terrorism" and the Spanish government entertains the idea of getting Batasuna, the political wing of the ETA, banned on its failure to condemn the car bomb attack carried out by the ETA on 4 August 2002.

II

India, at the primary level, maintains that the problem in Kashmir is of a domestic nature, to be solved within the framework of the Indian Constitution. At the secondary level, the Kashmir tangle is being projected as a bilateral problem between India and Pakistan, caused by the sponsorship of cross-border terrorism by the latter. India is always against the involvement of a third party in the issue. However, to convince the international community of the righteousness of its stand and to counter the false propaganda of Pakistan in this regard, India is constrained to discuss the Kashmir issue with the third parties, the oft-referred international community. On the other hand, on failing to arrive at a solution to the Kashmir imbroglio bilaterally, Pakistan tries to internationalize the issue by presenting its case on all available international platforms, both at bilateral and multilateral levels. To make its case more appealing to the Western democracies, which always harp on human rights protection and promotion, Pakistan has chosen to highlight the case as a human rights problem and as a struggle for self- determination of the Kashmiri people. This strategy too has invited the member states of the European Union, individually as well as collectively, to involve themselves in the Kashmir problem.

European Union's Response to Terrorism in Kashmir

Initially, in the Kashmir question, the EU tried to give an impression that it would like to maintain equi-distance between the contending parties. Of late, there is a change in the outlook of the EU. By March 2000, the EU has taken a stand akin to the Indian side and it was in favour of solving the problem bilaterally through dialogue between India and Pakistan on the basis of the Shimla Agreement and Lahore Declaration.

However, the EU has always been very particular that

the fight against terrorism must not violate human rights and it is quite cautious against the violation of human rights in the global "fixation" with the war against terrorism. Again, it holds the view that response to acts of terrorism should be measured, proportional, consistent with international legality and in keeping with the norms and processes defined by the UN. The EU 's obsession with human rights in its dealings with the developing world is well–reflected in the Commission's suggestion that India should proceed cautiously in dealing with Kashmir, without giving any scope for human rights violations of the people of the valley.[8] Later, the Europeans held the view that Pakistan-sponsored terrorists are the real perpetrators of human rights violations in Kashmir. The EU actually shares the Indian feelings that cross-border terrorism, aided and abetted by Pakistan is the root cause and support base of the insurgency in Kashmir and the stumbling bloc in finding a peaceful and enduring solution to the vexed Kashmir question.[9]

The European Parliament (EP) also shows extraordinary interest in the developments in South Asia. A delegation of the MEPs, responsible for relations with South Asia and SAARC, visited New Delhi in April 2000 as part of the regular inter-parliamentary meeting with their Indian counterparts. This is the 10th such meeting between the EU and India. The MEPs reiterated the stand adopted by the EP during its plenary session on 16 March 2000, condemning cross-border terrorism and reaffirming the need to capture the spirit of the Lahore Declaration of February 1999 in order to enhance the scope of stability and peaceful development in the South Asian region.[10]

In the EU-India summit in June 2000, India voiced its

concern over terrorism sponsored and abetted by Pakistan, which claimed the lives of thousands of its citizens and the EU responded positively. Both the parties resolved to bolster joint efforts to counter terrorism. Under the French Presidency, the EU issued a strongly-worded statement condemning the killing of over 100 pilgrims near Pahalgam in August 2000, calling it a 'terrorist attack'. This is for the first time that the EU referred to them as terrorist activities and also mentioned their backers and condemned them in unequivocal terms.[11]

The leaders of the EU have condemned the terrorist attack on the J & K Assembly in October 2001 in strong terms. Growing terrorist activities in the South Asian region and the consequent tension between India and Pakistan, attracted the attention of the European Parliament quite naturally and on 25 October 2001, Liz Lynne, a pro-Pakistani British MEP and the Chairman of the All Party Kashmir Group of MEPs, persuaded the Parliament to back an amendment to the CFSP for the EU to adopt an 'honest broker' role in the dispute and re-affirming the need to fight terrorism in all its forms. Echoing the sentiment and stand of the Pakistani leader Parvez Musharraf, Lynne advocated that external mediation is the only way out to break the log jam.[12]

Several factors have gone into the change in the EU's stand of the earlier misconception and misunderstanding to the present understanding and appreciation of the Indian stand. The fact that India continues to be a 'functioning democracy', an oasis amidst the 'democratically deficient' desert of the developing world, against heavy odds is well taken by the EU. On the other hand, it has not taken kindly to the military coup in Pakistan and indefinitely postponed the signing of the EU-Pakistan Cooperation Agreement, which was to be signed on 20 October 1999. The finalization of this agreement had been already postponed twice due to the concern of the EU regarding the lack of media freedom in Pakistan, its incendiary role in Kashmir issue and the nuclear tests.[13] The EU has taken a stand that the relations between them hinge on Pakistan's returning to democracy.

The member states of the EU like Britain and France in their individual capacity have also taken strong measures against the terrorist networks based in Pakistan. In early 2001, the UK banned Lashkar-e-Taiba and Jaish-e-Mohammad. France and India have formed a joint working group on counter-terrorism and its first meeting was held on 7 September 2001. France had included LeT on the terrorist list in October 2001. The UK has banned six more terrorist groups, which were active in India in November 2001.

Meanwhile, in their endeavour to prevent the deteriorating trend in Indo-Pakistan relations over Kashmir, the EU called upon both countries to show the utmost moderation on the ground. It also encouraged them to continue talking to each other, despite the lack of progress at the Agra Summit.

The post-11 September scenario has actually infused a new lifeline to Pakistan which was in the throes of a massive economic crisis, having accumulated a massive $ 40 billion foreign debt.[14] Musharraf was being praised for showing 'very considerable statesmanship' in the wake of the 11 September terrorist attack on the US Pakistan as a frontline state in the fight against terrorism has prompted the international community to confer "a halo of support" to Musharraf, who was treated as the *putschist* General earlier.

Recognizing the indispensable role of Pakistan in this endeavour, the EU reacted with great speed and alacrity in rewarding it with an impressive and liberal trade package from the European Commission worth about $1,350 million. It was aimed at helping Pakistan's economy and "bolstering" Musharraf's government in the face of growing protests against the war on Afghanistan. The EU considered that Pakistan's close ties with the Taliban regime and its long border with Afghanistan entitles it a crucial role in the military campaign launched by Western powers. Pakistan has also been offered an aid programme worth some $500 million to cope with the crises posed by the arrival of some five to six million Afghan refugees.

In November 2001, Pakistan-EU (Third Generation) Cooperation Agreement, the finalization of which was postponed thrice, as mentioned earlier, was signed envisaging an increased level of cooperation in diverse fields between the two sides. The EU promised to help Pakistan to cope with the losses suffered by its economy on account of the war in Afghanistan. It also abolished its 7 per cent customs duty on textiles from Pakistan and increased the quota for such goods by 15 per cent Member states of the EU like France followed suit and extended financial support to Pakistan generously.

The Comprehensive Convention against Terrorism proposed by India drew support from the EU and both French and British ambassadors urged the UN General Assembly member-states to accelerate work on it. However, the EU could not succeed in resolving the deadlock created by Pakistan and other countries over the definition of terrorism and in differentiating a terrorist from a freedom fighter.

During his visit to India in November 2001 to participate in the second India-EU summit meeting, Romono Prodi, President of the European Commission, accepted that India's warning about the growing threat of global terrorism, which the West ignored all through, had come true and stressed the joint fight against terrorism. "We in Europe will listen more closely to India in future," Prodi reassured and insisted that both the parties should work as "poles of stability in an unstable world situation". The Declaration against International Terrorism, signed at the end of the second India-EU summit on 23 November 2001, maintained that all states had a responsibility to refrain from providing moral, material or diplomatic support to acts of terrorism and preventing the use of their territory for sponsoring terrorist acts against other states. The declaration added that "there can be no religious, ethnic, ideological or any other justification of terrorism". It also projected that both the contracting parties should fight against international terrorism wherever it occurs and regardless of its motives. The declaration stressed the need to take decisive measures against all states, individuals and entities which render support, harbour or provide safe haven, finance, instigate or train terrorists or promote terrorism and called for an early adoption of the draft Comprehensive Convention on International Terrorism and the Convention for the Suppression of acts of Nuclear Terrorism.[15]

Philippe Douste – Blazer, sent by the French President Jacques Chirac as his special emissary to India by late December, too condemned the "cowardly terrorist attack on the Indian Parliament – all the more so as it hit the very heart of democratic institutions." "Terrorism had to be fought irrespective of the motive behind it." The fight against terrorism did not stop with Afghanistan but "should, on the contrary, be all comprehensive and sustained", Blazer observed.[16]

Jack Straw, the British Foreign Secretary, urged Pakistan to take "more effective" steps against terrorist groups which are operating "with impunity" on its territory. He rejected Islamabad's description of terrorist groups as Kashmiri freedom fighters and maintained that the attack on the very "heart of Indian democracy" must be seen as "an attack on democracy worldwide". Straw also stressed the need to have a single categorical approach towards terrorism. Britain "unreservedly" condemned those responsible for the attack on the Indian Parliament on 13 December 2001. During his visit to New Delhi in the first week, of January the British Premier Tony Blair declared "total solidarity with India in its outrage against the terrorist attack on its Parliament" and maintained that there was "no room in any civilized society for terrorist organizations already banned in the UK like Jaish-e-Mohammad or Lashkar-e-Taiba."[17]

Blair took a stand close to the Indian point of view and maintained that the starting point for any dialogue had to be complete and total rejection of terrorist attacks. In the New Delhi Declaration that was signed at the end of the visit, both the countries agreed that terrorism could not be justified on any grounds and must be condemned unambiguously and eradicated wherever it exists. There was also convergence of opinion that all those who support terrorism directly and indirectly must be condemned, including those individuals or groups that "finance, train, or provide support for terrorists." Both the contracting parties also resolved to support the UN Security Council

Resolution -1373 which makes a comprehensive case for rooting out terrorism globally and to collaborate in the counter terrorism exercise by including joint training under the framework of the UK-India Joint Working Group on Terrorism. Blair also echoed the Indian view that complete rejection of terrorism is a pre-condition for any dialogue process to begin between India and Pakistan.[18]

As mentioned earlier, in early May 2002, the EU has listed some of the terrorist groups active in India and confiscated their assets. The European Parliament too condemned the suicide attack on a passenger bus and army family quarters in Jammu by terrorist groups in mid-May in unequivocal terms and some members regretted that the EU paid more attention to China and Pakistan despite the fact that India is the biggest democracy in the world, and at present reeling under a series of atrocious terrorist attacks by Islamic *'jihadi'* extremists. During his visit to Pakistan on 23 May, Chris Patten, the European Commissioner in charge of External Affairs, insisted that the time had come for Islamabad to curb the extremism and restoration of democracy.

In June 2002, the EU's policy-setting Council of Ministers at its meeting in Luxembourg maintained that Pakistan needs to "take visible, decisive and verifiable steps" to seal the LoC, restrain militant groups violent activities and shut down militant training camps in Pakistan-occupied Kashmir. The European Council went a step ahead and called for further action to stop infiltration across the LoC in Kashmir by Pakistan and expected India to respond positively once Pakistan acts. It also stressed on the importance of holding "free, fair and inclusive" elections in J & K.[19] In spite of the dubious efforts of the pro-Pakistani lobby of British MEPs to put India and Pakistan at equal footing ignoring the negative role played by the latter, on 6 July 2002, the EP adopted a resolution putting the onus on Pakistan for the present stand off and called for positive measures from the Pakistani leadership.

During his recent visit to the Indian subcontinent, the EU 's Foreign Policy Chief, Javier Solana was forthright in maintaining that Pakistan needs to do more and sequentially the Indian response would be positive. To Islamabad's request to the EU to play the role of facilitator for a dialogue between India and Pakistan, Solana made it very clear that EU had no plan or desire to be a mediator. While EU did not consider that the recent elections in J & K as a solution to the Kashmir issue, Solana maintained that it was a process towards finding a solution. This is diametrically opposed to the Pakistani stand, which always described the elections in J & K as 'sham'. While participating in the conference of the Association of South East Asian Nations Regional Forum (ARF) on 1 August 2002, Solana went a step ahead and added that the international community would like to see Pakistan act in a manner that would help to end trans-border terrorism and facilitate a free poll in J & K. Foreign Ministers from the UK and France, whose visits to the Indian subcontinent preceded and followed Solana's trip respectively, took the same stand more or less vigorously.

III

Conclusion

The leaders of the EU always indicated that they wanted to create "a democratic and globally engaged

Europe", which would champion the cause of human rights, democracy, rule of law and development. As such, in its approach to terrorism in the Indian sub-continent, as elsewhere, the EU insisted that "an unremitting and uncompromising struggle against terrorism is and should at all times be compatible with human rights and fundamental freedoms."

There is a widespread feeling that Pakistani involvement in the global war against terrorism on the side of the US and its Western allies has brought an advantage to Pakistan at the cost of India in the Kashmir question. However, the foregoing arguments clearly show that it is not so. The British Premier Blair was quite forthright to be on record that no country had changed its position on the Kashmir issue on account of Pakistan's participation in the international coalition against international terrorism and he maintains that the campaign against terrorism would focus on all terrorist networks elsewhere, including Kashmir, which is close to the well-known and well-articulated Indian stand.

The ways and means by which the European countries try to curb and control the terrorist menace may offer a couple of lessons to the authorities of the South Asian governments. Creation of common judicial space to control the terrorist movements is a judicious move. Again, the cooperation and coordination prevalent among the EU member states in tackling the terrorist outfits is worth emulating. The traditional approach of the EU to international terrorism can very well help the international community in finding a solution to the vexing stalemate over the drafting of the Comprehensive Convention on Terrorism proposed by India in the UN. As mentioned earlier, the European Convention has adopted the pragmatic approach of identifying specific offences of a "predominately criminal character" most likely to be committed by terrorist offenders as extraditable, notwithstanding its so-called political motivation or political character, thus, moving away from attempting a definition of the term 'terrorism' with all its political complexities, which are used by some countries like Pakistan to stall the process. The Europeans should pull their weight to convince the international community and the UN to follow the example set by them in 1977. That could be the notable contribution of the EU to the international coalition and confrontation against terrorism in general and against cross-border terrorism sponsored and abetted by Pakistan in the Indian sub continent in particular.

Notes

1. See http://conventions.coe.int/Treaty/EN/Treaties/html/090/htm (26/01/02)
2. Amrith Rohan Perera, *International Terrorism* (New Delhi: Vikas Publishing House Pvt.Ltd, 1997), p.105.
3. *Ibid.*, p. 293.
4. See http://www.g7.utoronto.ca/g7/terrorism/terror 25.htm (14/6/02)
5. See http://www.ict.org.il/documents/documentdet. efm?docid=35, 9 December 1999 (14/6/02).
6. *The Hindu*, 13 October 2001.
7. http://conventions.coe.int/Treaty/EN/Treaties/Html/090.htm - Fight Against Terrorism-Acts Adopted

by the Council. 26 January 2002

8. *The Hindu*, 6 March 1992 and 13 February 1994. On the issue of human rights violations in Kashmir, the European Commission appealed to India, while accepting its sovereign and legitimate right to curb terrorism "appropriately", to ensure that "violations of human rights in the process are avoided". Still, the EU has refused to support a Pakistan sponsored resolution on Kashmir at the UN Human Rights Commission suggesting that India is "impervious to the human rights situation in the Kashmir valley."

9. *Ibid.*, 15 January & 29 June 2000.

10. *European Union News*, vol.10, no.2, March-April 2000, p.5.

11. Krzytof de Breza, "EU Criticizes Kashmir Attacks", 5 August 2000.

    See http://www.ofbjp.org/news/0800/7.html (29/5/02). Breza attributes this change of stand to the 'strategic dialogue. France continues to have with India. This is yet another case to prove that how the policy of an influential EU member state gets transformed into the policy of the EU as a whole.

12. See http://www.wmlibdems.org/Press_releases/liz.press/press2002/07_01_2002.asp (29/5/02)

13. *The Hindu*, 17 October 1999.

14. Chintamani Mahapatra, "Pakistan's Role in War against Terrorism: Costs and Benefits", 26 November 2001. http://www.ipcs.org/issues/newartcles/647-ter-chintamani.html (26/01002).

15. *Strategic Digest,* vol. 31, no.12, December 2001, p. 1637.

16. *The Hindu,* 25 December 2001.

17. *Ibid.,* 6 January 2002.

18. *Ibid.,* 7 January 2002.

19. *Deccan Chronicle,* 23 June 2002.

Section-VII: Women and Terrorism

Women and Terrorism in South Asia: Some Observations

A. Subramanyam Raju

South Asia is one of the regions, which has been affected by the terrorist activities in the world. India has been facing terrorism for more than two decades. Pakistan has been sponsoring terrorism and such efforts are seen as a part of Pakistan's long-term strategy of revenging India's support to the emergence of independent Bangladesh. Pakistan wanted to see the dismemberment of India by extending its support to a proxy war in Kashmir through Islamic militants.[1] In Sri Lanka, the LTTE is held responsible for the killing of thousands of people. Now it is engaged in negotiations with the government to resolve the ethnic crisis. Nepal has also been facing increasing strife from the Maoist insurgents. Terrorism is increasingly widening its base in Bangladesh. There are reports that the Al-Qaeda had taken shelter in Bangladesh and began its activities. In Bhutan overflow of terrorism from India's North-east and the Gurkha question are the destabilizing factors. People who are involved in these movements considered themselves as freedom fighters. Respective states considered the movements as sporadic violent events carried out by terrorists against the state.

In the conflicts between the extremists (terrorists) and the military forces in South Asia, people are exposed to serious hazardous problems. In such situations women are more vulnerable victims than men, as a mother, as a wife and as the one who takes responsibilities of the family. While the man joins the struggle, it is the woman who remains at home to look after the family. Women are socially disadvantaged. They become the worst sufferers in times of war, where they are not responsible for the conflict.

In South Asia there are women who became victims in the conflicts and some of them are directly or indirectly involved in the conflicts. In the following sections, an attempt is made to focus on the impact of violence on women and their involvement in the LTTE and Kashmir struggles and Maoist insurgency.

a) Sri Lanka

Sri Lanka was liberated from the British in 1948. It is a multi-ethnic society. The Sinhalese are predominantly Buddhists and they live in all the provinces outside the north and east. Sri Lankan Tamils live mostly in the northern and eastern provinces. The conflict between the state and Tamils and between the Sinhalese and Tamils has continued for the past two decades. The main factors that have led to the conflict are as follows:

- The declaration of Sinhala as the sole official language to replace English in 1956, which led to a serious reduction of opportunities for Tamils in state services;
- The enactment of the 1972 constitution removed minority safeguards and gave Buddhism foremost place; and
- State-aided settlement schemes in Tamil regions changed the demographic patterns.

Tamil people voiced against the discrimination and

demanded some degree of regional autonomy and power sharing but were ignored by the Sinhalese and the government. As a result, the TULF and the LTTE emerged as the dominant militant groups and fought for a separate state for Tamils. Later the LTTE has become the most powerful organization and spread from northern and eastern provinces to other parts of the country through sporadic attacks against the military establishments and Sinhalese. It has established its own army. It trained people and procured weapons. The various governments in power used force to tackle this struggle. In this brutal game, many of the civilians are affected. Among them women are the more affected. There were many attempts to resolve differences between them but failed. Recently peace process has been initiated and talks are being held to resolve the problem.

Women as Victims

Women constitute 50 per cent of the Tamil population. They are the victims in the hands of security forces. In Sri Lanka sexual violence is not only a personal trauma, but also has a social stigma.[2] Rape is a convenient and effective weapon to terrorize individuals and ethnic groups. The security forces raped women not only to satisfy their desire but also to take revenge against their own people who are involved in the conflict. The molested women are rejected by their families and their husbands. Women emerged from the war as widows. There are thousands of women who became widows and half-widows. Some lost their properties and some sold their properties. They are forced to leave their places. Some of them are internally displaced and some migrated to other countries particularly to India. They were kept in the refugee camps. They lived with many people and did not have any privacy. It was reported that more than 68,629 Tamil refugees lived in 130 refugee camps in Tamil Nadu (India) and nearly 30,000 lived elsewhere in India.[3]

Women are not only losing their beloved ones but are also not allowed to move away from their houses. They fear for their daughters' safety and sexual vulnerability and tend to confine themselves to the home. Some of them are hesitant to remarry because they think that their children may not be taken care of by their second husbands. There are also young girls who refuse to marry because of an uncertain future in case their husbands get killed. Being raped, being deprived of the company of their men, being alone, being deprived of property, some of them are forced to be involved in the conflict. Some are convinced that it is their duty to fight against the state establishment.

Women as Warriors

The ideal Tamil woman is expected to be a mother and a fighter, thus integrating the subject position of 'brave mother' with that of 'woman warrior' that is a 'warrior mother.'[4] The internal makeup of the LTTE woman is expected to be 'pure', 'chaste', and 'virginal', her outer body is marked as masculine; her hair is cut short and she wears a beret, combat fatigues, boots and a cyanide capsule around her neck. All members of the LTTE wear a cyanide capsule so that in the event of capture they can bite it and die instantly without betraying their movement under subsequent interrogation.[5] Since the 1980s there have been about 300 suicide attacks in the world and half of them occurred in Sri Lanka itself. Some 30 per cent to 40 per cent of the Tigers' suicide bombers have been women.[6] Suicide bombers are willing to die on behalf of his/her community/group. The LTTE is the first and the only group that killed two prominent national leaders in the world. Danu was one of the LTTE women who became responsible for the assassination of the former Indian Prime Minister, Rajiv Gandhi in May 1991 and another one assassinated the incumbent Sri Lankan President Ranasinghe Premadasa in May 1993.

Women warriors refused to use red kumkum on their foreheads and thali/jewellery around their necks. Their desire to transform their biological and cultural marked body to that of 'heroic' masculinity, can be seen in the following poem:

The ideal woman of Tamil Eelam
Her forehead shall be adorned not with red kumkum
but with blood
All that is seen in her eyes is not the sweetness of youth
but the tombs of the dead
On her neck will lay no tali
but a cyanide capsule
She has embraced not men
but weapons![7]

There are women who get actively involved in the LTTE operations. The LTTE has a separate wing for women's forces. It focused its recruitment on women to fill losses of its cadres.[8] There is equal representation from women in the LTTE. By joining the movement, women achieved a social status equal to men. For instance, Akila, the leader of the women's wing was considered top in the LTTE hierarchy before her death in 1996. Women wanted to become Black Tigers. In the LTTE, Black Tigers are given special status and respect. Women consist of one-third of the Black Tigers. They worship Prabakaran, the leader of the LTTE. They felt that by joining the movement, they could articulate their grievances and fight against oppression and exploitation exercised on them. It was reported that about 3,000 women were involved with the LTTE in the early 1990s. There are women who encouraged their male counterparts to participate in the war against the government. They were disappointed if their people refused to fight.[9]

b) Kashmir

The accession of Kashmir to India was never accepted by Pakistan on the ground that it was annexed by force. Since the majority of the people of Kashmir are Muslims, Pakistan argues, they belong to it. Pakistan has been trying to interfere in the internal affairs of Kashmir through ISI (Pakistan intelligence).[10] Kashmir also has an internal dimension. From the 1980s onwards, certain sections of the Kashmiri people have been involved in violence against the Indian state. Different groups are using people for various purposes. Violence, killings and molestation of women have become the order of the day. The voices are many and varied. One section believes in acceding Kashmir to Pakistan, another group articulates the idea of remaining independent both from India and Pakistan, while some other section desires to be a part of India. In this pluralistic game, guns are superseding politics. In the name of religion, secularism and Kashmiriyat, hundreds and thousands are being killed. Among them, women are more vulnerable.

Women as Victims

In the conflict, an estimated 60,000 people are killed

and more than 2,000 people either disappeared or are in illegal detention.[11] There are 15,000 widows and thousands of half-widows. There have been more than 250,000 people internally displaced and 100,000 migrated to other parts of India.[12] The majority of them are Hindu women. Most of them are from Ladakh and Jammu. It was reported that 23,611 people from Kargil, 300 families from Leh and 46,000 people from Jammu are displaced.[13] They have lost not only their counterparts but also lost their properties. They became homeless. Some of them are kept in the refugee camps. The government has failed to provide minimum facilities to them. Some of them lost their employment or opportunities. Some are dependent on their counterparts. But when their men are killed either by the security forces or by militants, they become vulnerable. There are reports that militants forced Muslim women to marry them or to live with them to fulfil their desires. The forced married women have become half-widows, because their husbands left them without informing them and were involved in the militant activities. Their future remains uncertain. Muslim women are not only harassed by the security forces but also by the militants. Militants forced them to wear purdah. They linked the wearing of purdah with the struggle for freedom and with Islam. Though many women refused to wear purdah, some who fear, wear purdah without their choice. There are incidents where some of the employed women are asked to pay money to the militant groups. Some times, women are forced to give shelter to the militants. These women are being attacked by the security forces suspecting that they are supporters of militants. They are treated as anti-nationals by the security forces. Women, who are behind burqa, are becoming vulnerable to the security forces. The forces are checking women, who are in burqa, because they suspect these women are involved in militant activities. They are convinced that every third burqa-clad person is a militant.[14] Many young girls stopped going to schools or college. They are vulnerable to sexual harassment from security personals. Having been harassed by the security forces, some Muslim women became violent and joined in the struggle either to take revenge against the security forces who killed their people or joined in the name of religion the and freedom struggle. They also encouraged and sent their people to join in the struggle. However, Hindu women, who are being harassed, did not take part in fighting against injustice done to them.

Muslim Women as Militants

In Kashmir some of the Muslim women are in the forefront of the struggle. They played a significant role in sending war material and worked as informers. They wanted to see their people to fight against the state. Women are preparing for jihad. The following poem explains how a woman sends her son to holy war and refuses to mourn at her son's funeral.

We danced over burning flames
Even the shadows danced, behind the doors, behind the walls,
In our frenzy, we broke all custom, we broke all traditions.
We danced over the withering flowers
We set our tents on fire
We danced to the music,
The music of the caravan bells
With love, we placed the dagger on our lips
We danced over the carpet of flowers
Was it a song or a melancholy lament, Who knows?
We never stopped dancing that entire night

We mourned with moistened eyes
We danced with an open heart,
The candle, the smoke, the flame, the moth and the gathering,
For you we danced, we danced.[15]

Another example is Akbar Bhai, who was killed by the security forces. At his funeral, his wife told her son that "If we're killed at his (husband) funeral, you will be able to hold your head high for our honour will no longer be at risk."[16] Women encouraged their sons and husbands to join in the armed conflict. They were glad if their beloved died in the struggle. They felt that they were being betrayed by India and were fighting against it to get freedom. They came out of their houses and demonstrate in support of the struggle. Though their culture does not allow them to come out of their homes, but they are allowed to participate in the struggle. They are strong and courageous to agitate against the state. Asiyah Andrabi, the leader of the Dukhtarane Millat, argues that "I would never say that the solution of Kashmir is possible through politics. Militancy is necessary. We need to strengthen militancy. If the struggle is limited to political means, the problem of Kashmir will not go away for 200 years. Many of the women lost their beloved people and how can they sit back?"[17] They are not only looking after their families but also looking after the welfare of militants. They hide militants. They take responsibilities of taking injured militants to hospitals and providing them with food..

c) Nepal

The Maoists in Nepal represent the poor and marginalized people. Through guerilla actions, these groups fight against the state. They called for land reforms, property rights for women, employment and protection of oppressed and disadvantaged people. They are spread in many parts of the country. Women joined the movement to fight for their rights.

Women as Victims

Women are being discriminated more in Nepal than in other countries of South Asia. They are most oppressed and marginalized. They suffer from 23 discriminatory laws.[18] For instance, they have no right over parent properties, unless they remain unmarried. Apart from these discriminations, they, like Kashmiri and Tamil women, are arrested, raped, harassed and killed by the police. If men are suspected as members of Maoist groups, the security forces not only attack them but also their female counterparts. For instance, Kumari Budha's father was suspected as a member of a Maoist group and arrested at the police station. When she came to see his father, she was raped and killed by the police. Women, who suffered at the hands of the security forces and who lost their beloved people, wanted to take revenge against injustice. Sita Kumari Puri's brother was killed by the police. He had no links with the Maoists. She joined the movement to take revenge against the security forces. In her words, "Yes, my brother has been killed. But we have another 1,000 brothers of the same kind. We will all come together and take revenge. We will not spare those responsible for our grief."[19] To cite another example: husband of Nanda Kumar Shrestha was killed by the police. She refused to mourn. She said, "I am ready to lift a gun to follow my husband's beliefs. I will make his dream come true."[20] In order to retaliate against the security forces and fight for their rights, women joined the movement.

Women as Militants

There are women who are actively involved in the Maoist insurgency in Nepal. They are either combatants or spies or informers. In the Maoist strongholds, every third guerilla is a woman and in the new areas, every tenth combatant is a woman. Hisila Yami says that "the people's war gives all of them (women) a meaningful life and a meaningful death; it allows them to prove their worth is equal to the men."[21] In the Maoist movement, women are concerned with issues such as property for women; punishing the rapists; preventing polygamy. Yami rightly pointed out that, "The women have more to gain than the men from the people's war. That is why the women, especially the Tibeto-Burman and non-Aryan women constitute such an important part of the movement."[22] They constitute nearly 70 per cent of the women who are involved in the movement. Women are projected as "formidable fighters, more committed, disciplined, reliable and militant."[23] They are exposed to the radical extremism. There are less chances for women militants to give up their activities. When they joined the movement, they became free from patriarchal bonds. They do not want to go back to live in their society, where they are being discriminated against. Women and girls have a high opinion about the movement. A young girl says that "Maoists grab the property of the rich and give to the poor." They are "fighting for justice for the poor." They are "tortured and killed by the police because they are working for the poor."[24] Insurgency, for a few, has become a business. There are a few who sent their sons to the conflict, not because to fight for a cause but for economic reasons. The son will bring money, which will help his mother to look after the family. However, most of them get involved seriously in the movement to fight against the state.

Conclusion

Women are more vulnerable than men in the conflicts in South Asia. They have directly or indirectly become victims. Most of them are mentally disturbed; either raped, harassed, displaced or lost their counterparts, who were killed either by the security forces or militants. Many of them (in Sri Lanka and Kashmir) are internally displaced or migrated to other parts of their countries or neighbouring countries. Women in the conflicts had played two roles: some women opposed violence that took away their sons, brothers and husbands, while some involved in the conflict and others, who could not actively participate in fighting, encouraged and sent their beloved to fight against injustice. There are many reasons for them to act violently and to join in the armed conflict like: forced to join; joined to take revenge against the security forces who killed their beloved; joined because they took it as a pride and joined in the name of nationalism or religion. On the other hand, there are reasons for a few not to join in the conflict because they did not want to see their beloved killing others or get killed by others. However, women are affected by violence on both sides: being involved in the conflict and not being associated with the violence.

Women should be given proper representation during the discussions in resolving the conflict. At the third round of talks held at Oslo in December 2002, it was agreed to set up a women's committee to look at gender issues in the peace process. Further, in the fourth round of talks held in Thailand, it announced the names of women who are in the committee. Among them, five would be from the LTTE. This could be a model for any peace processes any where in the world, particularly in Kashmir and Nepal.

Notes

1. See Olive Roy, "Why War is Going on in Afghanistan: The Afghan Crisis in Perspective", *Journal of International Affairs*, vol.5, no.4, December 2000-February 2001, p.11. The US officials acknowledged this. See also James Risen and Judith Miller, "Pakistani Intelligence Had Links to Al-Qaeda, US officials say," *New York Times*, 29 October 2001.

   Some of the militant organizations operating in Kashmir are: Jamaat-e-Islami (JI); Jamaat-e-Ulema Islam (JUI); Hizb-e-Islam (Hel); Hizbul Mujahideen (HM); Taliban-Religeous Scholars; Sioah-e-Sabha Pakistan (SSP); Lashkar-e-Jhangui (Leg); Harkat-Ul-Mujahideen (HUM); Markaz-e-Dawa Wal Irshad (MDI); Lashkar-e-Toyyaba (LeT); Tehrik-e-Jafaria Pakistan; Sipah-e-Mohd Pak (SMP)

2. Asha Hans, "Sri Lankan Tamil Refugee Women in India", *Refuge*, vol.16, no. 2, June 1997, p.5.

3. *The Hindu*, 2 March 2003, p.11.

4. Sitralega Maunaguru, "Gendering Tamil Nationalism: The Construction of 'Woman' in Projects of Protests and Control", in Pradeep Jeganathan and Qadri Ismail (eds), *Un-making the Nation: The Politics of Identity and History in Modern Sri* Lanka (Colombo: Social Scientists' Association, 1995), p.163 cited in Malathi de Alwis,

"Moral Mothers and Stalwart Sons: Reading Binaries in a Time of War" in Lois Ann Lorentzen and Jennifer Turpin (ed), *The Women War Reader* (New York: New York University Press, 1999), p. 265.

5. *Ibid.*, p. 266.

6. *New York Times*, 14 January 2003.

7. de Alwis, n. 4, p. 266.

8. See http://www.satp.org/satporgtp/southasia/samain.html.

9. See Elise Boulding, *The Underside of History: A View of Women through Time* (Boulder,Co: Westview Press, 1976); Jean Bethke Elshtaim, *Women and War* (New York: Basic Books, 1987); Sara Ruddick, *Maternal Thinking: Towards a Politics of Peace* (Boston,MA: Beacon Press, 1989).

10. Following are some of the activities of the ISI: "Religious fundamentalism was propagated in small but lethal doses to promote separatism and communal outlook. Training and indoctrination of settled leaders from the Kashmir Valley was arranged to create militant cadres. A large number of youths from the Kashmir Valley and Poonch Sector was given extensive training in the use of automatic weapons, sabotage and attacks on security forces. Automatic weapons and explosives were now issued to these people. Special teams were trained to organize disruption and engineer incidents to damage the democratic and secular image of India." Cited in Clifford E. Simonsen and Jeremy R. Spindlove, *Terrorism Today: The Past, the Players, the Future* (New Jersey: Prentice Hall, 2000), p. 217.

11. Rita Manchanda, "Guns and Burqa: Women in the Kashmir Conflict", in Rita Manchanda (ed), *Women, War and Peace in South Asia* (New Delhi: Sage Publications, 2001), p. 46.

12. See *The Hindu*, 2 March 2002, p. 11.

13. *Ibid.*

14. Manchanda, n.11, p. 59.

15. Shafaq Sopori's poem, cited by Manchanda, *ibid.*, p. 53.

16. Rita Manchanda, "Who is Afraid of Foreign Mercenaries?", *Sunday Observer*, 2 September 1993, cited in Manchanda, *ibid.*, p. 54.

17. *Ibid.*, p. 84.

18. Shobha Gautam, Amrita Banskota and Rita Manchanda, "Where There Are No Men: Women in the Maoist Insurgency in Nepal", in Manchanda (ed), n.11, p. 222.

19. *Ibid.*, p. 232.

20. *Ibid.*, p. 233.

21. *Ibid.*, p. 237.

22. *Ibid.*, p. 236.

23. *Ibid.*, p. 239.

24. *Ibid.*, p. 245.

Terrorism: The Enduring Saga of Women in Kashmir

Rashmi Bhure

Introduction

The canvass of terrorism is very wide in India, from the ethnic violence in the North- East and the terrorist violence in Jammu & Kashmir (J & K) to the Naxalite movement in the parts of Andhra Pradesh, Bihar, Jharkhand, Chhattisgarh, Maharashtra and Orissa. The causes and consequences of the conflict in each of these states is different. But one factor that is common to all the conflicts is the devastation of the civil society and amongst this the most significant group is of women and children. J & K remains the most troubled area in the South Asian region, though the world's attention is on Afghanistan. Since 1989 about 60,000 people have been killed and a greater number of people injured.[1] Terrorism in J & K is multi-dimensional, therefore it is not possible to put all vital and related issues of terrorism in this paper though they are equally important. Firstly, the paper discusses and analyzes the violation and discrimination against women in J & K since 1989. Secondly the paper focuses on the efforts made by women to live and struggle for peace in J & K.

Impact of Terrorism on Women in Kashmir

The decade long hostilities in J & K over the autonomous status and also dispute between India and Pakistan over territory, have left the women of this lush green sub- Himalayan region deeply traumatized and violated. Women are the biggest losers who have lost their children, husbands and homes. They are both psychologically and physically affected due to a near war-like situation.

Displacement

Displacement in the context of Kashmir can be broadly categorized into two: Forced Displacement and Voluntary Displacement. The decade long hostilities have displaced at least 30,000 people within J & K and around 60,000 families have migrated to other parts of India.[2] In many cases the displacement is piecemeal and for some their status is relegated to refugees. Of the world's total refugee and internally displaced population, women constitute the majority.[3] Those who take refuge a with family that lives elsewhere, may be displaced within the country. However, most of the women often find themselves in refugee camps. Falling prey to 'Post Traumatic Stress Disorders' (PTSD), these women enter the refugee camps, which are neither designed nor safe for women. The government has announced relief measures for refugee families – distribution of goods – nine litres of kerosene oil, two kilos of flour, seven kilos of rice and Rs.200 per head per month and ex gratia payment to victim. It has yet to offer relief to those who have lost their homes. It has been slow to provide relief and rehabilitation to the people in the refugee camp. Medical facilities are limited in these camps and education for the children is another casualty for the refugees. The government's approach to the malaise of the people in the refugee camp is clear with the fact that it was only in April 1999 that for the first time the Indian Prime Minister visited the refugee camps.

On the other side the Kashmiris who were forced out from their ancient indigenous habitat by terrorist and religious extremists also lost their land, property, homes, educational and employment opportunities, break–up of families, social and community ties. The continued state of homelessness, deprivation and insecurity has pushed the Kashmiri Pandit community to a state of chronic stress. While interviewing a college teacher, a displaced Kashmiri Pandit now living in Mumbai said, "her daughter is totally alienated with the ethos and culture of Kashmir. When she narrates to her daughter about the days they spent in Kashmir, the daughter feels it is some fairy tale story". [4] Another important problem faced by the displaced community has been the loss of their immovable property, which they left. In the case of people belonging to rural Kashmir who were dependent for their livelihood on land, orchards and cattle their situation is further worse as in most cases the land is encroached and orchards are destroyed. Many displaced people who left Kashmir in 1990 had to sell in distress their property almost after seven to eight years later as they felt the state government was unable to protect their property. Employment is a big problem for the Kashmiris who have moved out either forcefully or "voluntary" to other parts of India.

Women in the New Role as Bread Earners

Militancy and the terror of security forces in Kashmir have made thousands of women widows and half-widows. This has made extremely difficult for the women to perform the socially assigned responsibility to feed and care for the children and the aged in the family. The majority of widows are in circumstances of poverty and distress because of their sole bread earner was either killed or disappeared. These women are dependent on others and are striving for work.

The major sources of monetary support for the widows are:

- Government Relief.
- Parents' Support.
- Help from Non-Governmental Organizations.
- Handicraft/ Agricultural Activities.

But many women are availing no support from anybody. In many cases the support is irregular or came to the women almost after two or three years after they lost the only male earner in the family. What disturbed the women most was the education of their children and their future. Added to this was the feeling of insecurity, which was increasing with insufficient income. This feeling of insecurity forced many women in the new role that of the primary bread earner, which probably they never dreamt of (Kashmir generally being a traditional feudal society). At the same time there were also women who refused to seek financial help from anyone as this was against their principles. Despite her financial struggle, she would not complain but continuously struggle to get some or the other job.

But the major hurdle in getting employment is widespread illiteracy amongst women in Kashmir. Moreover, with security forces occupying school buildings in the valley there is a very high drop out rate – 58 per cent for girls and 45 per cent for boys.[5] These children have been forced into economic activities in farming and the labour intensive carpet industry. The middlemen generally exploit many women due to illiteracy and being unskilled in the handicraft sector. Alternative means of livelihood are not available which results in increased powerlessness amongst women.[6] Women have to undergo a hard time in search of employment. Bribes to get government jobs are said to be the rule and a source of income for the power brokers. All departments, organizations and institutions only focus on giving monetary aid which is of a temporary nature, what is a required is permanent source of income – employment. The government gives a compensation of rupees one lakh to families of 'innocent' victims of militancy but a lot of corruption is involved in getting the claims passed. The humiliation the women experience in running from pillar to post to get the compensation is quite demoralizing. Besides, the unemployment is rampant owing to the economic crisis, which further leads to emotional crisis.

Human Rights Violations

Women in Kashmir are caught in a situation of helplessness due to deprivation of their basic human rights like the right to livelihood. Kashmiris mainly depend for their livelihood on their agricultural land, orchards, cattle and the most important the tourism sector. Agricultural land in most cases is encroached, orchards are destroyed and tourism is essentially a peacetime activity. In addition to suffering of the general violations, women also suffer gender-specific violations like rape, forced marriage, right to dignity, right to privacy.

Rape, in particular, is used for various reasons. Rape in a conflicting situation is either done to humiliate or to degrade the masculinity in the society. Or another motivation for rape is to destroy the adversary's culture because women are linked with motherhood and transmission of cultural values within society; by abusing and raping women, the militants can deconstruct the purity of culture. Rape has been used as a strategy for "ethnic cleansing". Rape in this sense is not only a violation of one woman, but is considered a grave insult to the whole ethnic group. Rape is also used to satisfy sexual desires of the militants or the security forces, as they use rape as a weapon of genocide for which the women are caring and bonding throughout their lives. This suppression of women is derived from and reinforces the patriarchal structure of the society, which in turn obtains its power from gender oppression. Women are also subjected to rape from the security forces as a form of torture, to punish and subdue them so that they would give information on the whereabouts of their husbands or brothers or sons. The terror and humiliation faced by the victims of rape does not end with the physical and mental sufferings experienced at the time of the rape. But the punishment for the rape victims starts afterwards. The victims of rape are looked at as defile unclean and sinners by the society. Rape has long-term adverse effects on women, yet the violations are often left unattended. Actual incidents of rape are higher than those revealed because of the associated stigma. Due to this the real figures of rape are difficult to get and thus it becomes difficult to understand the intensity of the violation. Rape is not an accident of conflict but is used as an instrument, it poses a larger question of human security. Furthermore, women are predisposed to HIV and AIDS and other forms of sexually transmitted diseases (STD), which will be a significant problem in the coming years.

Forced marriage is another difficulty faced by women in Kashmir. In many cases the militants force the women to marry them for their personal desires and a number of them disappear within a few years. These women are then treated as 'half-widows'. Their future is uncertain, the remarriage laws are not clear. They don't know whether they can remarry? How long should they wait in hope for their husbands return?

S. Bano, 19-year-old college student, Tregam village, said, "India has not trained its forces properly. Can't the jawans make out the difference between a man's walk and a woman's walk? Why do they have to keep lifting burqas to check whether we are women or militants?"[7] The humiliation and abuse, which the women face at the hands of the security forces is tremendous. The treatment the women get at the time of search operation in the houses or even when the hospitals are raided by the security forces is extremely humiliating and forces the women to reflect on what happened to their right to live with dignity and privacy given to them by the Constitution.

Psychological Trauma

The terror, which was seen in the eyes of every Kashmiri in the early years of terrorism, has frozen in the past few years. People have got used to such terror tactics. They say it has become a way of life "Aadat pad gayee hai"(It is a habit now).[8] Terrorist activities and the presence of security forces in fact lead to the feeling of insecurity amongst people. People in fact go to the extreme and say that the security forces are only terrorist.[9] Women live in fear of humiliation, harassment, molestation, or rape. All this has developed 'Post Traumatic Stress Disorders' (PTSD) amongst the Kashmiris.

PTSD is seen both in Muslims and Pandits, even in those who have migrated to other parts. For the people living in the valley the PTSD is the result of continuous violence, bomb blasts, daily killings that have made this peaceful valley into hell. The case of Kashmiri Pandits who migrated from Kashmir, for them the loss of habitat, uprootedness, ness, alien way of life, different climatic conditions, language and a totally new culture lead to stress and psychological problems.

Another factor, which is important here, is the custodial disappearances that has especially left a tragic imprint on the minds of women. According to Muslim Personal law a person cannot be declared dead for seven years after disappearance. Till then his property cannot be disposed of and his wife cannot remarry during that time. A number of such women whose husbands are missing (taken for interrogation) is increasing and they have been denied the inheritance rights, which results in financial crisis for them and their children. These women reach a situation of helplessness. A few families have been awarded compensation from the High Courts and State Human Rights Commission. But what people want from the government is accountability and not compensation. The Psychiatric Diseases Hospital, Srinagar, points towards a manifold increase in the stress related disease among the people of the valley.[10] Such cases in large numbers prior to 1989 were beyond imagination as Kashmir was compared to Jannat(heaven). Further many people in Kashmir are threatened and abused by the perpetrators of "disappearances" to give up their search. Some have even risked their lives in the search for their dear ones. Amnesty International said " the law must also guarantee human rights defenders- including relatives of the disappeared- the freedom to document human rights violations and to campaign and protest without fear of reprisals."[11] Since 1990 it is estimated that up to 1000 people have "disappeared" after being arrested by police or armed or paramilitary forces in Kashmir.[12] Many cases of habeas corpus filed by families of the "disappeared" remained unresolved. The psychological trauma under which the women go also affect their health. Cases of high blood pressure amongst women are increasingly reported in the hospitals. Regular check-up of such women is important but treatment to such women is difficult because the health services in the state are thrown decades back. Added to this the militants terrorize the people, like in October 1989 some militant groups opposed sterilizations and abortion.

The acts of suppression as of rape on women also lead to PTSD. Sexual violence is physically, emotionally, and psychologically devastating the women. Further women in the double burdened role of sole bread earner and the traditional role of family maker puts her under immense stress and a feeling of insecurity and powerlessness and depression. Fear of her family's future in such an uncertain environment is a question of deep concern for the women. The psychological turmoil faced by the women can never be quantified and rectified by any medicine.

Women's Role in the Peace Process

Women in Kashmir for eleven long years had to face the guns of the militants and the security forces. It is she who had to keep the family and social values together at the time of crisis. Women had to enter in the new role as the sole economic supporter of the family, when they lost the male kin in the family; and it was only the women who had to groom a healthy future generation midst violence and uncertainties. There is no end to this long list of burdens on women in Kashmir. All these adversaries on women have forced them to enter yet, into another new role of peacemaker.

Women in their own ways are trying to fight positively with the grave situation in Kashmir because they know normal life and peace is the necessary condition for bringing up their children. The decade long militancy and the oppressive acts of security forces have made them adapt to the situation bravely, otherwise they know they will be at the mercy of the situation.

Women are generally not independently organized, or even included in the existing political organization. But they are trying to carve a place for themselves in their own ways. They formed Mahila Mandals to fight corruption in leadership. Nineteen committees have been formed by women in Jammu for the welfare of the migrants. There are also groups like the Dukhtarani Milat and the Khawateen Markaaz, both Srinagar-based. These organizations were among the first to reach Kunan Poshpora village in Kupwara district in 1991 after the mass rapes. Khawateen Markaaz, started in 1990, after the Gaunkadal massacre where security forces killed 60 people in a peaceful demonstration. There has been no effort on the part of the state to involve women in actual negotiations and non-participation of women in these processes has resulted in marginalizing women's needs and aspirations. The capacity of women to be good in peace building and conflict resolution stems from the very conditions of marginalization and invisibility in which they have been forced.

Conclusion

There is a need to sensitize people throughout the country to the trauma the Kashmiris are undergoing. Media can play a very important role in this matter by bringing out unbiased stories of Kashmir. For instance, the Hindi films in the last few years have started making an effort in this direction. Films like *Roja,* which showed the wife struggling with the government machinery to get her husband back who was kidnapped by the terrorist. In a film like *Mission Kashmir* the women caught in the crossfire of the terrorist son and the husband as a police officer and in the film *Fiza* mother along with sister convincing the son of not joining the terrorists group was portrayed. In all these films the problems faced by women while dealing with terrorist are effectively projected. There also is a need for an effective government action to de-escalate the violence rather than coming out with pro–tempore or ex-post facto policies which are unable to bring an enduring peace to Kashmir or stop the sufferings of women in Kashmir. This statement is supported by the fact that the Indian Prime Minister Atal Behari Vajpayee, on 19 March 1999, announced an outrageous insurance policy to "protect" potential rape victims between the age group of 10 to 75 at an annual premium of Rs.15. The state-run General Insurance Corporation will be the arbiter to decide how much compensation should be paid to the victim. A woman is entitled up to Rs.25, 200 if she suffers "permanent disability". The catch is that she needs to prove beyond a doubt that she has been raped. The plan is a component of a comprehensive insurance package for women that covers death, injuries, and disabilities caused by accidents, surgery, snake bites, drowning, murder and terrorism.[13] This policy is a clear example of how insensitively the government is handling such an important issue concerning women. In fact the rape insurance will eternize violence against women. This also shows that government looks at rape as an accident, but it is already mentioned in the paper, that rape is used as an instrument of terrorism. This confirms that instead of creating a safe environment for women to live, the government is coming out with ex-post facto policies.

There is an imperative need to listen to the voices of women in Kashmir. There is an urgent need to give representation to women in any peace processes, as that will bring a fresh and more sensitized approach to not only to women's problems in Kashmir but will definitely bring out a holistic approach in general to the problems of people in Kashmir.

Notes

1. Dabala Bashir, Ahmad, " Impact of Conflict Situation on Women and Children in Kashmir", A Report by the Department of Sociology, University of Kashmir, Srinagar, June 1999.
2. Vemuri Suchita, "Kashmir: Drenched in Women's Tears", *Women in Action*, no. 2, 2001

   Website on (http://www.isiswomen.org/pub/wia/wiawcar/kashmir.htm);

   Warikoo, K. "Internally Displaced Persons: Case Study of Displacement of Kashmiri Pandits, the Indigenous Minority Community of Kashmir", presentation made at the National Seminar on "Displacement and Emerging Humanitarian Concerns", University of Mumbai, 4-5 December 1999.

3. Susan Forbes-Martin, *Women and World Development Series* (London and New Jersey: Zed Books, 1992), p. 1.

4. In a personal interview with a Kashmiri Pandit now working in one of the colleges in Mumbai, in February 2002. Identity of the interviewee was not given on request.

5. Shafi Aneesa, "Women's Education: Practices and Challenges", *New Hope,* vol. 2, no.1, January- February 2001, pp. 55-59.

6. Ritu Dewan and Bashir Manzar, *Demystifying Kashmir: Developmental Potential of Horticulture and Tourism* (Srinagar: Kashmir Foundation for Peace and Developmental Studies, 2000).

7. See the Report " Women's Testimonies from Kashmir-The Green of the Valley is Khaki", *Women's Initiative,* 1994.

8. *Ibid.*

9. This view came out very clearly in a group discussion with the students of the Kashmir University, in Mumbai on 25 March 2002.

10. Rasool Raouf, "Psychological Impact of Violence", *New Hope,* vol. 1, no. 2, March- April 2000, pp.6- 11.

11. For Amnesty International Report, "If they are dead, tell us", 1999, see www.amnesty.org.

12. For Amnesty International Report, "India (Jammu and Kashmir): Day of the "Disappeared", 2000, see www.amnesty.org.

13. "Violence Against Women in South Asia: India", *Manavi Newsletter,* vol.11, no. 1, Spring 1999, p.5.

Appendices

UN Security Council Resolution No. 1368 (2001) Condemning the Terrorist Attacks on the US, Adopted on 12 September 2001

The Security Council,

Reaffirming the principles and purposes of the Charter of the United Nations,

Determined to combat by all means threats to international peace and security caused by terrorist acts, recognizing the inherent right of individual or collective self-defence in accordance with the Charter,

1. Unequivocally condemns in the strongest terms the horrifying terrorist attacks which took place on 11 September 2001 in New York, Washington, D C and Pennsylvania and regards such acts, like any act of international terrorism, as a threat to international peace and security;

2. Expresses its deepest sympathy and condolences to the victims and their families and to the people and Government of the United States of America;

3. Calls on all States to work together urgently to bring to justice the perpetrators, organizers and sponsors of these terrorist attacks and stresses that those responsible for aiding, supporting or harbouring the perpetrators, organizers and sponsors of these acts will be held accountable;

4. Calls also on the international community to redouble their efforts to prevent and suppress terrorist acts including by increased cooperation and full implementation of the relevant international anti-terrorist conventions and Security Council resolutions, in particular Resolution 1269 (1999) of 19 October 1999;

5. Expresses its readiness to take all necessary steps to respond to the terrorist attacks of 11 September 2001, and to combat all forms of terrorism, in accordance with its responsibilities under the Charter of the United Nations;

6. Decides to remain seized of the matter.

UN Security Council Resolution No. 1373 (2001) on Suppressing the Financing of Terrorism and Improving International Cooperation, Adopted on 28 September 2001

"The Security Council,

Reaffirming its resolutions 1269 (1999) of 19 October 1999 and 1368 (2001) of 12 September 2001,

Reaffirming also its unequivocal condemnation of the terrorist attacks which took place in New York, Washington, D C and Pennsylvania on 11 September 2001, and expressing its determination to prevent all such acts,

Reaffirming further that such acts, like any act of international terrorism, constitute a threat to international peace and security,

Reaffirming the inherent right of individual or collective self-defence as recognized by the Charter of the United Nations as reiterated in resolution 1368 (2001),

Reaffirming the need to combat by all means, in accordance with the Charter of the United Nations, threats to international peace and security caused by terrorist acts,

Deeply concerned by the increase, in various regions of the world, of acts of terrorism motivated by intolerance or extremism,

Calling on States to work together urgently to prevent and suppress terrorist acts, including through increased cooperation and full implementation of the relevant international conventions relating to terrorism,

Recognizing the need for States to complement international cooperation by taking additional measures to prevent and suppress, in their territories through all lawful means, the financing and preparation of any acts of terrorism,

Reaffirming the principle established by the General Assembly in its declaration of October 1970 (Resolution 2625 (XXV)) and reiterated by the Security Council in its resolution 1189 (1998) of 13 August 1998, namely that every State has the duty to refrain from organizing, instigating, assisting or participating in terrorist acts in another State or acquiescing in organized activities within its territory directed towards the commission of such acts,

Acting under Chapter VII of the Charter of the United Nations,

1. **Decides that all States shall:**

(a) Prevent and suppress the financing of terrorist acts;

(b) Criminalize the wilful provision or collection, by any means, directly or indirectly, of funds by their nationals or in their territories with the intention that the funds should be used, or in the knowledge that they are to be used, in order to carry out terrorist acts;

(c) Freeze without delay funds and other financial assets or economic resources of persons who commit, or attempt to commit, terrorist acts or participate in or facilitate the commission of terrorist acts; of entities owned or controlled directly or indirectly by such persons; and of persons and entities acting on behalf of, or at the direction of such persons and entities, including funds derived or generated from property owned or controlled directly or indirectly by such persons and associated persons and entities;

(d) Prohibit their nationals or any persons and entities within their territories from making any funds, financial assets or economic resources or financial or other related services available, directly or indirectly, for the benefit of persons who commit or attempt to commit or facilitate or participate in the commission of terrorist acts, of entities owned or controlled, directly or indirectly, by such persons and of persons and entities acting on behalf of or at the direction of such persons;

2. **Decides also that all States shall:**

(a) Refrain from providing any form of support, active or passive, to entities or persons involved in terrorist acts, including by suppressing recruitment of members of terrorist groups and eliminating the supply of weapons to terrorists;

(b) Take the necessary steps to prevent the commission of terrorist acts, including by provision of early warning to other States by exchange of information;

(c) Deny safe haven to those who finance, plan, support, or commit terrorist acts, or provide safe havens;

(d) Prevent those who finance, plan, facilitate or commit terrorist acts from using their respective territories for those purposes against other States or their citizens;

(e) Ensure that any person who participates in the financing, planning, preparation or perpetration of terrorist acts or in supporting terrorist acts is brought to justice and ensure that, in addition to any other measures against them, such terrorist acts are established as serious criminal offences in domestic laws and regulations and that the punishment duly reflects the seriousness of such terrorist acts;

(f) Afford one another the greatest measure of assistance in connection with criminal investigations or criminal proceedings relating to the financing or support of terrorist acts, including assistance in obtaining evidence in their possession necessary for the proceedings;

(g) Prevent the movement of terrorists or terrorist groups by effective border controls and controls on issuance of identity papers and travel documents, and through measures for preventing counterfeiting, forgery or fraudulent use of identity papers and travel documents;

3. Calls upon all States to:

(a) Find ways of intensifying and accelerating the exchange of operational information, especially regarding actions or movements of terrorist persons or networks; forged or falsified travel documents; traffic in arms, explosives or sensitive materials; use of communications technologies by terrorist groups; and the threat posed by the possession of weapons of mass destruction by terrorist groups;

(b) Exchange information in accordance with international and domestic law and cooperate on administrative and judicial matters to prevent the commission of terrorist acts;

(c) Cooperate, particularly through bilateral and multilateral arrangements and agreements, to prevent and suppress terrorist attacks and take action against perpetrators of such acts;

(d) Become parties as soon as possible to the relevant international conventions and protocols relating to terrorism, including the International Convention for the Suppression of the Financing of Terrorism of 9 December 1999;

(e) Increase cooperation and fully implement the relevant international conventions and protocols relating to terrorism and Security Council Resolutions 1269 (1999) and 1368 (2001);

(f) Take appropriate measures in conformity with the relevant provisions of national and international law, including international standards of human rights, before granting refugee status, for the purpose of ensuring that the asylum seeker has not planned, facilitated or participated in the commission of terrorist acts;

(g) Ensure, in conformity with international law, that refugee status is not abused by the perpetrators, organizers or facilitators of terrorist acts, and that claims of political motivation are not recognized as grounds for refusing requests for the extradition of alleged terrorists;

4. Notes with concern the close connection between international terrorism and transnational organized crime, illicit drugs, money-laundering, illegal arms-trafficking, and illegal movement of nuclear, chemical, biological and other potentially deadly materials, and in this regard emphasizes the need to enhance coordination of efforts on national, sub regional, regional and international levels in order to strengthen a global response to this serious challenge and threat to international security;

5. Declares that acts, methods, and practices of terrorism are contrary to the purposes and principles of the United Nations and that knowingly financing, planning and inciting terrorist acts are also contrary to the purposes and principles of the United Nations;

6. Decides to establish, in accordance with Rule 28 of its provisional rules of procedure, a Committee of the Security Council, consisting of all the members of the Council, to monitor implementation of this resolution, with the assistance of appropriate expertise, and calls upon all States to report to the Committee, no later than 90 days from the date of adoption of this resolution and thereafter according to a timetable to be proposed by the Committee, on the steps they have taken to implement this resolution;

7. Directs the Committee to delineate its tasks, submit a work

programme within 30 days of the adoption of this resolution, and to consider the support it requires, in consultation with the Secretary-General;

8. Expresses its determination to take all necessary steps in order to ensure the full implementation of this resolution, in accordance with its responsibilities under the Charter;

9. Decides to remain seized of this matter."

SAARC Regional Convention on Suppression of Terrorism
The Member States of the South Asian Association for Regional Cooperation (SAARC)

Mindful of the principles of cooperation enshrined in the SAARC Charter;

Recalling that at the Dhaka Summit on 7-8 December, 1985, the Heads of State or Government of the member States of the SAARC recognised the seriousness of the problem of terrorism as it affects the security and stability of the region;

Also Recalling the Bangalore Summit Declaration of 17 November 1986, in which the Heads of State or Government of SAARC agreed that cooperation among SAARC States was vital if terrorism was to be prevented and eliminated from the region; unequivocally condemned all acts, methods and practices of terrorism as criminal and deplored their impact on life and property, socio-economic development, political stability, regional and international peace and cooperation; and recognized the importance of the principles laid down in UN Resolution 2625 (XXV) which among others required that each state should refrain from organizing instigating, assisting or participating in acts of civil strife or terrorist acts in another state or acquiesing in organised activities within its territory directed towards the commission of such acts;

Aware of the danger posed by the spread of terrorism and its harmful effect on peace, cooperation, friendship and good neighbourly relations and which could also jeopardize the sovereignty and territorial integrity of states;

Have Resolved to take effective measures to ensure that perpetrators of terroristic acts do not escape prosecution and punishment by providing for their extradition or prosecution, and to this end,

***Have Agreed* as follows:**

Article 1

Subject to the overall requirements of the law of extradition, conduct constituting any of the following offences, according to the law of the Contracting State, shall be regarded as terroristic and for the purpose of extradition shall not be regarded as a political offence or as an offence connected with a political offence or as an offence inspired by political motives:

An offence within the scope of the Convention for the Suppression of Unlawful Seizure of Aircraft, signed at the Hague on 16 December 1970;

An offence within the scope of the Convention for the Suppression of Unlawful Acts against the Safety of Civil Aviation, signed at Montreal on 23 September 1971;

An offence within the scope of the Convention on the Prevention and Punishment of Crimes against Internationally Protected Persons, including Diplomatic Agents, signed at New York on 14 December 1973;

An offence within the scope of any Convention to which the SAARC member States concerned are parties and which obliges the parties to prosecute or grant extradition.

Murder, manslaughter, assault causing bodily harm, kidnapping, hostage-taking and offences relating to firearms, weapons, explosives and dangerous substances when used as a means to perpetrate indiscriminate violence involving death or serious bodily injury to persons or serious damage to property;

An attempt or conspiracy to commit an offence described in sub-paragraphs (a) to (e), aiding, abetting or counselling the commission of such an offence or participating as an accomplice in the offences so described.

Article II

For the purpose of extradition between SAARC member States, any two or more Contracting States may, by agreement, decide to include any other serious offence involving violence, which shall not be regarded as a political offence or an offence connected with a political offence or an offence inspired by political motives.

Article III

1. The provisions of all extradition treaties and arrangements applicable between Contracting States are hereby amended as between Contracting States to the extent that they are incompatible with the Convention.

2. For the purpose of this Convention and to the extent that any offence referred to in Article I or agreed to in terms of Article II is not listed

as an extraditable offence in any extradition treaty existing between Contracting States, it shall be deemed to be included as such therein.

3. Contracting States undertake to include these offences as extraditable offences in any future extradition treaty to be concluded between them.

4. If a Contracting State which makes extradition conditional on the existence of a treaty receives a request for extradition from another Contracting State with which it has no extradition treaty, the requested State may, at its option, consider this Convention as the basis for extradition in respect of the offences set forth in Article I or agreed to in terms of Article II. Extradition shall be subject to the law of the requested State.

5. Contracting States which do not make extradition conditional on the existence of a treaty, shall recognise the offences set forth in Article I or agreed to in terms of Article II as extraditable offences between themselves, subject to the law of the requested State.

Article IV

A Contracting State in whose territory a person suspected of having committed an offence referred to in Article I or agreed to in terms of Article II is found and which has received a request for extradition from another Contracting State, shall, if it does not extradite that person, submit the case without exception and without delay, to its competent authorities, so that prosecution may be considered. These authorities shall take their decisions in the same manner as in the case of any offence of a serious under the law of that State.

Article V

For the purpose of Article IV, each Contracting State may take such measures as it deems appropriate, consistent with its national laws, subject to reciprocity, to exercise its jurisdiction in the case of an offence under Article I or agreed to in terms of Article II.

Article VI

A Contracting State in whose territory an alleged offender is found, shall upon receiving a request for extradition from another Contracting State, take appropriate measures, subject to its national laws, so as to ensure his presence for purposes of extradition or prosecution. Such measures shall immediately be notified to the requesting State.

Article VII

Contracting States shall not be obliged to extradite, if it appears to the requested State that by reason of the trivial nature of the case or by reason of the request for the surrender or return of a fugitive offender not being made in good faith or in the interests of justice or for any other reason it is unjust or inexpedient to surrender or return the fugitive offender.

Article VIII

1. Contracting States shall, subject to their national laws, afford one another the greatest measure of mutual assistance in connection with proceedings brought in respect of the offences referred to in Article I or agreed to in terms of Article II, including the supply of all evidence at their disposal necessary for the proceedings.

2. Contracting States shall cooperate among themselves, to the extent permitted by their national laws, through consultations between appropriate agencies, exchange of information, intelligence and expertise and such other cooperative measures as may be appropriate, with a view to preventing terroristic activities through precautionary measures.

Article IX

1. The Convention shall be open for signature by the member States of SAARC at the SAARC Secretariat in Kathmandu.
2. It shall be subject to ratification. Instruments of Ratification shall be deposited with the Secretary-General of SAARC.

Article X

The Convention shall enter into force on the fifteenth day following the date of the deposit of the seventh Instrument of Ratification with the Secretary-General of SAARC.

Article XI

The Secretary-General of SAARC shall be depository of this Convention and shall notify member States of signatures to this Convention and all deposits of Instruments of Ratification. The Secretary-General shall transit certified copies of such Instruments to each member State. The Secretary-General shall also inform member States of the date on which this Convention will have entered into force in accordance with Article X.

In witness whereof the undersigned, being duly authorized thereto by their respective Governments, have signed this Convention.

Done at Kathmandu on this Fourth Day of November One Thousand Nine Hundred and Eighty-Seven, in eight originals, in the English language, all texts being equally authentic.

HUMAYUN RASHEED CHOUDHURY
Minister of Foreign Affairs People's Republic of
Bangladesh

DAWA TSERING
Minister of Foreign Affairs
Kingdom of Bhutan

K. NATWAR SINGH
Minister of State for External
Affairs Republic of India

FATHULLA JAMEEL
Minister of Foreign Affairs
Republic of Maldives

SHAILENDRA KUMAR
Minister for Foreign Affairs and Land Reforms
His Majesty's Government of Nepal

UPADHYAYA ZAIN NOORANI
Minister of State for Foreign Affairs
Islamic Republic of Pakistan

A.C. SHAHUL HAMEED
Minister of Foreign Affairs
Democratic Socialist Republic of Sri Lanka

Bangladesh-Suppression of Terrorist Offences Act, 1992
Act No. 44 of 1992: Dated 6 November 1992

Full text of the Anti-Terrorism Act passed by the Bangladesh parliament in November 1992. The Act defines terrorism and provides for institutional mechanism to deal with it

An Act to provide for the suppression of terrorist offences

Whereas it is expedient to provide for the suppression of terrorist offences;

Now, therefore, it is enacted as follows: -

1. Short title and commencement. - (1) This Act may be called the Suppression of Terrorist Offences Act, 1992.

(2) This Act shall come into force at once and it shall have effect for a period of two years unless such period is extended by Parliament. Notwithstanding the expiry of the period of this Act, any action done or any measure taken under this Act shall be deemed to have been done or taken under this Act.

2. Definitions. - Unless there is anything repugnant in the subject or context, in this Act-

(1) "Tribunal" means the Anti-Terrorism Tribunal established under Section 8;

(2) "Terrorist offence" means-

a) by holding out any kind of threat or applying any kind of illegal force-

i) to collect or acquire from any person or institution money or property as contributions, assistance or by whatever other name it may be called-

ii) to obstruct or impede the traffic by land, on railroads, by water or on air routes, or to alter the course of any vehicle against the wishes of the conductor of the vehicle-

b) to intentionally damage any vehicle;

c) to intentionally destroy or damage any property, whether movable or immovable, belonging to the Government or any institution under the control of the Government, or to any institute, authority or institution founded, established or created under the law, or to any company, firm or private non-governmental organization, any embassy or foreign institute or institution, or any person;

d) to steal or seize by force from any person any money, jewellery, valuable article or any other article or vehicle;

e) to outrage the modesty of, or to molest, any minor or adult woman, including any female child, adolescent and young woman on the streets or *ghats*, in vehicles, in educational institutions or in the vicinity thereof or in public places;

f) to create, alone or in a group, with or without premeditation, fear, terror, confusion or anarchy by ostentatiously displaying force or power at any place, in any building, shop, market and *bazar*, on any street or *ghat*, in any vehicle or in any institution;

g) to obstruct or impede by use of force the buying, accepting or entering of bills of sale by any institution or to illegally compel anybody to accept bills of sale;

(3) "Code of Criminal Procedure" means the Code of Criminal Procedure, 1898 (Act V of 1898).

3. Act to override other laws.- The provisions of this Act shall have effect, notwithstanding anything inconsistent contained in any other law for the time being in force.

4. Punishments for terrorist offences.- Whoever commits a terrorist offence shall be punishable with capital punishment or life imprisonment or rigorous imprisonment for a term which shall not exceed twenty years and not be less than five years, and shall also be liable to fine. Besides this, a Tribunal or the High Court Division may, in appropriate cases, in addition to the above-mentioned punishments, order the culprit to pay compensation to the injured person or institution.

5. Punishments for abatement of offences.- Whoever abets the commission of a terrorist offence shall be punishable with the punishments provided for in Section 4.

6. Provision regarding materials used or money collected in committing an offence.- A Tribunal may, if it thinks fit so to do, order any materials used or money collected in committing an

offence to be confiscated in favour of the Government or to be given back to the legal owner or possessor.

7. Trial of (terrorist) offences.- Notwithstanding anything to the contrary contained in any other law, offences under this Act are to be tried only by the Tribunals established under Section 8.

8. Establishment of Suppression of Terrorist Offences Tribunals.- (1) The Government may, for the purposes of this Act, establish, by notification in the official Gazette, in every Zila one or more Tribunals, which shall be called Suppression of Terrorist Offences Tribunals.

(2) There shall be one judge to each Tribunal and only a sitting or retired sessions judge or additional sessions judge shall be qualified to be a judge at such Tribunal.

(3) The judge of a Tribunal shall be appointed by the Government.

(4) The Government may, if necessary, appoint any sessions judge or additional sessions judge to any Tribunal beyond his jurisdiction.

(5) If more than one Tribunal is established in any Zila, the Government may, by notification in the official Gazette, determine the area of each Tribunal.

(6) Every Tribunal shall be situated in the headquarters of the Zila, but it may, on directions from the Government, conduct trials at any other place.

9. Jurisdiction of the Tribunal.- (1) No Tribunal shall take cognizance of an offence without a report in writing from a police officer not below the rank of an Inspector, or a person authorized, generally or in particular, in this behalf by the Government.

(2) If any other offence is connected with an offence under this Act in such way that it is necessary, in the interest of justice, to try both offences jointly or in one trial, such other offence and the offence under this Act shall be tried by the Tribunal jointly or in one trial.

(3) The proceedings required for a trial of an offence under this Act shall be taken by the Tribunal in the area of which such offence, or a part of it, has been committed, or by the Tribunal in the area of which the accused person or, in the case of there being more than one accused persons, any of the accused persons has been traced.

(4) A Tribunal may, if it thinks fit so to do, order any police officer or person referred to in sub-section (1) to make further investigations of an offence relating to any case pending before the Tribunal, and it may determine in the order the period, not exceeding fifteen days, within which the report of the investigation shall be produced.

Explanation.- The period referred to in the order under this section to make further investigations shall be included in the period referred to in sub-section (3) of Section 15.

(5) A Tribunal may award the punishments prescribed for offences under this Act as well as the punishments prescribed for the offences referred to in sub-section (2).

10. Procedure of trials.- (1) A Tribunal shall, when trying and deciding a case, follow the procedures prescribed by the Code of Criminal Procedure for the trial and decision of a case by a Sessions Court.

(2) A case brought up for trial before a Tribunal shall be conducted until its conclusion without any interruption from day to day, but a Tribunal may, if satisfied that it is, in the interest of justice, necessary to adjourn a trial, adjourn, after having recorded its reasons, a trial for a short period, which shall, however, under no circumstances exceed seven days.

(3) Where the Judge of a Tribunal has been transferred, the Judge succeeding him in office shall, if his predecessor has left the trial of any case, continue such trial from the stage at which it had been left, and if his predecessor has taken the testimony of a witness, such witness shall not be required to give his testimony again.

11. Trial in the absence of the accused.- (1) If a Tribunal has sufficient reason to believe that-

a) an accused person has absconded or is concealing himself in order to avoid being arrested or committed for trial, and

b) if there is no possibility of his imminent arrest, it may, by an order published in at least two Bengali daily newspapers, order the accused person to appear before the Tribunal within the period specified in the order, and may, if the accused person fails to appear before the Tribunal within such period, conduct the trial in his absence.

(2) The provision of sub-section (1) shall not apply in the case of an

accused person who absconds after appearing before a Tribunal or a Court, or after being produced before a Tribunal, and a Tribunal may, in such case, after recording reasons, conclude the trial against the accused person in the latter's absence.

12. Power of a Magistrate to take depositions.- (1) Where a police officer or any other person investigating an offence under this Act is of the opinion that it is necessary, in the interest of a prompt trial of the offence, to have, without any delay, a Magistrate take down in writing the deposition of a person who is well-informed about the occurrence, he may request, in written form, a Chief Metropolitan Magistrate or, as the case may be, a Zila Magistrate or any First Class Magistrate authorized in this behalf by the Government to take down in writing the deposition of such person.

(2) A Chief Metropolitan Magistrate or a Zila Magistrate shall, on receipt of a request under sub-section (2), without any delay, direct a Metropolita in Magistrate or, as the case may be, a First Class Magistrate to take the deposition of such person.

(3) The Magistrate who has received a direction under sub-section (2) or the Magistrate who has been authorized by the Government as mentioned in sub-section (1) shall take the deposition of the said person at the place of the occurrence or at any other appropriate place, and shall send the deposition thus taken to the police officer or person investigating the offence for being included in the report of the investigation.

(4) If, during the trial by a Tribunal of a person accused of an offence referred to in sub-section (1), it turns out that it is necessary to take the testimony of a person who made a deposition under sub-section (3), but such person has died, or is unable to give his testimony, or does not, in spite of being summoned, appear at the Tribunal, or cannot be traced, or cannot be produced at the tribunal without making efforts which involve such delays, expenditures or inconveniences as to make it undesirable under the circumstances so to do, the Tribunal may accept his deposition as a testimony in the trial.

13. Appeal and approval of death sentences.- (1) Any person aggrieved may, in accordance with the provisions of section 410 of the Code of Criminal Procedure, submit to the High Court Division an appeal against any sentence passed by the Tribunal within thirty days

after the date on which the sentence has been passed.

(2) A Tribunal, which has passed a death sentence, shall, in accordance with the provisions of Section 374 of the Code of Criminal Procedure, send without any delay the records of the proceeding to the High Court Division, and no death sentence shall be executed without the confirmation of such Division.

14. Offences to be cognizable and non-bailable.- (1) Offences under this Act shall be cognizable.

(2) Notwithstanding anything to the contrary contained in the Code of Criminal Procedure, no Magistrate or Tribunal nor any other Court may, at the stage of the investigations, order to release on bail any person accused of having committed an offence under this Act.

15. Code of Criminal Procedure to apply.- (1) Unless there is anything to the contrary contained in this Act, the provisions of the Code of Criminal Procedure shall apply in the case of instituting charges in connection with, investigating, trying, and in all other matters relating to, offences under this Act, and a Tribunal shall be deemed to be a Sessions Court.

(2) The investigation of an offence under this Act shall be concluded within thirty days after the date on which a statement about it has been received by the police:

Provided that an investigation which for any unavoidable reason cannot be concluded within such period shall, with the approval of the Tribunal, be concluded within an additional period of fifteen days.

(3) A Tribunal shall conclude the trial of any case within sixty days after the date on which the case came up for trial:

Provided that a Tribunal shall, if for any compelling reason a trial cannot be concluded within such period, conclude such trial, after recording such reason, within an additional period of thirty days.

16. Repeal and savings.- (1) The Suppression of Terrorist Offences Ordinance, 1992 (Ordinance No.7, 1992) stands hereby repealed.

(2) Notwithstanding such repeal, any action done or any measure taken under the repealed Ordinance shall be deemed to have been done or taken under this Act.

Bangladesh : Suppression of Terrorist Offences (Special Provisions) Act, 1994

Act No. 21 of 1994: Dated 1 December 1994

Full text of the Act which provides for settlement of unsettled issues which have been filed on or before November 5, 1994, when the Suppression of Terrorist Offences Act, 1992 expired.

An Act made to provide for the settlement of suits, appeals and other proceedings which are unsettled and which have been filed on or before the date on which expires the period of the Suppression of Terrorist Offences Act, 1992 and for the conduct of cases and other proceedings on the basis of completed investigations and incidental matters

Whereas the period of the Suppression of Terrorist Offences Act, 1992 (Act No.44 of 1992) has expired on 21st Kartik, 1401/fifth November, 1994, respectively, in accordance with section 1 (2) of the said Act;

and whereas it is expedient to provide for the settlement of suits, appeals and other proceedings which are unsettled and which have been filed on or before the date of expiry of the said period and for the conduct of cases and other proceeding on the basis of completed investigations and for matters ancillary thereto;

Now, therefore, it is enacted as follows:-

1. Short title and commencement.- (1) This Act may be called the Suppression of Terrorist Offences (Special Provisions) Act, 1994.

(2) This Act shall come into force on the 15th Kartik, 1401/31 October 1994, respectively.

2. Definition.- In this Act "completed investigation" shall mean the forwarding of a police report under section 173 of the Code of Criminal Procedure, 1898 (Act V of 1898), hereto after referred to as the said Code, at the end of an investigation in respect of any offence in accordance with the provisions of the Suppression of Terrorist Offences Act, 1992 (Act No.44 of 1992), hereto after referred to as the said Act.

3. Settlement of certain proceedings under Act No.44 of 1992.- Notwithstanding the expiry of the period of the said Act in accordance

with section 1 (2) of the said Act,-

a) all cases, appeals and other necessary proceedings including additional investigations in accordance with the said Act for the purpose of deciding on any offence the investigation in respect of which under the said Act has been completed on or before the date of expiry of the period of the said Act shall be taken and completed as if the period of the said Act had not expired.

b) all cases, appeals and other necessary proceedings under the said Act pending before any Tribunal established under the said Act or any other court immediately before the expiry of the period of the said Act and all additional investigations which have not been completed and which it is necessary to complete at the investigating authorities even after the expiry of the said period shall be taken and completed as if the period of the said Act had not expired;

c) all Tribunals established under the said Act shall, for the purpose of settling cases and any other proceedings under the clauses a) and b), be maintained until they are abolished by the Government through publication in the official Gazette.

4. Completing and deciding investigations in respect of offences under Act No.44 of 1992. Where the investigation of any offence under the said Act has not been completed before the expiry of the period of the said Act, the investigation shall be completed in accordance with the provisions of the said Code; and the trial of the offence and the other proceedings for this purpose shall be conducted in accordance with the Act and before the court or tribunal in accordance with which or before which they would have been conducted had the said Act not been made.

5. Repeal and savings.- (1) The Suppression of Terrorist Offences (Special Provisions) Ordinance, 1994 (Ordinance No.5 of 1994) stands herewith repealed.

(2) Notwithstanding such repeal, all actions done or measures taken under the repealed Ordinance shall be deemed to have been done or taken under this Act.

Bhutan: Thrimshung Chhenpo Tesa Wa Sum Law

Articles :

TSA 1: Matters regarding anti-nationals—those aversed to the development of the Kingdom of Bhutan and those who assist the enemies.

TSA 1-1: The King of Bhutan, the Kingdom of Bhutan and the Government of Bhutan are the three main elements of Bhutan.

TSA 1-2: Whether beneficial or harmful to one, whether big or small matters, whether high or low as mentioned at (O), any person who with the intention to cause harm, big or small, causes harm or is not able to cause harm to the three main elements or any of them as mentioned under the above clause TSA 1-1, if commits offences or does not commit or attempts to commit offences falling under the clause TSA 1-3 to TSA 1-10 shall be treated as a traitor and shall be liable to the punishment of treason as written under the clause TSA 1-11.

TSA 1-3: If death is caused to the three main elements of Bhutan or any of them or if such an attempt is made, if harm is caused to the body or the five organs or if such attempt is made.

TSA 1-4: If the three main elements or any one of them is challenged with weapons or without weapons.

TSA 1-5: If defamation is caused to the three main elements or any one of them within Bhutan or outside or if such an attempt is made.

TSA 1-6: If attempt is made to create differences between Bhutan and a foreign country.

TSA 1-7: If with the intention to cause harm to the three main elements or any one of them, the people within Bhutan or people of a foreign country are instigated or such an attempt is made.

TSA 1-8: If with the intention to cause serious harm to the three main elements or any one of them, correspondence is made or conversation is held (whatever, the topic may be) with persons within Bhutan or with foreign nationals or if correspondence is made or conversation is held with persons in Bhutan and foreign nationals (who are not supposed to be conversed with).

TSA 1-9: If any conspiracy is heard or seen with intentions to cause harm to the three main elements or any one of them, if someone known to be antinational, if such matter is concealed and not reported immediately to the Government.

TSA 1-10: If known to be rebels or enemies against the three main elements or any one of them (if known or recognized to be a rebel or an enemy), if arms are sold to them or given freely or given for use, if guided, if secrets are disclosed, if food-water is provided or if any help is given to increase the rebel manpower or earnings.

TSA 1-11: All those who commit offences or do not commit or attempt to commit them as described under the above clause TSA 1-3 to TSA 1-10 shall be treated as anti-national and shall be liable to punishment for treason.

India: The Anti - Hijacking Act, 1982, No. 65 OF 1982

(Received the assent of the President on 6 November 1982)

An Act to give effect to the Convention for the Suppression of Unlawful Seizure of Aircraft and for matters connected therewith.

WHEREAS a Convention for the Suppression of Unlawful Seizure of Aircraft was, on the 16th day of December 1970, signed at The Hague;

AND WHEREAS it is expedient that India should accede to the said Convention and make provisions for giving effect thereto and for matters connected there with;

BE it enacted by Parliament in the Thirty-third Year of the Republic of India as follows:-

CHAPTER I - PRELIMINARY

1. Short title, extent application and commencement

(1) This Act may be called the Anti-Hijacking Act, 1982.

(2) It extends to the whole of India and, save as otherwise provided in this Act, it applies also to any offence thereunder committed outside India by any Person.

(3) It shall come into force on such date as the Central Government may, by notification in the Official Gazette, appoint.

2. Definitions

In this Act, unless the context otherwise requires,-

a "aircraft" means any aircraft, whether or not registered in India, other than a military aircraft or an aircraft used in customs or police service;

b "aircraft registered in India" means an aircraft which is for the time being registered in India;

c. "Convention country" means a country in which The Hague Convention is for the time being in force;

d. "Hague Convention" means the Convention for the Suppression of Unlawful Seizure of Aircraft signed at The Hague on the 16th day of December, 1970;

e. "military aircraft" means an aircraft of the naval, military, air force or any other armed forces of any country and includes every aircraft commanded for the time being by a person in any such force detailed for the purpose.

CHAPTER II - HIJACKING AND CONNECTED OFFENCES

3. Hijacking

(1) Whoever on broad an aircraft in flight, unlawfully, by force or threat of force or by any other form of intimidation, seizes or exercises control of that aircraft, commits the offence of hijacking of such aircraft.

(2) Whoever attempts to commit any of the acts referred to in sub-section (I) in relation to any aircraft, or abets the commission of any such act, shall also be deemed to have committed the offence of hijacking of such aircraft.

(3) For the purposes of this section, an aircraft shall be deemed to be in flight at any time from the moment when all its external doors are closed following embarkation until the moment when any such door is opened for disembarkation, and in the case of a forced landing, the fight shall be deemed to continue until the competent authorities of the country in which such forced lading takes place take over the responsibility for the aircraft and for persons and property on board.

4. Punishment for hijacking

Whoever commits the offence of hijacking shall be punished with imprisonment for life and shall also be liable to fine.

5. Punishment for acts to violence connected with hijacking

Whoever, being a person committing the offence of hijacking of an aircraft, commits, in connection with such offence, any act of violence against any passenger or member of the crew of such aircraft, shall be punished with the same punishment with which he would have been punishable under any law for the time being in force in India if such act had been committed in India.

6. Jurisdiction

(1) Subject to the provision of Sub-section (2), where an offence under Section 4 or Section 5 is committed outside India, the person

committing such offence may be dealt with in respect thereof as if such offence had been committed at any place within India at which he may be found.

2. No court shall take cognizance of an offence punishable under Section 4 or Section 5 which is committed outside India unless –

(a) such offence is committed on board an aircraft registered in India;

(b) such offence is committed on board an aircraft which is for the time being leased without crew to a lessee who has his principal place of business or where he had no such place of business, his permanent residence in India; or

(c) the alleged offender is a citizen of India or is on board the aircraft in relation to which such offence is committed when it lands in India or is found in India.

CHAPTER III - MISCELLANEOUS

7. Provisions as to extradition

1. The offences under Section 4 and Section 5 shall be deemed to have been included as extraditable offences and provided for in all the extradition treaties made by India with Convention countries and which extend to, and are binding on, India on the date of commencement of this Act.

2. For the purposes of the application of the Extradition Act, 1962 (34 of 1962) the offences under this Act, any aircraft registered in a Convention country shall, at any time while that aircraft is in flight, be deemed to be within the jurisdiction of that country, whether or not it is for the time being also within the jurisdiction of any other country.

8. Contracting parties of Convention

The Central Government may, by notification in the Official Gazette, certify as to who are the contracting parties to The Hague Convention and to what extent they have availed themselves of the provisions of the Convention, and any such notification shall be conclusive evidence of the matters certified therein.

9. Power to treat certain aircraft to be registered in Convention countries

If the Central Government is satisfied that the requirements of Article 5 of The Hague Convention have been satisfied in relation to any aircraft, it may, by notification in the Official Gazette, direct that such aircraft shall, for the purposes of this Act, be treated as registered in such Convention country as may be specified in the notification.

10. Previous sanction necessary for prosecution

No prosecution for an offence under this Act shall be instituted except with the previous sanction of the Central Government.

11. Protection of action taken in good faith

1. No suit, prosecution or other legal proceeding shall lie against any person for anything which is in good faith done or intended to be done in pursuance of the provisions of this Act.

2. No suit or other legal proceedings shall lie against the Central Government for any damage caused or likely to be caused for anything which is in good faith done or intended to be done in pursuance of the provisions of this Act.

India: The Prevention of Terrorism Act, 2002

The Prevention of Terrorism Act, enacted on 28 March 2002, replaced the ***Prevention of Terrorism Ordinance (POTO) 2001****. The Act has now come into force after the President of India gave his assent.*

THE PREVENTION OF TERRORISM ACT, 2002
Act No. 15 of 2002

Objective: An Act to make provisions for the prevention of, and for dealing with, terrorist activities and for matters connected therewith. BE it enacted by Parliament in the Fifty-third Year of the Republic of India as follows: -

CHAPTER I
PRELIMINARY

1. Short title, application, commencement, duration and savings.-(1) This Act may be called the Prevention of Terrorism Act, 2002.

(2) It extends to the whole of India.

(3) Every person shall be liable to punishment under this Act for every act or omission contrary to the provisions thereof, of which he is held guilty in India.

(4) Any person who commits an offence beyond India which is punishable under this Act shall be dealt with according to the provisions of this Act in the same manner as if such act had been committed in India.

(5) The provisions of this Act apply also to-

(a) citizens of India outside India;

(b) persons in the service of the Government, wherever they may be; and

(c) persons on ships and aircrafts, registered in India, wherever they may be.

(6) Save as otherwise provided in respect of entries at serial numbers 24 and 25 of the Schedule to this Act, it shall be deemed to have come into force on the 24th day of October, 2001 and shall remain in force for a period of three years from the date f its commencement,

but its expiry under the operation of this sub-section shall not affect-

(a) the previous operation of, or anything duly done or suffered under this Act, or

(b) any right, privilege, obligation or liability acquired, accrued or incurred under this Act, or

(c) any penalty, forfeiture or punishment incurred in respect of any offence under this Act, or

(d) any investigation, legal proceeding or remedy in respect of any such right, privilege, obligation, liability, penalty, forfeiture or punishment as aforesaid, and, any such investigation, legal proceeding or remedy may be instituted, continued or enforced and any such penalty, forfeiture or punishment may be imposed as if this Act had not expired.

2. Definitions.-(1) In this Act, unless the context otherwise requires,-

(a) "Code" means the Code of Criminal Procedure, 1973 (2 of 1974);

(b) "Designated Authority" shall mean such officer of the Central Government not below the rank of Joint Secretary to the Government, or such officer of the State Government not below the rank of Secretary to the Government, as the case may be, as may be specified by the Central Government or, as the case may be, the State Government, by a notification published in the Official Gazette;

(c) "proceeds of terrorism" shall mean all kinds of properties which have been derived or obtained from commission of any terrorist act or have been acquired through funds traceable to a terrorist act, and shall include cash irrespective of person in who e name such proceeds are standing or in whose possession they are found;

(d) "property" means property and assets of every description, whether corporeal or incorporeal, movable or immovable, tangible or intangible and deeds and instruments evidencing title to, or interest in, such property or assets and includes bank account

(e) "Public Prosecutor" means a Public Prosecutor or an Additional Public Prosecutor or a Special Public Prosecutor appointed under Section 28 and includes any person acting under the directions of the Public Prosecutor;

(f) "Special Court" means a Special Court constituted under Section 23;

(g) "terrorist act" has the meaning assigned to it in sub-section (1) of Section 3, and the expression "terrorist" shall be construed accordingly;

(h) "State Government", in relation to a Union territory, means the Administrator thereof;

(i) words and expressions used but not defined in this Act and defined in the Code shall have the meanings respectively assigned to them in the Code.

(2) Any reference in this Act to any enactment or any provision thereof shall, in relation to an area in which such enactment or such provision is not in force, be construed as a reference to the corresponding law or the relevant provision of the corresponding law, if any, in force in that area.

CHAPTER II
PUNISHMENT FOR, AND MEASURES FOR DEALING WITH, TERRORIST ACTIVITIES

3. Punishment for terrorist acts.-(1) Whoever,-

(a) with intent to threaten the unity, integrity, security or sovereignty of India or to strike terror in the people or any section of the people does any act or thing by using bombs, dynamite or other explosive substances or inflammable substances or firearms or other lethal weapons or poisons or noxious gases or other chemicals or by any other substances (whether biological or otherwise) of a hazardous nature or by any other means whatsoever, in such a manner as to cause, or likely to cause, death of, r injuries to any person or persons or loss of, or damage to, or destruction of, property or disruption of any supplies or services essential to the life of the community or causes damage or destruction of any property or equipment used or intended to be used for the defence of India or in connection with any other purposes of the Government of India, any State Government or any of their agencies, or detains any person and threatens to kill or injure such person in order to compel the Government or any o her person to do or abstain from doing any act;

(b) is or continues to be a member of an association declared unlawful under the Unlawful Activities (Prevention) Act, 1967 (37 of 1967), or voluntarily does an act aiding or promoting in any manner the objects of such association and in either case is i possession of any unlicensed firearms, ammunition, explosive or other instrument or substance capable of causing mass destruction and commits any act resulting in loss of human life or grievous injury to any person or causes significant damage to any property, commits a terrorist act.

Explanation.-For the purposes of this sub-section, "a terrorist act" shall include the act of raising funds intended for the purpose of terrorism.

(2) Whoever commits a terrorist act, shall,-

(a) if such act has resulted in the death of any person, be punishable with death or imprisonment for life and shall also be liable to fine;

(b) in any other case, be punishable with imprisonment for a term which shall not be less than five years but which may extend to imprisonment for life and shall also be liable to fine.

(3) Whoever conspires or attempts to commit, or advocates, abets, advises or incites or knowingly facilitates the commission of, a terrorist act or any act preparatory to a terrorist act, shall be punishable with imprisonment for a term which shall not b less than five years but which may extend to imprisonment for life and shall also be liable to fine.

(4) Whoever voluntarily harbours or conceals, or attempts to harbour or conceal any person knowing that such person is a terrorist shall be punishable with imprisonment for a term which shall not be less than three years but which may extend to imprisonment for life and shall also be liable to fine:

Provided that this sub-section shall not apply to any case in which the harbour or concealment is by the husband or wife of the offender.

(5) Any person who is a member of a terrorist gang or a terrorist organization, which is involved in terrorist acts, shall be punishable with imprisonment for a term which may extend to imprisonment for life or with fine which may extend to rupees ten lakhs or with both.

Explanation.-For the purposes of this sub-section, "terrorist organization" means an organization which is concerned with or involved in terrorism.

(6) Whoever knowingly holds any property derived or obtained from commission of any terrorist act or has been acquired through the terrorist funds shall be punishable with imprisonment for a term which may extend to imprisonment for life or with fine which may extend to rupees ten lakh or with both.

(7) Whoever threatens any person who is a witness or any other person in whom such witness may be interested, with violence, or wrongfully restrains or confines the witness, or any other person in whom the witness may be interested, or does any other unlawful act with the said intent, shall be punishable with imprisonment which may extend to three years and fine.

4. Possession of certain unauthorized arms, etc.-Where any person is in unauthorised possession of any-

(a) arms or ammunition specified in columns (2) and (3) of Category I or Category III (a) of Schedule I to the Arms Rules, 1962, in a notified area,

(b) bombs, dynamite or hazardous explosive substances or other lethal weapons capable of mass destruction or biological or chemical substances of warfare in any area, whether notified or not, he shall be guilty of terrorist act notwithstanding anything contained in any other law for the time being in force, and be punishable with imprisonment for a term which may extend to imprisonment for life or with fine which may extend to rupees ten lakh or with both.

Explanation.-In this section, "notified area" means such area as the State Government may, by notification in the Official Gazette, specify.

5. Enhanced penalties.-(1) If any person with intent to aid any terrorist contravenes any provision of, or any rule made under the Explosives Act, 1884 (4 of 1884), the Explosive Substances Act, 1908 (6 of 1908), the Inflammable Substances Act, 1952 (20 f 1952) or the Arms Act, 1959 (54 of 1959), he shall, notwithstanding anything contained in any of the aforesaid Acts or the rules made thereunder, be punishable with imprisonment for a term which may extend to imprisonment for life and shall also be liable to fine.

(2) For the purposes of this section, any person who attempts to contravene or abets, or does any act preparatory to the contravention of any provision of any law, rule or order, shall be deemed to have contravened that provision, and the provisions of s b-section (1) shall, in relation to such person, have effect subject to the modification that the reference to "imprisonment for life" shall be construed as a reference to "imprisonment for ten years".

6. Holding of proceeds of terrorism illegal.-(1) No person shall hold or be in possession of any proceeds of terrorism.

(2) Proceeds of terrorism, whether held by a terrorist or by any other person and whether or not such person is prosecuted or convicted under this Act, shall be liable to be forfeited to the Central Government or the State Government, as the case may be, in the manner provided under this Chapter.

7. Powers of investigating officers and appeal against order of Designated Authority.-(1) If an officer (not below the rank of Superintendent of Police) investigating an offence committed under this Act, has reason to believe that any property in relation to which an investigation is being conducted, represents proceeds of terrorism, he shall, with the prior approval in writing of the Director General of the Police of the State in which such property is situated, make an order seizing such property and w ere it is not practicable to seize such property, make an order of attachment directing that such property shall not be transferred or otherwise dealt with except with the prior permission of the officer making such order, or of the Designated Authority before whom the properties seized or attached are produced and a copy of such order shall be served on the person concerned.

(2) For the removal of doubts, it is hereby provided that where an organization is declared as a terrorist organization under this Act and the investigating officer has reason to believe that any person has custody of any property which is being used or s intended to be used for the purpose of such terrorist organisation, he may, by an order in writing, seize or attach such property.

(3) The investigating officer shall duly inform the Designated Authority within forty-eight hours of the seizure or attachment of such property.

(4) It shall be open to the Designated Authority before whom the seized or attached properties are produced either to confirm or revoke the order of attachment so issued:

Provided that an opportunity of making a representation by the person whose property is being attached shall be given.

(5) In the case of immovable property attached by the investigating officer, it shall be deemed to have been produced before the Designated Authority, when the investigating officer notifies his report and places it at the disposal of the Designated Authority.

(6) The investigating officer may seize and detain any cash to which this Chapter applies if he has reasonable grounds for suspecting that-

(a) it is intended to be used for the purposes of terrorism;

(b) it forms the whole or part of the resources of an organisation declared as terrorist organization under this Act:

Provided that the cash seized under this sub-section by the investigating officer shall be released not later than the period of forty-eight hours beginning with the time when it is seized unless the matter involving the cash is before the Designated Authority and such Authority passes an order allowing its retention beyond forty-eight hours.

Explanation.-For the purposes of this sub-section, "cash" means-

(a) coins and notes in any currency;

(b) postal orders;

(c) traveller's cheques;

(d) banker's drafts; and

(e) such other monetary instruments as the Central Government or, as the case may be, the State Government may specify by an order made in writing.

(7) Any person aggrieved by an order made by the Designated Authority may prefer an appeal to the Special Court and the Special Court may either confirm the order of attachment of property or seizure so made or revoke such order and release the property.

8. Forfeiture of proceeds of terrorism.-Where any property is seized or attached on the ground that it constitutes proceeds of terrorism and the Special Court is satisfied in this regard under sub-Section (7) of section 7, it may order forfeiture of such property, whether or not the person from whose possession it is seized or attached, is prosecuted in a Special Court for an offence under this Act.

9. Forfeiture of proceeds of terrorism.-Where any property is seized or attached on the ground that it constitutes proceeds of terrorism and the Special Court is satisfied in this regard under sub-section (7) of section 7, it may order forfeiture of such property, whether or not the person from whose possession it is seized or attached, is prosecuted in a Special Court for an offence under this Act.

10. Issue of show cause notice before forfeiture of proceeds of terrorism.-(1) No order forfeiting any proceeds of terrorism shall be made under section 8 unless the person holding or in possession of such proceeds is given a notice in writing informing h m of the grounds on which it is proposed to forfeit the proceeds of terrorism and such person is given an opportunity of making a representation in writing within such reasonable time as may be specified in the notice against the grounds of forfeiture an is also given a reasonable opportunity of being heard in the matter.

(2) No order of forfeiture shall be made under sub-section (1), if such person establishes that he is a bona fide transferee of such proceeds for value without knowing that they represent proceeds of terrorism.

(3) It shall be competent for the Special Court to make an order in respect of property seized or attached,-

(a) directing it to be sold if it is a perishable property and the provisions of Section 459 of the Code shall, as nearly as may be practicable, apply to the net proceeds of such sale;

(b) nominating any officer of the Central or State Government, in the case of any other property, to perform the function of the Administrator of such property subject to such conditions as may be specified by the Special Court.

11. Appeal.-(1) Any person aggrieved by an order of forfeiture under section 8 may, within one month from the date of the receipt of such order, appeal to the High Court within whose jurisdiction,

the Special Court, who passed the order appealed against, is situated.

(2) Where an order under section 8 is modified or annulled by the High Court or where in a prosecution instituted for the contravention of the provisions of this Act, the person against whom an order of forfeiture has been made under Section 8 is acquitted, such property shall be returned to him and in either case if it is not possible for any reason to return the forfeited property, such person shall be paid the price therefor as if the property had been sold to the Central Government with reasonable interest calculated from the day of seizure of the property and such price shall be determined in the manner prescribed.

12. Order of forfeiture not to interfere with other punishments.-The order of forfeiture made under this Act by the Special Court, shall not prevent the infliction of any other punishment to which the person affected thereby is liable under this Act

13. Claims by third party.-(1) Where any claim is preferred, or any objection is made to the seizure of any property under Section 7 on the ground that such property is not liable to seizure, the Designated Authority before whom such property is produced shall proceed to investigate the claim or objection:

Provided that no such investigation shall be made where the Designated Authority considers that the claim or objection is designed to cause unnecessary delay.

(2) In case claimant or objector establishes that the property specified in the notice issued under section 9 is not liable to be forfeited under the Act, the said notice shall be withdrawn or modified accordingly.

14. Powers of Designated Authority.-The Designated Authority, acting under the provisions of this Act, shall have all the powers of a civil court required for making a full and fair enquiry into the matter before it.

15. Obligation to furnish information.-(1) Notwithstanding anything contained in any other law, the officer investigating any offence under this Act, with prior approval in writing of an officer not below the rank of a Superintendent of Police, may require any officer or authority of the Central Government or a State Government or a local authority or a bank, or a company, or a firm

or any other institution, establishment, organisation or any individual to furnish information in their possession in relation to such offence, on points or matters, where the investigating officer has reason to believe that such information will be useful for, or relevant to, the purposes of this Act.

(2) Failure to furnish the information called for under sub-section (1), or deliberately furnishing false information shall be punishable with imprisonment for a term which may extend to three years or with fine or with both.

(3) Notwithstanding anything contained in the Code, the offence under sub-section (1) shall be tried as a summary case and the procedure prescribed in Chapter XXI of the said Code [except sub-section (2) of Section 262] shall be applicable thereto.

16. Certain transfers to be null and void.-Where, after the issue of an order under Section 7 or issue of a notice under Section 9, any property referred to in the said order or notice is transferred by any mode whatsoever, such transfer shall, for the purpose of the proceedings under this Act, be ignored and if such property is subsequently forfeited, the transfer of such property shall be deemed to be null and void.

17. Forfeiture of property of certain persons.-(1) Where any person is accused of any offence under this Act, it shall be open to the Special Court trying him to pass an order that all or any of the properties, movable or immovable or both belonging to h m, shall, during the period of such trial, be attached, if not already attached under this Act.

(2) Where a person has been convicted of any offence punishable under this Act, the Special Court may, in addition to awarding any punishment, by order in writing, declare that any property, movable or immovable or both, belonging to the accused and specified in the order, shall stand forfeited to the Central Government or the State Government, as the case may be, free from all encumbrances.

18. Company to transfer shares to Government.-Where any shares in a company stand forfeited to the Central Government or the State Government, as the case may be, under this Act, then, the company shall, on receipt of the order of the Special Court, notwithstanding

anything contained in the Companies Act, 1956 (1 of 1956), or the articles of association of the company, forthwith register the Central Government or the State Government, as the case may be, as the transferee of such shares.

CHAPTER III
TERRORIST ORGANISATIONS

19. Declaration of an organization as a terrorist organization.-(1) For the purposes of this Act, an organization is a terrorist organization if-

(a) it is listed in the Schedule, or

(b) it operates under the same name as an organization listed in that Schedule.

(2) The Central Government may by order, in the Official Gazette,-

(a) add an organization to the Schedule;

(b) remove an organization from that Schedule;

(c) amend that Schedule in some other way.

(3) The Central Government may exercise its power under clause (a) of sub-section (2) in respect of an organization only if it believes that it is involved in terrorism.

(4) For the purposes of sub-section (3), an organization shall be deemed to be involved in terrorism if it-

(a) commits or participates in acts of terrorism,

(b) prepares for terrorism,

(c) promotes or encourages terrorism, or

(d) is otherwise involved in terrorism.

20. Denotification of a terrorist organization.-(1) An application may be made to the Central Government for the exercise of its power under clause (b) of sub-section (2) of section 18 to remove an organization from the Schedule.

(2) An application may be made by-

(a) the organization, or

(b) any person affected by inclusion of the organization in the Schedule as a terrorist organization.

(3) The Central Government may make rules to prescribe the procedure for admission and disposal of an application made under this section.

(4) Where an application under sub-section (1) has been refused, the applicant may apply for a review to the Review Committee constituted by the Central Government under sub-section (1) of section 60 within one month from the date of receipt of the order by the applicant.

(5) The Review Committee may allow an application for review against refusal to remove an organization from the Schedule, if it csonsiders that the decision to refuse was flawed when considered in the light of the principles applicable on an application for judicial review.

(6) Where the Review Committee allows review under sub-section (5) by or in respect of an organization, it may make an order under this sub-section.

(7) Where an order is made under sub-Section (6), the Central Government shall, as soon as the certified copy of the order is received by it, make an order removing the organization from the list in the Schedule.

21. Offence relating to membership of a terrorist organization.-(1) A person commits an offence if he belongs or professes to belong to a terrorist organization:

Provided that this sub-section shall not apply where the person charged is able to prove-

(a) that the organization was not declared as a terrorist organization at the time when he became a member or began to profess to be a member; and

(b) that he has not taken part in the activities of the organization at any time during its inclusion in the Schedule as a terrorist organization.

(2) A person guilty of an offence under this section shall be liable, on conviction, to imprisonment for a term not exceeding ten years or with fine or with both.

22. Offence relating to support given to a terrorist organization.-(1) A person commits an offence if-

(a) he invites support for a terrorist organization, and

(b) the support is not, or is not restricted to, the provision of money or other property within the meaning of Section 22.

(2) A person commits an offence if he arranges, manages or assists in arranging or managing a meeting, which he knows is-

(a) to support a terrorist organization, or

(b) to further the activities of a terrorist organization, or

(c) to be addressed by a person who belongs or professes to belong to a terrorist organization.

(3) A person commits an offence if he addresses a meeting for the purpose of encouraging support for a terrorist organization or to further its activities.

(4) A person guilty of an offence under this section shall be liable on conviction, to imprisonment for a term not exceeding ten years or with fine or with both.

Explanation.-For the purposes of this section, the expression "meeting" means a meeting of three or more persons whether or not the public are admitted.

23. Fund raising for a terrorist organization to be an offence.-(1) A person commits an offence if he-

(a) invites another to provide money or other property, and

(b) intends that it should be used, or has reasonable cause to suspect that it may be used, for the purposes of terrorism.

(2) A person commits an offence if he-

(a) receives money or other property, and

(b) intends that it should be used, or has reasonable cause to suspect that it may be used, for the purposes of terrorism.

(3) A person commits an offence if he-

(a) provides money or other property, and

(b) knows or has reasonable cause to suspect that it will or may be used for the purposes of terrorism.

(4) In this section, a reference to the provision of money or other property is a reference to its being given, lent or otherwise made available, whether or not for consideration.

(5) A person guilty of an offence under this section shall be liable on conviction, to imprisonment for a term not exceeding fourteen years or with fine or with both.

CHAPTER IV
SPECIAL COURTS

24. Special Courts.-(1) The Central Government or a State Government may, by notification in the Official Gazette, constitute one or more Special Courts for such area or areas, or for such case or class or group of cases, as may be specified in the notification.

(2) Where a notification constituting a Special Court for any area or areas or for any case or class or group of cases is issued by the Central Government under sub-section (1), and a notification constituting a Special Court for the same area or areas o for the same case or class or group of cases has also been issued by the State Government under that sub-section, the Special Court constituted by the Central Government, whether the notification constituting such Court is issued before or after the issue of the notification constituting the Special Court by the State Government, shall have, and the Special Court constituted by the State Government shall not have, jurisdiction to try any offence committed in that area or areas or, as the case may be, th case or class or group of cases and all cases pending before any Special Court constituted by the State Government shall stand transferred to the Special Court constituted by the Central Government.

(3) Where any question arises as to the jurisdiction of any Special Court, it shall be referred to the Central Government whose decision in the matter shall be final.

(4) A Special Court shall be presided over by a judge to be appointed by the Central Government or, as the case may be, the State Government, with the concurrence of the Chief Justice of the High Court.

(5) The Central Government or, as the case may be, the State Government may also appoint, with the concurrence of the Chief Justice of the High Court, additional judges to exercise jurisdiction of a Special Court.

(6) A person shall not be qualified for appointment as a judge or an additional judge of a Special Court unless he is, immediately before such appointment, a sessions judge or an additional sessions judge in any State.

(7) For the removal of doubts, it is hereby provided that the attainment, by a person appointed as a judge or an additional judge of a Special Court, of the age of superannuation under the rules applicable to him in the service to which he belongs, shall not affect his continuance as such judge or additional judge.

(8) Where any additional judge or additional judges is or are appointed in a Special Court, the judge of the Special Court may, from time to time, by general or special order, in writing, provide for the distribution of business of the Special Court among all judges including himself and the additional judge or additional judges and also for the disposal of urgent business in the event of his absence or the absence of any additional judge.

25. Place of sitting.-A Special Court may, on its own motion, or on an application made by the Public Prosecutor and if it considers it expedient or desirable so to do, sit for any of its proceedings at any place other than its ordinary place of sitting:

Provided that nothing in this section shall be construed to change the place of sitting of a Special Court constituted by a State Government to any place outside that State.

26. Jurisdiction of Special Courts.-(1) Notwithstanding anything contained in the Code, every offence punishable under any provision of this Act shall be triable only by the Special Court within whose local jurisdiction it was committed or, as the case may be, by the Special Court constituted for trying such offence under Section 23.

(2) If, having regard to the exigencies of the situation prevailing in

a State,-

(a) it is not possible to have a fair, impartial or speedy trial; or

(b) it is not feasible to have the trial without occasioning the breach of peace or grave risk to the safety of the accused, the witnesses, the Public Prosecutor and a judge of the Special Court or any of them; or

(c) it is not otherwise in the interests of justice, the Supreme Court may transfer any case pending before a Special Court to any other Special Court within that State or in any other State and the High Court may transfer any case pending before a Special Court situated in that State to any other Special court within the State.

(3) The Supreme Court or the High Court, as the case may be, may act under this section either on the application of the Central Government or a party interested and any such application shall be made by motion, which shall, except when the applicant is he Attorney-General of India, be supported by an affidavit or affirmation.

27. Power of Special Courts with respect to other offences.-(1) When trying any offence, a Special Court may also try any other offence with which the accused may, under the Code, be charged at the same trial if the offence is connected with such other o fence.

(2) If, in the course of any trial under this Act of any offence, it is found that the accused person has committed any other offence under this Act or under any other law, the Special Court may convict such person of such other offence and pass any sentence or award punishment authorised by this Act or such rule or, as the case may be, under such other law.

28. Power to direct for samples, etc.-(1) When a police officer investigating a case requests the Court of a Chief Judicial Magistrate or the Court of a Chief Metropolitan Magistrate in writing for obtaining samples of handwriting, finger-prints, foot-prints, photographs, blood, saliva, semen, hair, voice of any accused person, reasonably suspected to be involved in the commission of an offence under this Act, it shall be lawful for the Court of a Chief Judicial Magistrate or the Court of a Chief Metropolitan Magistrate to direct that such samples be given by the accused person to the police officer either through a medical practitioner or otherwise, as the case may be.

(2) If any accused person refuses to give samples as provided in sub-

section (1), the Court shall draw adverse inference against the accused.

29. Public Prosecutors.-(1) For every Special Court, the Central Government or, as the case may be, the State Government, shall appoint a person to be the Public Prosecutor and may appoint one or more persons to be the Additional Public Prosecutor or Additional Public Prosecutors:

Provided that the Central Government or, as the case may be, the State Government, may also appoint for any case or class or group of cases, a Special Public Prosecutor.

(2) A person shall not be qualified to be appointed as a Public Prosecutor or an Additional Public Prosecutor or a Special Public Prosecutor under this section unless he has been in practice as an Advocate for not less than seven years or has held any post, for a period of not less than seven years, under the Union or a State, requiring special knowledge of law.

(3) Every person appointed as a Public Prosecutor or an Additional Public Prosecutor or a Special Public Prosecutor under this section shall be deemed to be a Public Prosecutor within the meaning of clause (u) of Section 2 of the Code, and the provision of the Code shall have effect accordingly.

30. Procedure and powers of Special Courts.-(1) Subject to the provisions of section 50, a Special Court may take cognizance of any offence, without the accused being committed to it for trial, upon receiving a complaint of facts that constitute such offence or upon a police report of such facts.

(2) Where an offence triable by a Special Court is punishable with imprisonment for a term not exceeding three years or with fine or with both, the Special Court may, notwithstanding anything contained in sub-Section (1) of Section 260 or Section 262 of he Code, try the offence in a summary way in accordance with the procedure prescribed in the Code and the provisions of Sections 263 to 265 of the Code, shall so far as may be, apply to such trial:

Provided that when, in the course of a summary trial under this sub-section, it appears to the Special Court that the nature of the case is such that it is undesirable to try it in a summary way, the Special Court shall recall any witnesses who may have been examined and proceed to re-hear the case in the manner provided by the provisions of the Code for the trial of such offence and the said provisions shall apply to and in relation to a Special Court as they apply to and in relation to a Magistrate:

Provided further that in the case of any conviction in a summary trial under this section, it shall be lawful for a Special Court to pass a sentence of imprisonment for a term not exceeding one year and with fine which may extend to rupees five lakh.

(3) Subject to the other provisions of this Act, a Special Court shall, for the purpose of trial of any offence, have all the powers of a Court of Session and shall try such offence as if it were a Court of Session so far as may be in accordance with the procedure prescribed in the Code for the trial before a Court of Session.

(4) Subject to the other provisions of this Act, every case transferred to a Special Court under section 25 shall be dealt with as if such case had been transferred under section 406 of the Code to such Special Court.

(5) Notwithstanding anything contained in the Code, but subject to the provisions of Section 299 of the Code, a Special Court may, if it thinks fit and for reasons to be recorded by it, proceed with the trial in the absence of the accused or his pleader and record the evidence of any witness, subject to the right of the accused to recall the witness for cross-examination.

31. Protection of witnesses.-(1) Notwithstanding anything contained in the Code, the proceedings under this Act may, for reasons to be recorded in writing, be held in camera if the Special Court so desires.

(2) A Special Court, if on an application made by a witness in any proceeding before it or by the Public Prosecutor in relation to such witness or on its own motion, is satisfied that the life of such witness is in danger, it may, for reasons to be recorded in writing, take such measures as it deems fit for keeping the identity and address of such witness secret.

(3) In particular, and without prejudice to the generality of the provisions of sub-section (2), the measures which a Special Court may take under that sub-section may include-

(a) the holding of the proceedings at a place to be decided by the Special

Court;

(b) the avoiding of the mention of the names and addresses of the witnesses in its orders or judgments or in any records of the case accessible to public;

(c) the issuing of any directions for securing that the identity and address of the witnesses are not disclosed;

(d) a decision that it is in the public interest to order that all or any of the proceedings pending before such a Court shall not be published in any manner.

(4) Any person who contravenes any decision or direction issued under sub-section (3) shall be punishable with imprisonment for a term which may extend to one year and with fine which may extend to one thousand rupees.

32. Trial by Special Courts to have precedence.-The trial under this Act of any offence by a Special Court shall have precedence over the trial of any other case against the accused in any other court (not being a Special Court) and shall be concluded in preference to the trial of such other case and accordingly the trial of such other case shall remain in abeyance.

33. Certain confessions made to police officers to be taken into consideration.-(1) Notwithstanding anything in the Code or in the Indian Evidence Act, 1872 (1 of 1872), but subject to the provisions of this section, a confession made by a person before police officer not lower in rank than a Superintendent of Police and recorded by such police officer either in writing or on any mechanical or electronic device like cassettes, tapes or sound tracks from out of which sound or images can be reproduced, s all be admissible in the trial of such person for an offence under this Act or the rules made thereunder.

(2) A police officer shall, before recording any confession made by a person under sub-section (1), explain to such person in writing that he is not bound to make a confession and that if he does so, it may be used against him:

Provided that where such person prefers to remain silent, the police officer shall not compel or induce him to make any confession.

(3) The confession shall be recorded in an atmosphere free from threat

or inducement and shall be in the same language in which the person makes it.

(4) The person from whom a confession has been recorded under sub-section (1), shall be produced before the Court of a Chief Metropolitan Magistrate or the Court of a Chief Judicial Magistrate along with the original statement of confession, written or r corded on mechanical or electronic device within forty-eight hours.

(5) The Chief Metropolitan Magistrate or the Chief Judicial Magistrate, shall, record the statement, if any, made by the person so produced and get his signature or thumb impression and if there is any complaint of torture, such person shall be directed o be produced for medical examination before a Medical Officer not lower in rank than an Assistant Civil Surgeon and thereafter, he shall be sent to judicial custody.

34. Power to transfer cases to regular courts.-Where, after taking cognizance of any offence, a Special Court is of the opinion that the offence is not triable by it, it shall, notwithstanding that it has no such offence to any court having jurisdiction under the Code and the Court to which the case is transferred may proceed with the trial of the offence as if it had taken cognizance of the offence. jurisdiction to try such offence, transfer the case for the trial of

35. Appeal.-(1) Notwithstanding anything contained in the Code, an appeal shall lie from any judgment, sentence or order, not being an interlocutory order, of a Special Court to the High Court both on facts and on law.

Explanation.-For the purposes of this section, "High Court" means a High Court within whose jurisdiction, a Special Court which passed the judgment, sentence or order, is situated.

(2) Every appeal under sub-section (1) shall be heard by a bench of two Judges of the High Court.

(3) Except as aforesaid, no appeal or revision shall lie to any court from any judgment, sentence or order including an interlocutory order of a Special Court.

(4) Notwithstanding anything contained in sub-section (3) of Section 378 of the Code, an appeal shall lie to the High Court against an order of the Special Court granting or refusing bail.

(5) Every appeal under this section shall be preferred within a period of thirty days from the date of the judgment, sentence or order appealed from:

Provided that the High Court may entertain an appeal after the expiry of the said period of thirty days if it is satisfied that the appellant had sufficient cause for not preferring the appeal within the period of thirty days.

36. Transitional provisions and transfer of pending proceedings.-(1) The jurisdiction conferred by this Act on a Special Court, shall, until a Special Court is constituted under Section 23, in the case of any offence punishable under this Act, notwithstanding anything contained in the Code, be exercised by the Court of Session of the division in which such offence has been committed and it shall have all the powers and follow the procedure provided under this Chapter.

(2) On and from the date when the Special Court is constituted under Section 23, every trial under the provisions of this Act, which would have been required to be held before the Special Court, shall stand transferred to that Court on the date on which it is constituted.

CHAPTER V
INTERCEPTION OF COMMUNICATION IN CERTAIN CASES

37. Definitions.-In this Chapter, unless the context otherwise requires,-

(a) "electronic communication" means any transmission of signs, signals, writings, images, sounds, data or intelligence of any nature transmitted in whole or in part by a wire, radio, electromagnetic, photo electronic or photo optical system that affects inland or foreign commerce but does not include-

(i) the radio portion of a cordless telephone communication that is transmitted between the wireless telephone hand-set and the base unit; or

(ii) any wire or oral communication; or

(iii) any communication made through a tone only paging device; or

(iv) any communication from a tracking device;

(b) "intercept" means the aural or other acquisition of the contents by wire, electronic or oral communication through the use of any electronic, mechanical or other device;

(c) "oral communication" means any oral communication uttered by a person exhibiting an expectation that such communication is not subject to interception under circumstances justifying such expectation but such term does not include any electronic communication;

(d) "wire communication" means any aural transmission made in whole or part through the use of facilities for the transmission of communications by the aid of wire, cable or other like connection between the point of origin and the point of connection, b tween the point of origin and the point of reception (including the use of such connection in switching station) and such term includes any electronic storage of such communication.

38. Appointment of Competent Authority.-The Central Government or the State Government, as the case may be, may appoint an officer not below the rank of Secretary to the Government in the case of State Government and not below the rank of Joint Secretary to the Government in the case of Central Government, to be the Competent Authority for the purposes of this Chapter

39. Application for authorization of interception of wire, electronic or oral communication.-(1) A police officer not below the rank of Superintendent of Police supervising the investigation of any terrorist act under this Act may submit an application i writing to the Competent Authority for an order authorising or approving the interception of wire, electronic or oral communication by the investigating officer when he believes that such interception may provide, or has provided evidence of any offence involving a terrorist act.

(2) Each application shall include the following information:-

(a) the identity of the investigating officer making the application, and the head of the department authorizing the application;

(b) a statement of the facts and circumstances relied upon by the applicant to justify his belief that an order should be issued, including-

(i) details as to the offence of terrorist act that has been, is being, or is about to be committed;

(ii) a particular description of the nature and location of the facilities from which or the place where the communication is to be intercepted;

(iii) a particular description of the type of communications sought to be intercepted; and

(iv) the identity of the person, if known, committing the terrorist act whose communications are to be intercepted;

(c) a statement of the period of time for which the interception is required to be maintained, if the nature of the enquiry is such that the authorization of interception should not automatically terminate after the described type of communication has be n first obtained;

(d) a particular description of facts establishing probable cause to believe that additional communications of the same type will occur thereafter; and

(e) where the application is for the extension of an order, a statement setting forth the results thus far obtained from the interception, or a reasonable explanation of the failure to obtain such results.

(3) The Competent Authority may require the applicant to furnish additional oral or documentary evidence in support of the application.

40. Decision by Competent Authority on application for interception.- (1) Upon such application, the Competent Authority may reject the application, or issue an order, as requested or as modified, authorising or approving interception of wire, electronic or oral communications, if the Competent Authority determines on the basis of the facts submitted by the applicant that-

(a) there is a probable cause for belief that an individual is committing, has committed, or is about to commit, a particular offence described and made punishable under Sections 3 and 4 of this Act;

(b) there is a probable cause of belief that particular communications concerning that offence may be obtained through such interception;

(c) there is probable cause of belief that the facilities from which, or the place where, the wire, electronic or oral communications are to be intercepted are being used or are about to be used, in connection with the commission of such offence, leased to, or are listed in, the name of or commonly used by such person.

(2) Each order by the Competent Authority authorising or approving the interception of any wire, electronic or oral communication under this section shall specify-

(a) the identity of the person, if known, whose communications are to be intercepted;

(b) the nature and location of the communication facilities as to which, or the place where, authority to intercept is granted;

(c) a particular description of the type of communication sought to be intercepted, and a statement of the particular offence to which it relates;

(d) the identity of the agency authorized to intercept the communications, and the person authorising the application; and

(e) the period of time during which such interception is authorized, including a statement as to whether or not the interception shall automatically terminate after the described communication has been first obtained.

41. Submission of order of interception to Review Committee.-(1) The Competent Authority shall, immediately after passing the order under sub-section (1) of section 39, but in any case not later than seven days from the passing of the order, submit a cop of the same to the Review Committee constituted under section 60 along with all the relevant underlying papers, record and his own findings, in respect of the said order, for consideration and approval of the order by the Review Committee.

(2) An order authorizing the interception of a wire, electronic or oral communication under this section shall, upon request of the applicant, direct that a provider of wire or electronic communication applicant forthwith all information, facilities and technical assistance necessary to accomplish the interception unobtrusively and with a minimum of interference with the services that such service provider, landlord, custodian or person is service, landlord, custodian or other person shall furnish to the providing to the person whose communications are to be intercepted.

42. Duration of an order of inception, etc.-(1) No order issued under this section may authorise or approve the interception of any wire,

electronic or oral communication for any period longer than is necessary to achieve the objective of the authorization, nor in any event longer than sixty days and such sixty days period shall begin on the day immediately preceding the day on which the investigating officer first begins to conduct an interception under the order or ten days after order is issued whichever is earlier.

(2) The extension of an order may be granted, but only upon an application for an extension made in accordance with sub-section (1) of Section 38 and the Competent Authority making the findings required by sub-section (1) of section 39, and the period of such extension shall be no longer than the Competent Authority deems necessary to achieve the purposes for which it was granted and in no event for longer than sixty days at a time.

(3) Every order and extension thereof shall contain a provision that the authorization to intercept shall be executed as soon as practicable and shall be conducted in such manner as to minimise the interception of communications not otherwise subject to nterception under this section and shall terminate upon attainment of the authorized objective, or in any event on the expiry of the period of said order or extension thereof.

43. Authority competent to carry out interception.-(1) An interception under this Chapter may be conducted in whole or in part by a public servant, acting under the supervision of the investigating officer authorized to conduct the interception.

(2) Whenever an order authorizing an interception is issued pursuant to this section, the order may require reports to be made to the Competent Authority who issued the order showing that progress has been made towards achievement of the authorized objective and the need for continued interception and such report shall be made at such intervals as the Competent Authority may require.

44. zInterception of communication in emergency.-(1) Notwithstanding anything contained in any other provision of this Chapter, an officer not below the rank of Additional Director General of Police or a police officer of equivalent rank who reasonably de ermines that-

(a) an emergency situation exists that involves-

(i) immediate danger of death or serious physical injury to any person; or

(ii) conspiratorial activities threatening the security or interest of the State; or

(iii) conspiratorial activities, characteristic of a terrorist act, that requires a wire, electronic or oral communication to be intercepted before an order from the Competent Authority authorizing such interception can, with due diligence, be obtained; and

(b) there are grounds on which an order should be issued under this section to authorise such interception, may authorize, in writing, the investigating officer to intercept such wire, electronic or oral communication, if an application for an order approving the interception is made in accordance with the provisions of sub-sections (1) and (2) of Section 38 w thin forty-eight hours after the interception has occurred, or begins to occur.

(2) In the absence of an order approving the interception made under sub-section (1), such interception shall immediately terminate when the communication sought is obtained or when the application for the order is rejected, whichever is earlier; and in he event of an application for permitting interception being rejected under sub-section (1) of Section 39 or an application under sub-section (1) of this section for approval being rejected, or in any other case where the interception is terminated without an order having been issued, the contents of any wire, electronic or oral communication intercepted shall be treated as having been obtained in violation of this section.

45. Protection of information collected.-(1) The contents of any wire, electronic or oral communication intercepted by any means authorized by this Chapter shall, as far as possible, be recorded on tape or wire or other comparable device and shall be don in such manner as to protect the recording from editing or other alterations.

(2) Immediately upon the expiration of the period of order, or extension thereof, such recording shall be made available to the Competent Authority issuing such order and shall be sealed under his directions and kept in the custody of such person or authority as the Competent Authority orders, and such recordings shall not be destroyed except upon an order of the Competent Authority and in any event shall be kept for ten years.

(3) Applications made and orders issued under this Chapter shall be

sealed by the Competent Authority and custody of the applications and orders shall be kept in such manner as the Competent Authority directs, and shall not be destroyed except on an order of the Competent Authority, and in any event shall be kept for ten years.

46. Admissibility of evidence collected through the interception of communications.-Notwithstanding anything in the Code or in any other law for the time being in force, the evidence collected through the interception of wire, electronic or oral communication under this Chapter shall be admissible as evidence against the accused in the Court during the trial of a case:

Provided that, the contents of any wire, electronic or oral communication intercepted pursuant to this Chapter or evidence derived therefrom shall not be received in evidence or otherwise disclosed in any trial, hearing or other proceeding in any court u less each accused has been furnished with a copy of the order of the Competent Authority, and accompanying application, under which the interception was authorized or approved not less than ten days before trial, hearing or proceeding:

Provided further that, the period of ten days may be waived by the judge trying the matter, if he comes to the conclusion that it was not possible to furnish the accused with the above information ten days before the trial, hearing or proceeding and that the accused will not be prejudiced by the delay in receiving such information.

47. Review of authorization order.-(1) The Review Committee constituted by the Central Government or the State Government, as the case may be, shall review every order passed by the Competent Authority under Section 39.

(2) Every order passed by the Competent Authority under Section 39, or disapproved by the officer under Section 43, shall be placed before the Review Committee, which shall be considered by the Review order was necessary, reasonable and justified. Committee within ten days after its receipt, to decide whether the

(3) The Review Committee, after examining the entire record and holding such enquiry, if any, deemed necessary may, by order in writing, either approve the order passed by the Competent Authority or may issue order disapproving the same.

(4) On issue of an order of disapproval by the Review Committee, the interception, if any, already commenced shall be forthwith

discontinued and the intercepted communication, if any, in the form of tape, wire or other device shall, thereupon, not be admissible as evidence in any case and shall be directed to be destroyed

48. Interception and disclosure of wire, electronic or oral communications prohibited.-Except as otherwise specifically provided in Section 39, any police officer who-

(a) intentionally intercepts, endeavours to intercept, or procures any other person to intercept or endeavour to intercept any wire, electronic or oral communication;

(b) intentionally uses, endeavours to use, or procures any other person to use or endeavours to use any electronic, mechanical or other device to intercept any oral communication when-

(i) such device is affixed to, or otherwise transmits a signal through a wire, cable, or other like connection used in wire communication; or

(ii) such device transmits communications by radio, or interferes with the transmission of such communication;

(c) intentionally discloses, or endeavours to disclose, to any other person the contents of any wire, electronic or oral communication, knowing or having reason to know that the information was obtained through the interception of a wire, electronic or oral communication in violation of this Chapter;

(d) intentionally uses, or endeavours to use, the contents of any wire, electronic or oral communication, knowing or having reason to know that the information was obtained through the interception of a wire, electronic or oral communication in violation of this Chapter;

(e) intentionally discloses, or endeavours to disclose, to any other unauthorised person the contents of any wire, electronic or oral commur ication, intercepted by means authorized by Section 39; (f) intentionally continues the interception of wire, electronic or oral communication after the issue of an order of rejection by the Competent Authority under this Chapter;

(g) intentionally continues the interception of wire, electronic or oral communication after the issue of an order of disapproval by the Review Committee under sub-section (3) of Section 46, shall for such violation be punishable with imprisonment for a term which may extend to one year and with fine up to rupees fifty thousand.

49. Annual report of interceptions.-(1) The Central Government and the State Government, as the case may be, shall cause an annual report to be prepared giving a full account of-

(a) the number of applications for authorisation of interceptions received by the Competent Authority from the Police Department in which prosecutions have been launched;

(b) the number of such applications permitted or rejected;

(c) the number of interceptions carried out in emergency situations and the number of approvals granted or rejected in such matters;

(d) the number of prosecutions launched based on such interceptions and convictions resulting from such interceptions, along with an explanatory memorandum giving general assessment of the utility and importance of the interceptions authorised.

(2) An annual report shall be laid by the State Government before the State Legislature within three months of the completion of every calendar year:

Provided that, if the State Government is of the opinion that the inclusion of any matter in the annual report would be prejudicial to the security of the State or to the prevention or detection of any terrorist act, the State Government may exclude such matter from being included in such annual report.

(3) An annual report shall be laid by the Central Government before each House of Parliament within three months of the completion of every calendar year:

Provided that, if the Central Government is of the opinion that the inclusion of any matter in the annual report would be prejudicial to the security of the country or to the prevention or detection of any terrorist act, the Central Government may exclude such matter from being included in such annual report.

CHAPTER VI
MISCELLANEOUS

50. Modified application of certain provisions of the Code.-(1) Notwithstanding anything contained in the Code or any other law,

every offence punishable under this Act shall be deemed to be a cognizable offence within the meaning of clause (c) of Section 2 of the Code, and "cognizable case" as defined in that clause shall be construed accordingly.

(2) Section 167 of the Code shall apply in relation to a case involving an offence punishable under this Act subject to the modification that in sub-section (2),-

(a) the references to "fifteen days", "ninety days" and "sixty days", wherever they occur, shall be construed as references to "thirty days", "ninety days" and "ninety days", respectively; and

(b) after the proviso, the following provisos shall be inserted, namely:-

"Provided further that if it is not possible to complete the investigation within the said period of ninety days, the Special Court shall extend the said period up to one hundred and eighty days, on the report of the Public Prosecutor indicating the progress of the investigation and the specific reasons for the detention of the accused beyond the said period of ninety days:

Provided also that if the police officer making the investigation under this Act, requests, for the purposes of investigation, for police custody from judicial custody of any person from judicial custody, he shall file an affidavit stating the reasons for doing so and shall also explain the delay, if any, for requesting such police custody.".

(3) Section 268 of the Code shall apply in relation to a case involving an offence punishable under this Act subject to the modification that-

(a) the reference in sub-section (1) thereof-

(i) to "the State Government" shall be construed as a reference to "the Central Government or the State Government",

(ii) to "order of the State Government" shall be construed as a reference to "order of the Central Government or the State Government, as the case may be"; and

(b) the reference in sub-section (2) thereof, to "the State Government" shall be construed as a reference to "the Central Government or the State Government, as the case may be".

(4) Sections 366, 367 and 371 of the Code shall apply in relation to a

case involving an offence triable by a Special Court subject to the modification that the reference to "Court of Session", wherever occurring therein, shall be construed as the reference to "Special Court".

(5) Nothing in Section 438 of the Code shall apply in relation to any case involving the arrest of any person accused of having committed an offence punishable under this Act.

(6) Notwithstanding anything contained in the Code, no person accused of an offence punishable under this Act shall, if in custody, be released on bail or on his own bond unless the Court gives the Public Prosecutor an opportunity of being heard.

(7) Where the Public Prosecutor opposes the application of the accused to release on bail, no person accused of an offence punishable under this Act or any rule made thereunder shall be released on bail until the Court is satisfied that there are grounds for believing that he is not guilty of committing such offence:

Provided that after the expiry of a period of one year from the date of detention of the accused for an offence under this Act, the provisions of sub-section (6) of this section shall apply.

(8) The restrictions on granting of bail specified in sub-sections (6) and (7) are in addition to the restrictions under the Code or any other law for the time being in force on granting of bail.

(9) Notwithstanding anything contained in sub-sections (6), (7) and (8), no bail shall be granted to a person accused of an offence punishable under this Act, if he is not an Indian citizen and has entered the country unauthorizedly or illegally except in very exceptional circumstances and for reasons to be recorded in writing.

51. Cognizance of offences.-No court shall take cognizance of any offence under this Act without the previous sanction of the Central Government or, as the case may be, the State Government.

52. Officers competent to investigate offences under this Act.- Notwithstanding anything contained in the Code, no police officer,-

(a) in the case of the Delhi Special Police Establishment, below the rank of a Deputy Superintendent of Police or a police officer of equivalent rank;

(b) in the metropolitan areas of Mumbai, Kolkata, Chennai and Ahmedabad and any other metropolitan area notified as such under sub-section (1) of section 8 of the Code, below the rank of an Assistant Commissioner of Police;

(c) in any other case not relatable to clause (a) or clause (b), below the rank of a Deputy Superintendent of Police or a police officer of an equivalent rank, shall investigate any offence punishable under this Act.

53. Arrest.-(1) Where a police officer arrests a person, he shall prepare a custody memo of the person arrested.

(2) The person arrested shall be informed of his right to consult a legal practitioner as soon as he is brought to the police station.

(3) Whenever any person is arrested, information of his arrest shall be immediately communicated by the police officer to a family member or in his absence to a relative of such person by telegram, telephone or by any other means and this fact shall be recorded by the police officer under the signature of the person arrested.

(4) The person arrested shall be permitted to meet the legal practitioner representing him during the course of interrogation of the accused person:

Provided that nothing in this sub-section shall entitle the legal practitioner to remain present throughout the period of interrogation

54. Presumption as to offences under Section 3.-(1) In a prosecution for an offence under sub-section (1) of section 3, if it is proved-

(a) that the arms or explosives or any other substances specified in Section 4 were recovered from the possession of the accused and there is reason to believe that such arms or explosives or other substances of a similar nature, were used in the commission of such offence; or

(b) that the finger-prints of the accused were found at the site of the offence or on anything including arms and vehicles used in connection with the commission of such offence, the Special Court shall draw adverse inference against the accused.

(2) In a prosecution for an offence under sub-section (3) of Section 3, if

it is proved that the accused rendered any financial assistance to a person, having knowledge that such person is accused of, or reasonably suspected of, an offence under that sec ion, the Special Court shall draw adverse inference against the accused.

55. Bar of jurisdiction of courts, etc.-No civil court or other authority shall have or, be entitled to, exercise any jurisdiction, powers or authority in relation to the matters referred to in Sections 19 and 40 of the Act 55. Saving.-(1) Nothing in this Act shall affect the jurisdiction exercisable by, or the procedure applicable to, any court or other authority under any law relating to the naval, military or air forces or other armed forces of the Union.

(2) For the removal of doubts, it is hereby declared that for the purposes of any such law as is referred to in sub-section (1) a Special Court shall be deemed to be a court of ordinary criminal justice.

56. Overriding effect.-The provisions of this Act shall have effect notwithstanding anything inconsistent therewith contained in any enactment other than this Act or in any instrument having effect by virtue of any enactment other than this Act.

57. Protection of action taken in good faith.-No suit, prosecution or other legal proceeding shall lie against the Central Government or a State Government or any officer or authority of the Central Government or State Government or any other authority o whom powers have been conferred under this Act, for anything which is in good faith done or purported to be done in pursuance of this Act:

Provided that no suit, prosecution or other legal proceedings shall lie against any serving member or retired member of the armed forces or other para-military forces in respect of any action taken or purported to be taken by him in good faith, in the c urse of any operation directed towards combating terrorism.

58. Punishment and compensation for malicious action.-(1) Any police officer who exercises powers corruptly or maliciously, knowing that there are no reasonable grounds for proceeding under this Act, shall be punishable with imprisonment which may extend to two years, or with fine, or with both.

(2) If the Special Court is of the opinion that any person has been corruptly or maliciously proceeded against under this Act, the Court

may award such compensation as it deems fit to the person, so proceeded against and it shall be paid by the officer, erson, authority or Government, as may be specified in the order.

59. Impounding passport and arms license of person chargesheeted under the Act.-Notwithstanding anything contained in any other law for the time being in force, the passport and the arms license of a person, who is charge-sheeted for having committed any offence under this Act, shall be deemed to have been impounded for such period as the Special Court may deem fit.

60. Review Committees.-(1) The Central Government and each State Government shall, whenever necessary, constitute one or more Review Committees for the purposes of this Act.

(2) Every such Committee shall consist of a Chairperson and such other members not exceeding three and possessing such qualifications as may be prescribed.

(3) A Chairperson of the Committee shall be a person who is, or has been, a Judge of a High Court, who shall be appointed by the Central Government, or as the case may be, the State Government, so however, that the concurrence of the Chief Justice of the High Court shall be obtained in the case of a sitting Judge:

Provided that in the case of a Union territory, the appointment of a person who is a Judge of the High Court of a State shall be made as a Chairperson with the concurrence of the Chief Justice of the concerned High Court.

61. Power of High Courts to make rules.-The High Court may, by notification in the Official Gazette, make such rules, if any, as they may deem necessary for carrying out the provisions of this Act relating to Special Courts within their territories.

62. Power to make rules.-(1) Without prejudice to the powers of the High Courts to make rules under section 61, the Central Government may, by notification in the Official Gazette, make rules for carrying out the provisions of this Act.

(2) In particular, and without prejudice to the generality of the foregoing powers, such rules may provide for all or any of the following matters, namely:-

(a) regulating the conduct of persons in respect of areas the control of which is considered necessary or expedient and the removal of such persons from such areas;

(b) the entry into, and search of-

(i) any vehicle, vessel or aircraft; or

(ii) any place, whatsoever, reasonably suspected of being used for committing the offences referred to in section 3 or section 4 or for manufacturing or storing anything for the commission of any such offence;

(c) conferring powers upon-

(i) the Central Government;

(ii) a State Government;

(iii) an Administrator of a Union territory under article 239 of the Constitution;

(iv) an officer of the Central Government not lower in rank than that of a Joint Secretary; or

(v) an officer of a State Government not lower in rank than that of a District Magistrate, to make general or special orders to prevent or deal with terrorist acts;

(d) the arrest and trial of persons contravening any of the rules or any order made thereunder;

(e) the punishment of any person who contravenes or attempts to contravene or abets or attempts to abet the contravention of any rule or order made thereunder with imprisonment for a term which may extend to one year or fine or both;

(f) providing for the seizure and detention of any property in respect of which such contravention, attempt or abetment as is referred to in clause (e) has been committed and for the adjudication of such seizure and detention, whether by any court or by any other authority;

(g) determination of the price of the forfeited property under sub-section (2) of section 10;

(h) the procedure of making application under sub-section (3) of section 19; and

(i) the qualifications of the members of the Review Committee under sub-section (2) of section 60.

63. Orders and rules to be laid before Houses of Parliament.-Every order and every rule made by the Central Government under this Act shall be laid, as soon as may be after it is made, before each House of Parliament, while it is in session, for a total period of thirty days which may be comprised in one session or in two or more successive sessions, and if, before the expiry of the session immediately following the session or the successive sessions aforesaid, both Houses agree in making any modification in the order or rule or both Houses agree that the order or rule should not be made, the order or rule shall thereafter have effect only in such modified form or be of no effect, as the case may be; so, however, that any such modification or annulment s all be without prejudice to the validity of anything previously done under that order or rule

64. Repeal and saving.-(1) The Prevention of Terrorism (Second) Ordinance, 2001 is hereby repealed.

(2) Notwithstanding the repeal of the said Ordinance, anything done or any action taken under the said Ordinance shall be deemed to have been done or taken under the corresponding provisions of this Act.

THE SCHEDULE

(See Section 18)

TERRORIST ORGANIZATIONS

1. BABBAR KHALSA INTERNATIONAL.
2. KHALISTAN COMMANDO FORCE.
3. KHALISTAN ZINDABAD FORCE.
4. INTERNATIONAL SIKH YOUTH FEDERATION.
5. LASHKAR-E-TAIBA/PASBAN-E-AHLE HADIS.
6. JAISH-E-MOHAMMED/TAHRIK-E-FURQAN.
7. HARKAT-UL-MUJAHIDEEN/HARKAT-UL-ANSAR/KARKAT-UL-JEHAD-E-ISLAMI.

8. HIZB-UL-MUJAHIDEEN/HIZB-ULMUJAHIDEEN PIR PANJAL REGIMENT.

9. AL-UMAR-MUJAHIDEEN.

10. JAMMU AND KASHMIR ISLAMIC FRONT.

11. UNITED LIBERATION FRONT OF ASSAM (ULFA).

12. NATIONAL DEMOCRATIC FRONT OF BODOLAND (NDFB).

13. PEOPLE'S LIBERATION ARMY (PLA).

14. UNITED NATIONAL LIBERATION FRONT (UNLF).

15. PEOPLE'S REVOLUTIONARY PARTY OF KANGLEIPAK (PREPAK).

16. KANGLEIPAK COMMUNIST PARTY (KCP).

17. KANGLEI YAOL KANBA LUP (KYKL).

18. MANIPUR PEOPLE'S LIBERATION FRONT (MPLF).

19. ALL TRIPURA TIGER FORCE.

20. NATIONAL LIBERATION FRONT OF TRIPURA.

21. LIBERATION TIGERS OF TAMIL EELAM (LTTE).

22. STUDENTS ISLAMIC MOVEMENT OF INDIA.

23. DEENDAR ANJUMAN.

24 COMMUNIST PARTY OF INDIA (MARXIST-LENINIST)-PEOPLE'S WAR, ALL ITS FORMATIONS AND FRONT ORGANIZATIONS.

25 MAOIST COMMUNIST CENTRE (MCC), ALL ITS FORMATIONS AND FRONT ORGANIZATIONS.

Explanation.-For the purposes of this Schedule, serial numbers 24 and 25 shall be deemed to have been included with effect from the date of publication of S.O. No. 1194(E), dated 5 December 2001.

Nepal: Terrorist and Destructive Activities (Control and Punishment) Ordinance

Reproduced below are the main features of the Terrorist and Destructive Activities (Control and Punishment) Ordinance promulgated by the King of Nepal on the advice of the Cabinet on 26 November 2001. The government resorted to this measure on 26 November 2001 after the Maoist insurgents, brought to an end, the cease-fire being observed by them and the government since 23 July 2001, with a series of attacks across the country on 23 November.

The Ordinance has described the following acts as terrorism and disruptive activities:

1. Any act or plan of using any kinds of arms, grenades, or explosives, or any other equipment or goods with the objective of affecting or hurting sovereignty or the security and law and order of the Kingdom of Nepal or any part thereof or the property of the Nepalese diplomatic missions abroad thereby causing damage to property at any place or any act causing loss of life or dismemberment or injury or setting fire or hurting physically and mentally or any act of poising goods of daily consumption causing loss of life or injury, or any other aforesaid acts thereby causing panic among the people in motion or assembled; acts of intimidation or terrorizing individuals at any place or in any vehicle or abducting them or creating terror among them by threatening to abduct them from vehicles and places or abduction of people traveling on such vehicles as well as activities like taking the life of others, causing physical mutilation, injury and harm or causing other types of damage by using substances mentioned in the relevant section in that connection or by threatening to use such substances or any other substances other than those mentioned in that section or threatening to use them, or, Acts like the production, distribution, accumulation, peddling, import and export, marketing or possession or installation of any kind of arms and ammunition or bombs or explosive substances or poisonous substances or any assistance in this connection, and;

Acts of gathering people or giving training for this purpose;

Any other acts aimed at creating and spreading fear and terror in public life;

Act such as extortion of cash or kind or looting of property for this purpose, forcibly raising cash or kind or looting property in pursuit of the said purpose.

Any attempt or conspiracy to engage in terrorist or disruptive activity, or to encourage of force anyone to take up such activity, gathering more than one individual for such purpose, constituting any group to the same end, or assigning anyone to such activity or participating in such activity with or without pay or engaging in publicity for such activity, causing obstruction to government communications systems, or giving refuse to any individual engaged in terrorist or disruptive activity, or hiding any person doing any of this things.

Other main features are:

2. Anyone indulging in crime in Nepal while residing abroad will also be subject to punishment

3. The government can declare a terrorist affected area or terrorist individuals.

4. House arrest can be used to prevent any terrorist and disruptive act.

5. Cases will be heard in a court constituted or designed by His Majesty's Government.

6. Arrangements will be made for reasonable expenses for treatment and compensation in case of the maiming or death of security personnel or police assigned to control or investigate terrorist and disruptive activities.

7. Cases instituted under this ordinance will not be subject to any statute of limitations.

8. Individuals arresting or helping in the arrest of any terrorist will be suitably awarded.

9. Despite the State of Emergency, expression of views, running of presses and publications, migration and operation of communications systems can take place as usual without however, infringing the Terrorist and Disruptive Crimes Control and Punishment Act and the Constitution of the Kingdom of Nepal.

Pakistan: Anti-Terrorism (Amendment) Ordinance, 1999

Full text of Anti-terrorism (Amendment) Ordinance 1999, promulgated by President Rafiq Tarar on 29 April 1999

The original Anti-terrorism Act was promulgated by then President Farooq Ahmed Leghari on 18 August 1997

Whereas it is expedient to amend the Anti-terrorism Act, (XXVII of 1997), for the purposes hereinafter appearing;

And whereas the National Assembly is not in session and the President is satisfied that circumstances exist which render it necessary to take immediate action;

Now, therefore, in exercise of the powers conferred by clause (1) of Article 89 of the Constitution of the Islamic Republic of Pakistan, the President is pleased to make and promulgate the following Ordinance:-

1. Short title and commencement — (1) This Ordinance may be called the Anti-terrorism (Amendment) Ordinance, 1999.

   (2) It shall come into force at once and shall be deemed to have taken effect on the twenty-fourth day of February, 1999.

2. General Amendments, Act XXVII of 1997 — In the Anti-terrorism Act, 1997 (XXVII of 1997), hereinafter referred to as the said Act,—

(a) for the words "Special Court", "a Special Court" or "the Special Court" wherever occurring the words "Anti-terrorism Court", "an Anti-terrorism Court" or "the Anti-terrorism Court" shall be substituted respectively; and

(b) for the words "Appellate Tribunal", "an Appellate Tribunal" or "the Appellate Tribunal" wherever occurring the words "High Court," "a High Court" or "the High Court" shall be substituted respectively.

3. Amendment of Section 2, Act XXVII of 1997 — In the said Act, in Section 2,—

(a) after clause (d) the following new clause shall be inserted, namely:—

(d, a)" "High Court" means the High Court having territorial jurisdiction in respect of the area for which an anti-terrorism court has been established; and

(b) for clause (e), the following shall be substituted, namely:-

(e) "scheduled offence" means a terrorist or sectarian related offence as set out in this Act or the Schedule hereto."

4. Amendment of Section 5, Act XXVII of 1997 — In the said Act, in Section 5, in sub-section (2), in clause (i), the comma and words", or in all probability is likely to commit" shall be omitted.

5. Amendment of section 6, Act XXVII of 1997 — In the said Act, for Section 6, the following shall be substituted, namely:—

6. Terrorist Act — A person is said to commit a terrorist act if he,

(a) in order to, or if the effect of his actions will be to, strike terror or create a sense of fear and insecurity in the people, or any section of the people, does any act or thing by using bombs, dynamite or other explosive or inflammable substances, or such fire-arms or other lethal weapons as may be notified, or poisons or noxious gases or chemicals, in such a manner as to cause, or be likely to cause, the death of, or injury to, any person or persons, or damage to, or destruction of, property on a large scale, or a widespread disruption of supplies of services essential to the life of the community, or threatens with the use of force public servants in order to prevent them from discharging their lawful duties; or

(b) commits a scheduled offence, the effect of which will be, or be likely to be, to strike terror, or create a sense of fear and insecurity in the people, or any section of the people, or to adversely affect harmony among different sections of the people; or

(c) commits an act of gang rape, child molestation, or robbery coupled with rape as specified in the Schedule to this Act; or

(d) commits an act of civil commotion as specified in Section &A."

7. Amendment of Section 7, Act XXVII of 1997 — In the said Act, for Section 7, the following shall be substituted, namely:—

8. Punishment for terrorist act — Whoever commits a terrorist act,—

(i) referred to in paragraph (a) of Section 6, shall—

(a) if such act has resulted in the death of any person be punished with death; and

(b) in any other case, be punishable with imprisonment for a term which shall not be less than seven years but may extend to life imprisonment, and shall also be liable to fine; and

(ii) referred to in paragraphs (b) and (c) of Section 6 be liable to the punishment prescribed under the relevant law."

9. Insertion of Sections 7A and 7B, Act XXVII of 1997 — In the said Act, after Section 7, the following new sections shall be inserted, namely:—

9A. Creation of civil commotion — "Civil commotion" means creation of internal disturbances in violation of law or intended to violate law, commencement or continuation of illegal strikes, go-slows, lock-outs, vehicles snatching or lifting, damage to or destruction of State or private property, random firing to create panic, charging *bhatta*, acts of criminal trespass (illegal *qabza*), distributing, publishing or pasting of a handbill or making graffiti or wall-chalking intended to create unrest or fear or create a threat to the security of law and order or to incite the commission of an offence punishable under Chapter VI of the Pakistan Penal Code (Act (XLV of 1860).

9B. Punishment for creating civil commotion — Whoever commits an act of civil commotion shall be punished with rigorous imprisonment for a term which may extend to seven years, or with fine, or with both."

10. Amendment of Section 10, Act XXVII of 1997 — In the said Act, in section 10, the full stop at the end shall be replaced by a colon and thereafter the following proviso shall be added, namely:—

"Provided that the concerned officer shall first record in writing his reasons for such belief and serve a copy thereof either on the person or on the premises".

11. Amendment of Section 13, Act XXVII of 1997 — In the said Act, for Section 13, the following shall be substituted, namely:—

"13 Establishment of Anti-terrorism Court —

(1) For the purpose of providing for the speedy trial of the cases referred to in sub-section (2) and sub-section (3) of Section 39A, as

well as of scheduled offences, the Federal Government, or if so directed by the Government, the Provincial Government may establish by notification one or more anti-terrorism courts in relation to each area.

(2) Notwithstanding anything contained in sub-section (1), if, having regard to the exigencies of the situation prevailing in a Province, the Government is of the opinion that it is expedient to establish in relation to an area, or in relation to two or more areas, in the Province, an anti-terrorism court outside the said area or areas, for the trial of offences committed in the area, or areas, it may, by notification, establish in relation to such area or areas an anti-terrorism court at such place outside the said area, or areas as may be specified in the notification.

(3) Where more anti-terrorism courts than one have been established in any area, the Government in consultation with the Chief Justice of the High Court shall designate a judge of any such court to be an administrative judge and all cases triable under this Act pertaining to the said area shall be filed before the said court and such judge may either try the cases himself, or assign any case, or cases, for trial to any other anti-terrorism court at any time prior to the framing of the charge. The cases shall be assigned to a court one case at a time:

Provided that in order to ensure that the time of the court is not wasted if for some reason a given case cannot proceed more than one case can be assigned to it at any time or from time to time.

(4) In respect of a case assigned to a court under sub-section (3), all orders made or proceedings taken before the assignment shall be deemed to have been made or taken by the court to which the case has been assigned."

12. Amendment of Section 14, Act XXVII of 1997. — In the said Act, in section 14, —

(a) in sub-section (1), in clause (iii) after the word "advocate" at the end the words "of a High Court" shall be added; and

(b) for sub-section (2), the following shall be substituted, namely:-

(2) A Judge shall be appointed for a period of two and a half years after consultation with the Chief Justice of the High Court:.

Provided that the Judge may be removed from office prior to the expiry of the said period in consultation with the Chief Justice."

13. Amendment of Section 16, Act XXVII of 1997. — In the said Act, in section 16, for the words "his faith to the effect that he will decide the case honestly, faithfully according to his conscience and belief" the words "the Constitution, law and his conscience" shall be substituted.

14. Amendment of Section 19, Act XXVII of 1997. — In the said Act, in Section 19, — (i) for sub-section (10), the following shall be substituted, namely:-

(10) Any accused person may be tried in his absence if the anti-terrorism court, after such inquiry as it deems fit, is satisfied that such absence is deliberate and brought about with a view to impeding the course of justice:

Provided that the accused person shall not be tried under this sub-section unless a proclamation has been published in respect of him in at least three national daily newspapers out of which one shall be in the Urdu language requiring him to appear at a specified place within seven days failing which action may also be taken against him under Section 88 of the Code:

Provided further that the Court shall proceed with the trial after taking the necessary steps to appoint an advocate at the expense of the State to defend the accused person who is not before the Court.

Explanation. — An accused who is tried in his absence under this sub-section shall be deemed not to have admitted the commission of any offence for which he has been charged."; and (ii) after sub-section (11), the following new sub-section shall be inserted, namely:-

"... Nothing contained in sub-section (10) or sub-section (11) shall be ...trued to deny the accused the right to consult or be defended ...legal practitioner of his own choice."

15. Amendment of Section 24, Act XXVII of 1997. — In the said Act, Section 24 shall be omitted.

16. Amendment of Section 25, Act XXVII of 1997. — In the said Act, in Section 25, sub-section (6) and (7) shall be omitted.

17. Amendment of Section 26, Act XXVII of 1997. — In the said Act,

Section 26 shall be omitted.

18. Amendment of Section 28, Act XXVII of 1997. — In the said Act, in Section 28, in sub-section (2) the full stop at the end shall be replaced by a colon and thereafter the following proviso shall be added, namely:-

"Provided that nothing herein contained shall affect the powers of the presiding officer of the Special Court to call any witness as is available under the law."

19. Substitution of Section 37, Act XXVII of 1997. — In the said Act, for Section 37, the following shall be substituted, namely;-

37. Contempt of Court. — An anti-terrorism court shall have the power to punish with imprisonment for a term which may extend to six months and with fine any person who- (a) abuses, interferes with or obstructs the process of the Court in any way or disobeys and order or direction of the Court; (b) scandalizes the Court otherwise does anything which tends to bring the court or a person constituting the Court into hatred, ridicule or contempt; (c) does anything which tends to prejudice the determination of a matter pending or most likely to come up before the Court; or (d) does anything which, by any other law, constitutes contempt of court.

Explanation. — In this section, "Court" means anti-terrorism court."

20. Insertion of Section 39A, Act XXVII of 1997. — In the said Act, after Section 39, the following new section shall be inserted, namely:-

39A. Repeal — (1) The Pakistan Armed Forces (Acting in Aid of the Civil Power) Ordinance 1998 (XII of 1998), as amended by the Pakistan Armed Forces (Acting in aid of the Civil Power) (Amendment) Ordinance, 1998 (XIII of 1998), and the Pakistan Armed Forces (Acting in Aid the Civil Power) Second Amendment) Ordinance, 1998 (XVII of 1997) (hereinafter referred to as the repealed Ordinance), is hereby repealed.

(2) All cases, including cases before a court of appeals, which were pending under the repealed Ordinance shall stand transferred to the anti-terrorism court having jurisdiction under the Act and such court shall, (a) in cases which have been transferred from a trial court, continue the trial from the stage which the cases had reached; and (b) in cases which have been transferred from a court of appeals

decide the same other basis of the evidence earlier recorded after hearing the parties.

(3) Any judgement given or sentence passed by a trial court or a court of appeals convened under section 3 of the repealed Ordinance, except cases in which sentence of death was passed and has been executed, shall have no effect and all such cases shall stand transferred to the anti-terrorism court having jurisdiction under the Act for decision after hearing the parties on the basis of the evidence earlier recorded.

(4) In respect of a case transferred to a court by virtue of sub-section (2) or sub-section (3), the court shall not, by reason of the said transfer, be bound to recall and rehear any witness who have given evidence before the transfer and may act on the evidence already recorded by or produced before the court from which the case is so transferred.

(5) Nothing contained in sub-section (4) shall affect the power of the court to recall any witness or rehear any evidence as is available under the law."

21. Amendment of the Schedule Act XXVII of 1997. — In the said Act, in the Schedule, after entry at serial No. 4, the following new entry shall be added, namely:-

5. Any offence including an offence punishable under the Pakistan Arms Ordinance, 1965 (W. P. Ord. XX of 1965), committed conjointly with any other offence punishable under this Act."

Sri Lanka: Prevention of Terrorism (Temporary Provisions) Act No. 48 of 1979

[Certified on 20 July 1979]

AN ACT TO MAKE TEMPORARY PROVISION FOR THE PREVENTION OF ACTS OF TERRORISM IN SRI LANKA, THE PREVENTION OF UNLAWFUL ACTIVITIES OF ANY INDIVIDUAL, GROUP OF INDIVIDUALS, ASSOCIATION, ORGANIZATION OR BODY OF PERSONS WITHIN SRI LANKA OR OUTSIDE SRI LANKA AND FOR MATTERS CONNECTED THEREWITH OR INCIDENTAL THERETO.

WHEREAS the Parliament of the Democratic Socialist Republic of Sri Lanka continues to affirm that men and institutions remain free only when freedom is founded upon respect for the Rule of Law and that grievances should be redressed by constitutional methods:

AND WHEREAS public order in Sri Lanka continues to be endangered by elements or groups of persons or associations that advocate the use of force or the commission of crime as a means of, or as an aid in, accomplishing governmental change within Sri Lanka, and who have resorted to acts of murder and threats of murder of members of Parliament and of local authorities, police officers, and witnesses to such acts and other law abiding and innocent citizens, as well as the commission of other acts of terrorism such as armed robbery, damage to State property and other acts involving actual or threatened coercion, intimidation and violence:

AND WHEREAS other democratic countries have enacted special legislation to deal with acts of terrorism:

BE it enacted by the Parliament of the Democratic Socialist Republic of Sri Lanka as follows:-

1. This Act may be cited as the Prevention of Terrorism (Temporary Provisions) Act, No 48 of 1979, and shall come into operation in respect of all or any of its provisions on such date or dates as the Minister may appoint by Order published in the Gazette.

PART I - OFFENCES

2. (1) Any person who –

(a) causes the death of any specified person, or kidnaps or abducts a specified person, or commits any other attack upon any such person, which act would, under the provisions of the Penal Code, be punishable with death or a term of imprisonment of not less than seven years; or

(b) causes the death of any person who is a witness to any offence under this Act, or kidnaps or abducts or commits any other attack upon any such person, which act would, under the provisions of the Penal Code, be punishable with death or a term of imprisonment of not less than seven years; or

(c) commits criminal intimidation of any special person or a witness referred to in paragraph (b); or

(d) commits the offence of robbery of the property of the Government, any department, statutory board, public corporation, bank, cooperative union or cooperative society; or

(e) commits the offence of mischief to the property of the Government, any department, statutory board, public corporation, bank, cooperative union or cooperative society or to any other public property; or

(f) without lawful authority imports, manufactures or collects any firearms, offensive weapons, ammunition or explosives or any article or thing used, or intended to be used, in the manufacture of explosives; or

(g) possesses without lawful authority, within any security area, any firearms or any offensive weapon, ammunition or explosives or any article or thing used, or intended to be used, in the manufacture of explosives;or

(h) by words either spoken or intended to be read or by signs or by visible representations or otherwise causes or intends to cause commission of acts of violence or religious, racial or communal disharmony or feelings of ill-will or hostility between different communities or racial or religious groups; or

(i) without lawful authority erases, mutilates, defaces or otherwise interferes with any words, inscriptions, or lettering appearing on any board or other fixture on, upon or adjacent to, any highway, street, road or any other public place; or

(j) harbours, conceals or in any other manner prevents, hinders or interferes with the apprehension of, a proclaimed person or any other person, knowing or having reason to believe that such person has committed an offence under this Act, shall be guilty of an offence under this Act.

(2) Any person guilty of an offence specified in -

(i) paragraph (a) or (b) of subsection (1) shall on conviction be liable to imprisonment for life, and

(ii) paragraphs (c), (d), (e), (f), (g), (h), (i) or (j) of subsection (1) shall on conviction be liable to imprisonment of either description for a period not less than five years but not exceeding twenty years.

(3) In this section -

(i) "proclaimed person" means any person proclaimed by the Inspector-General of Police by Proclamation published in the Gazette to be a person wanted in connection with the commission of any offence under this Act; and

(ii) "security area" means any area declared by the Minister by Order published in the Gazette to be a security area if he is satisfied that by reason of any unlawful activity there is in such area a reasonable apprehension of organised violence.

3. Any person who -

(a) does any act preparatory to the commission of an offence; or

(b) abets, conspires, attempts, exhorts or incites the commission of an offence; or

(c) causes the death of any person, or commits any attack upon any person whomsoever in the course of committing any offence under this Act, which act would, under the provisions of the Penal Code, be punishable with death or with a term of imprisonment of not less than seven years, shall be guilty of an offence and shall on conviction be liable to imprisonment of either description for a period of not less than five years but not exceeding twenty years where the offence is one specified in paragraph (a) or (b), or to imprisonment for life where the offence is one specified in paragraph (c).

4. Where any person is convicted by any court of any offence under Section 2 or Section 3, then, in addition to any other penalty that the court shall impose for such offence -

(a) all property movable and immovable, of that person shall, by virtue of such conviction, be deemed to be forfeited to the Republic; and

(b) any alienation or other disposal of such property effected by such person after the date of coming into operation of this Part shall be deemed to have been, and to be, null and void.

5. Any person who -

(a) knowing or having reasonable cause to believe that any person -

(i) has committed an offence under this Act, or

(ii) is making preparation or is attempting to commit an offence under this Act, fails to report the same to a police officer; or

(b) having in his possession any information relating to the movements or whereabouts of any person who has committed or is making preparations or is attempting to commit an offence under this Act fails to report the same to a police officer, shall be guilty of an offence and shall, on conviction be liable to imprisonment of either description for period not exceeding seven years.

PART II - INVESTIGATION OF OFFENCES

6.(1) Any police officer not below the rank of Superintendent or any other police officer not below the rank of Sub-Inspector authorized in writing by him in that behalf may, without a warrant and with or without assistance and notwithstanding anything in any other law to the contrary -

(a) arrest any person;

(b) enter and search any premises;

(c) stop and search any individual or any vehicle, vessel, train or aircraft; and

(d) seize any document or thing, connected with or concerned in or reasonably suspected of being connected with or concerned in any unlawful activity.

(2) Any person who obstructs or hinders any police officer lawfully exercising any power conferred on him by or under subsection (1), shall be guilty of an offence and shall on conviction be liable to imprisonment of either description or a period not exceeding seven years.

7.(1) Any person arrested under subsection(1) of section 6 may be kept in custody for a period not exceeding seventy-two hours and shall, unless a detention order under Section 9 has been made in respect of such person, be produced before a Magistrate before the expiry of such period and the Magistrate shall, on an application made in writing in that behalf by a police officer not below the rank of Superintendent, make order that such person be remanded until the conclusion of the trial of such person: Provided that, where the Attorney-General consents to the release of such person before custody before the conclusion of the trial, the Magistrate shall release such person from custody.

(2) Where any person connected with or concerned in or reasonably suspected to be connected with or concerned in the commission of any offence under this Act appears or is produced before any court other than in the manner referred to in subsection (1), such court shall order the remand of such person until the conclusion of the trial: Provided that, if an application is made under the hand of a police officer not below the rank of Superintendent to keep such person in police custody for a period not exceeding seventy-two hours, the Magistrate shall authorize such custody and thereupon the order of remand made by the Magistrate shall remain suspended for the period during which such person is in police custody.

(3) A police officer conducting an investigation under this Act in respect of any person arrested under subsection (1) of Section 6 or remanded under subsection (1) or subsection (2) of this section -

(a) shall have the right of access to such person and the right to take such person during reasonable hours to any place for the purpose of interrogation and from place to place for the purposes of investigation; and

(b) may obtain a specimen of the handwriting of such person and do all such acts as may reasonably be necessary for fingerprinting or otherwise identifying such person.

8. Any police officer may at any stage of an investigation or trial produce before any Magistrate any person conversant with any fact relating to the commission of any offence under this Act, and the Magistrate shall thereupon record the statement of such person upon oath.

PART III - DETENTION AND RESTRICTION ORDERS

9.(1) Where the Minister has reason to believe or suspect that any person is connected with or concerned in any unlawful activity, the Minister may order that such person be detained for a period not exceeding three months in the first instance, in such place and subject to such conditions as may be determined by the Minister, and any such order may be extended from time to time for a period not exceeding three months at a time: Provided, however, that the aggregate period of such detention shall not exceed a period of eighteen months.

(a) At any time after an order has been made in respect of any person under subsection (1), the Minister may direct that the operation of such order be suspended and may make an order under subsection (1) of section 11.

(b) The Minister may revoke any such direction if he is satisfied that the person in respect of whom the direction was made has failed to observe any condition imposed or that the operation of the order can no longer remain suspended without detriment to public safety.

10. An order made under Section 9 shall be final and shall not be called in question in any court or tribunal by way of writ or otherwise

11.(1) Where the Minister has reason to believe or suspect that any person is connected with or concerned in the commission of any unlawful activity referred to in subsection (1) of section 9, he may make an order in writing imposing on such person such prohibitions or restrictions as may be specified in such order in respect of -

(a) his movement outside such place of residence as may be specified; or

(b) the places of residence and of employment of such person; or

(c) his travel within or outside Sri Lanka; or

(d) his activities whether in relation to any organisation, association or body of persons of which such person is a member, or otherwise; or

(e) such person addressing public meetings or from holding office in, or taking part in the activities of or acting as adviser to, any organization, association or body of persons, or from taking part in any political activities, and he may require such person to notify his movements to such authority, in such manner and at such times as may be specified in the order.

(2) Where the Minister makes a restriction order in respect of any person while an order of detention in respect of such person is in force, such restriction order shall, unless otherwise specified, take effect upon the expiry of the detention order.

(3) Every order made under subsection (1) shall be in force for such period, not exceeding three months, as may be specified therein: Provided, that the Minister may, by order in writing, extend such period from time to time for periods not exceeding three months at a time so however that the aggregate of such periods does not exceed eighteen months.

(4) Where an order is made under subsection (1), the Minister may by notice in writing served on the person to whom such order relates, vary, cancel or add to any prohibitions or restrictions imposed by such order on such person and the prohibitions or restrictions so varied or added to shall, unless earlier cancelled, continue in force for the unexpired portion of the period specified in such order or the period as extended under subsection (3).

(5) An order made by the Minister under subsection (1) shall be final and shall not be called in question in any court or tribunal by way of writ or otherwise.

12. Any person who contravenes or acts in breach of any prohibition or restriction imposed on him by an order under Section 11 shall be guilty of an offence and shall on conviction be liable to a term of imprisonment of either description for a period of five years.

PART IV - ADVISORY BOARD

13.(1) There shall, for the purposes of this Act, be established an Advisory Board consisting of not less than three persons appointed by the President.

(2) Any person in respect of whom any detention order or restriction order has been made shall be informed of the unlawful activity in connection with which such order has been made and such person or any other person on his behalf may make representations to the Advisory Board.

(3) Every meeting of the Advisory Board held to consider such representations shall be presided over by a Chairman nominated from among the members by the Minister and it shall be the duty of the Chairman to advise the Minister in respect of such representations.

(4) The Minister may make rules in relation to the hearing and disposal of any representations that may be made by any person in respect of any such order.

PART V - PROHIBITION OF PUBLICATIONS

14.(1) Notwithstanding any Order made under section 1, the provisions of subsection (2) shall come into operation only upon an Order made in that behalf by the Minister from time to time and published in the Gazette for such period as may be specified in the Order.

(2)

(a) No person shall, without the approval in writing of a competent authority, print or publish in any newspaper any matter relating to -

(i) the commission of any act which constitute an offence under this Act or the investigation of any such offence; or

(ii) incitement to violence, or which is likely to cause religious, racial or communal disharmony or feeling of ill-will or hostility between different communities or racial or religious groups.

(b) No person shall, without the approval in writing of a competent authority, distribute or be concerned in the distribution of any newspaper printed or published in Sri Lanka or outside Sri Lanka in respect of any matter the printing and publication of which is prohibited under paragraph (a).

(3) Any person who commits any act in contravention of any of the provisions of subsection (2) shall be guilty of an offence and shall on conviction be liable to imprisonment of either description for a period not exceeding five years.

(4)

(a) Where any person is convicted of an offence under this section, the court may, in addition to the punishment it may impose for that offence under subsection (3), order that no person shall print, publish or distribute or in any way be concerned in the printing, publication or distribution of any such newspaper for such period as is specified in such order and that the printing press in which such newspaper was printed shall, for such period as shall be specified in such order, not be used for any purpose whatsoever or for any such purpose as is specified in the order.

(b) Where any proceedings have been instituted against any person for the commission of any offence under this section, it shall be competent for the court to make an interim order that the printing press in which it is alleged that such newspaper or publication was printed shall not be used for any purpose whatsoever or for any such purpose as is specified in the order, until the conclusion of the trial.

15. (1) Every person who commits an offence under this Act shall be triable without a preliminary inquiry, on an indictment before a Judge of the High Court sitting alone without a jury or before a High Court at Bar by three Judges without a jury, as may be decided by the Chief Justice. The provisions of Sections 450 and 451 of the Code of Criminal Procedure Act, No. 15 of 1979, shall, mutatis mutandis, apply to the trial of offences under this Act by the High Court at Bar and to appeals from judgments, sentences and orders pronounced at any such trial held by the High Court at Bar. [The above sub-section was introduced by Amending Act 22 of 1988]

(2) Upon the indictment being received in the High Court against any person in respect of any offence under this Act or any offence to which the provisions of Section 23 shall apply, the court shall, in every case, order the remand of such person until the conclusion of the trial.

15A.(1) Where any person is on remand under the provisions of sub-section (2) of section 15, or section 19(a), notwithstanding any other provision of this Act or any other law, the Secretary to the Ministry of the Minister in charge of the subject of Defence may, if he is of the opinion that it is necessary or expedient so to do, in the interests of national security or public order, make Order, subject to such directions as may be given by the High Court to ensure a fair trial of such person, that such person be kept in the custody of any authority, in such place and subject to such conditions as may be determined by him having regard to such interests.

(2) Any Order made by the Minister under sub-section (1) shall be communicated to the High Court and to the Commissioner of Prisons and it shall be the duty of such Commissioner, to deliver the custody of such person to the authority specified in such order and the provisions of the Prisons Ordinance shall cease to apply in relation to the custody of such person. [Note: Section 15A was inserted by Amending Act 10 of 1982 w.e.f. 24 July 1979]

PART VI - TRIAL

16.(1) Notwithstanding the provisions of any other law, where any person is charged with any offence under this Act, any statement made by such person at any time, whether -

(a) it amounts to a confession or not;

(b) made orally or reduced to writing;

(c) such person was or was not in custody or presence of a police officer;

(d) made in the course of an investigation or not;

(e) it was or was not wholly or partly in answer to any question, against such person if such statement is not irrelevant under Section 24 of the Evidence Ordinance: Provided, however, that no such statement shall be proved as against such person if such statement was made to a police officer below the rank of an Assistant Superintendent.

(2) The burden of proving that any statement referred to in subsection (1) is irrelevant under Section 24 of the Evidence Ordinance shall be on the person asserting it to be irrelevant.

(3) Any statement admissible under subsection (1) may be proved as against any other person charged jointly with the person making the statement, if, and only if, such statement is corroborated in material particulars by evidence other than the statements referred to in subsection (1).

17. Notwithstanding anything to the contrary in any other law, the provisions of Sections 25, 26 and 30 of the Evidence Ordinance shall have no application in any proceedings under this Act.

18.(1) Notwithstanding anything to the contrary in any other law -

(a) a statement recorded by a Magistrate, or made at an identification parade by a person who is dead or who cannot be found, shall be admissible in evidence notwithstanding that such person is not present or cannot or has not been cross-examined; and

(b) any document found in the custody, control or possession of a person accused of any offence under this Act or of an agent or representative of such person may be produced in court as evidence against such person without the maker of such document being called as a witness and the contents of such document shall be evidence of the facts stated therein.

(2) If in the course of a trial for an offence under this Act, any witness shall, on any material point, contradict either expressly or by necessary implication a statement made by him and recorded by a Magistrate or a statement made by him at any identification parade, it shall be lawful for the presiding Judge-

(a) to act upon such statement; and

(b) to have such witness at the conclusion of such trial arraigned and tried on an indictment which shall be prepared and signed by the Registrar of such court, for intentionally giving false evidence in a stage of a judicial proceeding.

(3) At any trial referred to in subsection (2)(b), it shall be sufficient to prove that the witness made the contradictory statement and it shall not be necessary to prove which of the statements is false.

19. Notwithstanding the provisions of any other written law -

(a) every person convicted by any court of any offence under this Act shall, notwithstanding that he has lodged a petition of appeal against his conviction or the sentence imposed on him, be kept on remand until the determination of the appeal;

(b) any order made under the provisions of subsection (4) of Section 14 shall, notwithstanding any appeal made against such order, continue in force until the determination of such appeal: Provided, however, that the Court of Appeal may in exceptional circumstances release on bail any such person referred to in paragraph (a) subject to such conditions as the Court of Appeal may deem fit, or vary or suspend any order referred to in paragraph (b).

20. Notwithstanding anything in the Code of Criminal Procedure Act, No 15 of 1979 -

(a) the provisions of Section 303 of that Act shall not apply in the case of any person who is convicted;

(b) the provisions of Section 306 of that Act shall not apply in the case of any person who pleads or is found guilty, by or before any court of any offence under this Act.

21. Every court shall give priority to the trial of any person charged with, or indicted for, any offence under this Act and to the hearing of any appeal from the conviction of any such offence and sentence imposed on such conviction.

PART VII - SPECIAL PROVISIONS

22. Any person who has committed any offence under Section 296 or Section 297 or Section 300 of the Penal Code prior to the date of coming into operation of Part VI of this Act or has abetted or has conspired to abet the commission of any such offence prior to such date, in relation to any person who is a specified person or a person who was a witness to any offence which if such offence had been committed after the date of coming into operation of Part I of this Act would have constituted an offence under this Act shall, notwithstanding the provisions of any other law to the contrary, be triable without a preliminary inquiry, on an indictment before a Judge of the High Court sitting alone without a jury.

23. The provision of Sections 8, 16, 17 and 18 of this Act shall, mutatis mutandis, apply to and in relation to any act, or the trial for the commission of an offence in respect of any act, committed before the date of coming into operation of Parts I, II and VI of this Act, which act would, if committed after such date, have constituted an offence under this Act: Provided, however, that no statement referred to in any such section shall be admissible unless such statement was made after the coming into operation of the aforesaid Parts of this Act.

24. Any person who commits an act in or in relation to any vessel or aircraft registered in Sri Lanka shall, if such act constitutes an offence under this Act, be guilty of an offence under this Act.

PART VIII - MISCELLANEOUS

25. Where an offence under this Act is committed by a body of persons, then if that body of persons is -

(a) a body corporate, every director and officer of that body corporate; or

(b) a firm, every partner of that firm; or

(c) a body unincorporate other than a firm, every officer of that body responsible for its management and control, shall be deemed to be guilty of such offence: Provided that no such person shall be deemed to be guilty of such offence if he proves that such offence was committed without his knowledge or that he exercised all due diligence to prevent the commission of such offence.

26. No suit, prosecution or other proceeding, civil or criminal, shall lie against any officer or person for any act or thing in good faith done or purported to be done in pursuance or supposed pursuance of any order made or direction given under this Act.

27.(1) The Minister may make regulations under this Act for the purpose of carrying out or giving effect to the principles and provisions of this Act.

(2) Every regulation made by the Minister shall be published in the Gazette and shall come into operation on the date of such publication or on such later date as may be specified in the regulation.

(3) Every regulation made by the Minister shall as soon as convenient after its publication in the Gazette be brought before Parliament for its approval. Any regulation, which is not so approved, shall be deemed to be rescinded as from the date of disapproval but without prejudice to anything previously done there under. Notification of the date on which a regulation is deemed to be rescinded shall be published in the Gazette

28. The provisions of this Act shall have effect notwithstanding anything contained in any other written law and accordingly in the event of any conflict or inconsistency between the provisions of this Act and such other written law, the provisions of this Act shall prevail.

[Section 29 was repealed by Amending Act 10 of 1982, w.e.f. 24 July 1979]

30. The Proscribing of Liberation Tigers of Tamil Eelam and Other Similar Organisations Law, No 16 of 1978, is hereby repealed.

PART IX - INTERPRETATION

31.(1) In this Act, unless the context otherwise requires -

"competent authority" means any person appointed by the Minister by name or by office to be a competent authority for the purposes of this Act;

"cooperative union or cooperative society" includes any society registered or deemed to be registered under the Cooperative Societies Law, No 5 of 1972;

"document" has the same meaning as in the Penal Code;

"explosives" has the same meaning as in the Explosives Act;

"firearms" has the same meaning as in the Firearms Ordinance;

"local authority" means any Municipal Council, Urban Council, Town Council or Village Council and includes any Authority created and established by or under any law to exercise, perform and discharge powers, duties and functions corresponding to or similar to the powers, duties and functions exercised, performed and discharged by any such Council;

"newspaper" includes any journal, magazine, pamphlet or other publication; "offensive weapon" has the same meaning as in the Offensive Weapons Act, No 18 of 1966;

"organization" includes any movement, society, party, association or body or group of persons;

"printing press" includes any machinery, apparatus or plant capable of being used for printing, lithography, photography or other mode of representing or reproducing words in a visible form, or any type or other article belonging to such machinery, apparatus or plant;

"public corporation" means any corporation, board or other body which was or is established by or under any written law other than the Companies Ordinance, with funds or capital wholly or partly provided by the Government by way of grant, loan or otherwise;

"specified person" means -

(a) the President;

(b) a Judge of the Supreme Court, Court of Appeal, High Court, District Court, Magistrate's Court, Primary Court or any other Court of First Instance;

(c) any representative or official of a foreign State or any official or other agent of an international organisation of an inter-governmental character;

(d) a member of Parliament or of a local authority;

(e) any member of a commission established under the Special Presidential Commissions of Inquiry Law, No 7 of 1978, or under the Commissions of Inquiry Act;

(f) juror, counsel or officer of court; and

(g) any member of the Armed Forces, Police Force and any other Forces charged with the maintenance of public order.

"unlawful activity" means any action taken or act committed by any means whatsoever, whether within or outside Sri Lanka, and whether such action was taken or act was committed before or after the date of coming into operation of all or any of the provisions of this Act in the commission or in connection with the commission of any offence under this Act or any act committed prior to the date of passing of this Act, which act would, if committed after such date, constitute an offence under this Act.

[This definition was inserted by Amending Act 10 of 1982, w.e.f. 24 July 1979]

(2) All words and expressions used herein and defined in the Penal Code and not hereinbefore defined shall be deemed to have the meanings respectively attributed to them by that Code.

Background Information on Terrorist Groups in South Asia

1. Harakat ul-Mujahidin (HUM)

Description Formerly known as the Harakat al-Ansar, the HUM is an Islamic militant group based in Pakistan that operates primarily in Kashmir. Long-time leader of the group, Fazlur Rehman Khalil, in mid-February stepped down as HUM emir, turning the reins over to the popular Kashmiri commander and his second-in-command, Farooq Kashmiri. Khalil, who has been linked to Bin Ladin and signed his fatwa in February 1998 calling for attacks on US and Western interests, assumed the position of HUM Secretary General. Continued to operate terrorist training camps in eastern Afghanistan.

Activities Has conducted a number of operations against Indian troops and civilian targets in Kashmir. Linked to the Kashmiri militant group al-Faran that kidnapped five Western tourists in Kashmir in July 1995; one was killed in August 1995 and the other four reportedly were killed in December of the same year. The new millennium brought significant developments for Pakistani militant groups, particularly the HUM. Most of these sprang from the hijacking of an Indian airliner on 24 December by militants believed to be associated with the HUM. The hijackers negotiated the release of Masood Azhar, an important leader in the former Harakat ul-Ansar imprisoned by the Indians in 1994. Azhar did not, however, return to the HUM, choosing instead to form the Jaish-e-Mohammed (JEM), a rival militant group expressing a more radical line than the HUM.

Strength Has several thousand armed supporters located in Azad Kashmir, Pakistan, and India's southern Kashmir and Doda regions. Supporters are mostly Pakistanis and Kashmiris and also include Afghans and Arab veterans of the Afghan war. Uses light and heavy machineguns, assault rifles, mortars, explosives, and rockets. HUM lost some of its membership in defections to the JEM.

Location/Area of Operation

Based in Muzaffarabad, Rawalpindi, and several other towns in Pakistan and Afghanistan, but members conduct insurgent and terrorist activities primarily in Kashmir. The HUM trains its militants in Afghanistan and Pakistan.

External Aid

Collects donations from Saudi Arabia and other Gulf and Islamic states and from Pakistanis and Kashmiris. The sources and amount of HUM's military funding are unknown.

2. Liberation Tigers of Tamil Eelam (LTTE)

Other known front organizations: World Tamil Association (WTA), World Tamil Movement (WTM), the Federation of Associations of Canadian Tamils (FACT), the Ellalan Force, the Sangilian Force.

Description Founded in 1976, the LTTE is the most powerful Tamil group in Sri Lanka and uses overt and illegal methods to raise funds, acquire weapons, and publicize its cause of establishing an independent Tamil state. The LTTE began its armed conflict with the Sri Lankan Government in 1983 and relies on a guerrilla strategy that includes the use of terrorist tactics.

Activities The Tigers have integrated a battlefield insurgent strategy with a terrorist programme that targets not only key personnel in the countryside but also senior Sri Lankan political and military leaders in Colombo and other urban ceatres. The Tigers are most notorious for their cadre of suicide bombers, the Black Tigers. Political assassinations and bombings are commonplace. The LTTE has refrained from targeting foreign diplomatic and commercial establishments.

Strength Exact strength is unknown, but the LTTE is estimated to have 8,000 to 10,000 armed combatants in Sri Lanka, with a core of trained fighters of approximately 3,000 to 6,000. The LTTE also has a significant overseas support structure for fundraising, weapons procurement, and propaganda activities.

Location/Area of Operations

The Tigers control most of the northern and eastern coastal areas of Sri Lanka but have conducted operations throughout the island. Headquartered in northern Sri Lanka, LTTE leader Velupillai Prabhakaran has established an extensive network of checkpoints and informants to keep track of any outsiders who enter the group's area of control.

External Aid

The LTTE's overt organizations support Tamil separatism by lobbying foreign governments and the United Nations. The LTTE also uses its international contacts to procure weapons, communications, and any other equipment and supplies it needs. The LTTE exploits large Tamil communities in North America, Europe, and Asia to obtain funds and supplies for its fighters in Sri Lanka. Information obtained since the mid-1980s indicates that some Tamil communities in Europe are also involved in narcotics smuggling. Tamils historically have served as drug couriers moving narcotics into Europe.

3. Al-Qaeda

Description Established by Osama bin Ladin in the late 1980s to bring together Arabs who fought in Afghanistan against the Soviet invasion. Helped finance, recruit, transport, and train Sunni Islamic extremists for the Afghan resistance. Current goal is to establish a pan-Islamic Caliphate throughout the world by working with allied Islamic extremist groups to overthrow regimes it deems "non-Islamic" and expelling Westerners and non-Muslims from Muslim countries. Issued statement under banner of "the World Islamic Front for Jihad Against the Jews and Crusaders" in February 1998, saying it was the duty of all Muslims to kill US citizens—civilian or military--and their allies everywhere.

Activties Plotted to carry out terrorist operations against US and Israeli tourists visiting Jordan for millennial celebrations. (Jordanian authorities thwarted the planned attacks and put 28 suspects on trial.) Conducted the bombings in August 1998 of the US Embassies in Nairobi, Kenya, and Dares Salaam, Tanzania, that killed at least 301 persons and injured more than 5,000 others. Claims to have shot down US helicopters and killed US servicemen in Somalia in 1993 and to have conducted three bombings that targeted US troops in Aden, Yemen, in December 1992. Linked to the following plans that were not carried out: to assassinate Pope John Paul II during his visit to Manila in late 1994, simultaneous bombings of the US and Israeli Embassies in Manila and other Asian capitals in late 1994, the midair bombing of a dozen US trans-Pacific flights in 1995, and to kill President Clinton during a visit to the Philippines in early 1995. Continues to train, finance, and provide logistic support to terrorist groups in support of these goals.

Strength May have several hundred to several thousand members. Also serves as a focal point or umbrella organization for a worldwide network that includes many Sunni Islamic extremist groups such as Egyptian Islamic Jihad, some members of al-Gama'at al-Islamiyya, the Islamic Movement of Uzbekistan, and the Harakat ul-Mujahidin.

Location/Area of Operation

Al-Qaeda has a worldwide reach, has cells in a number of countries, and is reinforced by its ties to Sunni extremist networks. Bin Ladin and his key lieutenants reside in Afghanistan, and the group maintains terrorist training camps there.

External Aid

Bin Ladin, son of a billionaire Saudi family, is said to have inherited approximately $300 million that he uses to finance the group. Al-Qaeda also maintains moneymaking front organizations, solicits donations from like-minded supporters, and illicitly siphons funds from donations to Muslim charitable organizations

4. Jaish-e-Mohammed (JEM) (Army of Mohammed)

Description The Jaish-e-Mohammed (JEM) is an Islamist group based in Pakistan that has rapidly expanded in size and capability since Maulana Masood Azhar, a former ultrafundamentalist Harakat ul-Ansar (HUA) leader, announced its formation in February. The group's aim is to unite Kashmir with Pakistan. It is politically aligned with the radical, pro-Taliban, political party, Jamiat-i Ulema-i Islam (JUI-F).

Activities The JEM's leader, Masood Azhar, was released from Indian imprisonment in December 1999 in exchange for 155 hijacked Indian Airlines hostages in Afghanistan. The 1994 HUA kidnappings of US and British nationals in New Delhi and the July 1995 HUA/Al Faran kidnappings of Westerners in Kashmir were two of several previous HUA efforts to free Azhar. Azhar organized large rallies and recruitment drives across Pakistan throughout 2000. In July, a JEM rocket-grenade attack failed to injure the Chief Minister at his office in Srinagar, India, but wounded four other persons. In December, JEM militants launched grenade attacks at a bus stop in Kupwara, India, injuring 24 persons, and at a marketplace in Chadoura, India, injuring 16 persons. JEM militants also planted two bombs that killed 21 persons in Qamarwari and Srinagar.

Strength Has several hundred armed supporters located in Azad Kashmir, Pakistan, and in India's southern Kashmir and Doda regions. Following Maulana Masood Azhar's release from detention in India, a reported three quarters of Harakat ul-Mujahedin (HUM) members defected to the new organization, which has managed to attract a large number of urban Kashmiri youth. Supporters are mostly Pakistanis and Kashmiris and also include Afghans and Arab veterans of the Afghan war. Uses light and heavy machineguns, assault rifles, mortars, improvised explosive devices, and rocket grenades.

Location/Area of Operation

Based in Peshawar and Muzaffarabad, but members conduct terrorist activities primarily in Kashmir. The JEM maintains training camps in Afghanistan.

External Aid

Most of the JEM's cadre and material resources have been drawn from the militant groups Harakat ul-Jihad al-Islami (HUJI) and the Harakat ul-Mujahedin (HUM). The JEM has close ties to Afghan Arabs and the Taliban. Usama Bin Ladin is suspected of giving funding to the JEM.

5. Lashkar-e-Tayyiba (LT) (Army of the Righteous)

Description The LT is the armed wing of the Pakistan-based religious organization, Markaz-ud-Dawa-wal-Irshad (MDI)—a Sunni anti-US missionary organization formed in 1989. One of the three largest and best-trained groups fighting in Kashmir against India, it is not connected to a political party. The LT leader is MDI chief, Professor Hafiz Mohammed Saeed.

Activities Has conducted a number of operations against Indian troops and civilian targets in Kashmir since 1993. The LT is suspected of eight separate attacks in August that killed nearly 100, mostly Hindu Indians. LT militants are suspected of kidnapping six persons in Akhala, India, in November 2000 and killing five of them. The group also operates a chain of religious schools in the Punjab.

Strength Has several hundred members in Azad Kashmir, Pakistan, and in India's southern Kashmir and Doda regions. Almost all LT cadres are foreigners—mostly Pakistanis from seminaries across the country and Afghan veterans of the Afghan wars. Uses assault rifles, light and heavy machineguns, mortars, explosives, and rocket propelled grenades.

Location/Area of Operation

Based in Muridke (near Lahore) and Muzaffarabad. The LT trains its militants in mobile training camps across Pakistan-administered Kashmir and Afghanistan.

External Aid

Collects donations from the Pakistani community in the Persian Gulf and United Kingdom, Islamic NGOs, and Pakistani and Kashmiri businessmen. The amount of LT funding is unknown. The LT maintains ties to religious/military groups around the world, ranging from the Philippines to the Middle East and Chechnya through the MDI fraternal network.

CONTRIBUTORS

Shibashis Chatterjee, Lecturer, Department of International Relations, Jadavpur University, Kolkata-700 032

T. Sreedhar, Visiting Professor, School of International Studies, Jawaharlal Nehru University, New Delhi

Kousar J. Azam, Professor, Department of Political Science, Osmania University, Hyderabad-500 007

Mohd. Moazzam Ali, Reader, Department of Political Science, University of Hyderabad, Hyderabad-500 046

Pushpa M. Bhargava, Former Director of Centre for Cellular and Molecular Biology, Hyderabad.

A. Ravinder Nath, Director, Centre for Studies in Bio-Terrorism and Public Health Policy, Osmania University, Hyderabad-500 007

P.V. Rao, Director, Centre for Indian Ocean Studies, Osmania University, Hyderabad-500 007

J..Laxmi Narasimha Rao, Reader, Department of Political Science, Osmania University, Hyderabad-500 007

M. J. Vinod, Reader, Department of Political Science, Bangalore University, Bangalore-560 056

Suba Chandran, Research Officer, Institute of Peace and Conflict Studies, New Delhi-110 057

V.Nageswara Rao, Professor (Rtd), University College of Law, Osmania University, Hyderabad-500 007

G.B.Reddy, Lecturer, University College of Law, Osmania University, Hyderabad-500 007

Satya Narayan Pradhan, IPS, Assistant Director, SVP National Police Academy, Hyderabad-500 052

P.Sanjay, Advocacy Associate, Lok Satta, Hyderabad-500 082

B.Krishnamurthy, Reader, School of International Studies, Pondicherry University, Pondicherry-605 014

A.Subramanyam Raju, Scholar of Peace Fellow, Women in Security Conflict Management & Peace (WISCOMP), New Delhi-110 003

Rasmhi Bhure, Lecturer, Department of Politics, SIES College, University of Mumbai, Mumbai-400 022

INDEX